I0326079

মহৎসঙ্গ প্রসঙ্গ

On Associating with Great Ones

মহৎসঙ্গ প্রসঙ্গ

On Associating with Great Ones

Śrī Kanupriya Goswami

Based on lectures collected and edited in Bengali
by Śrī Gauraraydas Goswami

Introduced, translated, and annotated
by
Neal Delmonico

Blazing Sapphire Press
715 E. McPherson
Kirksville, Missouri 63501
2014

ISBN 978-0-9817902-9-9 (0-9817902-9-1)

Library of Congress Control Number: 2009908627

Published by:
Blazing Sapphire Press
715 E. McPherson
Kirksville, Missouri 63501

Available at:
Nitai's Bookstore
715 E. McPherson
Kirksville, Missouri, 63501
Phone: (660) 665-0273
http://www.nitaisbookstore.com
http://www.blazing-sapphire-press.com
Email: neal@blazing-sapphire-press.com

Image Credits

Image on front cover:
Sarang Raga from the Sirohi Ragamala
c.a. 1680-1690

Opague watercolor on paper
H: 23.2 W: 17.8 cm
Sirohi, India

Freer Gallery of Art, Smithsonian Institution, Washington, D.C.: Purchase: F1992.18

Contents

Preface ix

Translator's Introduction xi
A Short Biography of the Author xvii
Theology in the Caitanya Vaiṣṇava Context xxi
The Theologies of Caitanya Vaiṣṇavism xxv
The Theology of Kanupriya Goswami xlix
The Power and Provenance of Saṅga l
Conventions Observed in this Translation lv
Works Cited and Consulted lviii

Bengali Editor's Introduction lix

I On Associating with Great Ones 1

Chapter One 3

Chapter Two 19

Chapter Three 33

Chapter Four 41

Chapter Five 51

II Appendices 65

Appendix 1 67

Appendix 2: On the Author (by Rasikamohana Śarmā) 91

Appendix 3: The Guru and Divine Name 101
Taking Shelter with a Guru 106
The Greatness of the Divine Name 118

Introduction to the Devanāgarī Script 139
Vowels: Svara 139
Consonants: Viṣṇu/Vyañjana 140
The ka-varga (ka-group) 140
The ca-varga (ca-group) 141
The ṭa-varga (ṭa-group) 141
The ta-varga (ta-group) 141
The pa-varga (pa-group) 142
The Semivowels 142
The Sibilants 143
Combining Vowels and Consonants 143

Other Books by Blazing Sapphire Press 147
Coming soon: 150
Introducing Golden Avatar Press 151

প্রভুপাদ শ্রীল কানুপ্রিয় গোস্বামী

Prabhupāda Śrīla Kānupriya Gosvāmī

Preface

Reading this book has made me personally realize a number of things. One is how great a secret this specialized *rasik* tradition of pure *bhakti* is. Another is how high a level of intelligence is behind this path, and how important it is for us to apply our intelligences to appreciating more fully the rarified air we ascend into as we read and study this book. (Note to self: read this book over several times, let yourself be enraptured by it, and let yourself be deeply affected by it as well!).

Yet another realization is that the best way to truly benefit all beings, in an exalted way, is to genuinely attain the pure *bhakti* discussed in this book, within this lifetime! The type of loving devotion to God that is without desire for personal gain, without desire for any kind of personal life-fulfillment—other than, of course, to please God in a very real and tangible way, is indeed rarely mentioned in spiritual circles, let alone devoutly understood and practiced. Yet in India, I was fortunate enough to have witnessed it and lived with many great ones who had realized this most pure path in their lives. Having witnessed such *mahats*, I feel impelled to try to make it known—the depth and truth of their profound way of life and their supreme spiritual attainment.

This is the first of many *siddha* (perfected) Vaiṣṇava authors to be translated by Blazing Sapphire Press for presentation to a sincere and interested public for the enrichment of their personal lives. As a result there will be great benefit—the kind of benefit talked about by Siddha Kanupriya Gosvami himself, I believe. It is my firm belief that by reading this book with great respect and concentration, one will get the blessings needed to be introduced to *Bhagavad-bhakti* (God's own special energy of loving devotion to God), herself.

With the hope, then, that this book itself becomes *mahat saṅga* (association with a great one) for us readers, over and over again, may it lead us all to further *mahat saṅga* in this and every future life!

Jagadish Dass
Gurubār
24-1-2014

Translator's Introduction

The twentieth century was an extraordinary century for writers writing about Caitanya Vaiṣṇavism, the religious tradition that developed around the sixteenth century saint/reformer/ecstatic, Śrī Kṛṣṇacaitanya (1486-1533 C.E.). During the final decades of the 19th century and the first half of the 20th century, the tradition underwent an exhubrant literary renaissance and flowering during which it succeeded in bursting out of India and appearing on the world stage as a religious tradition to be recognized and reckoned with. While a few of those early works were written in English,[1] the vast majority were written in Bengali.[2] Bengal, the birth place of Śrī Caitanya, naturally witnessed among its citizens of that period the greatest share of renewed interest in his life and religious insights. Of the enormous number of works on Caitanya Vaiṣṇavism written in Bengali during that period, few have ever been translated into English. Forget about translation, even the scope and contents of this vast field of literature have not been surveyed in Bengali, English or any other language that I am aware of. Just the few quick glances at this literature that I have managed over the years suggest that it is filled with many rich and innovative theological reflections that would be of value to general readers as well as to scholars who

[1]Some of the English works of note are Premānanda Bhāratī's *Sree Krishna: the Lord of Love* (New York, 1904), Shishir Kumar Ghosha's *Lord Gouranga, or, Salvation for All* (2 vols., Calcutta, 1923), Bhagavat Kumar Śāstrī's *The Bhakti Cult in Ancient India* (Calcutta, 1924), and Dr. Mahanamabrata Brahmacari's *Vaiṣṇava Vedānta* (Dissertation, University of Chicago, 1937, and later published separately.).

[2]Writers like Rasikamohana Vidyābhūṣaṇa, Haridāsa Gosvāmī, Haridāsa Dāsa Bābājī, Dr. Radhagovinda Nath, Sundarānanda (Dāsa) Vidyāvinoda, and the present author, Kanupriya Gosvāmī, are some examples of prolific and learned writers who wrote in Bengali on the Caitanya tradition.

have an interest in the diverse views and insights of the religions of India and the world.

Why there was such a proliferation of Caitanya Vaiṣṇava literature during that period of seventy or so years (roughly 1880-1950 C.E.) is hard to say. Certainly, the fact that more printing presses were in the hands and under the control of affluent Bengalis was an important factor. The first printing presses in India were established by the Baptist Mission Press at Shreerampur (Serampur) on the Ganges north of Calcutta in the last few decades of the 18th century. The primary purpose of the Baptist Mission was to spread the "good news" of the Christian gospels among the Indian populace and Sreerampur, as the headquarters of the Baptist Mission in India, was an influential part of that program throughout the 19th century. But by the second half of that century many Bengalis had acquired their own presses and were busily publishing Bengali and Sanskrit titles and numerous, one might even say countless, periodical journals. It is in the context of this publishing frenzy, sometimes refered to as the Bengal Renaissance, that the literary flowering and output of Caitanya Vaiṣṇavism should be seen.

Another factor was the rather forward-looking policy adopted by the British of educating young Bengalis for posts in the civil service. By encouraging education and creating the facilities for good educations by establishing schools and colleges, a large, highly educated and widely literate population developed in Bengal by the end of the 19th century. Of course, the government-sponsored education was largely in English and was highly based on Western models. Nevertheless (despite Macaulay's famous ``minute'' on education), traditional subjects like Sanskrit and Bengali literature were also taught at the government-established institutions. Even Christian church-established institutions made room for traditional subjects, as was the case at Scottish Churches College, for instance. This rather enlightened British policy, it should be noted, was in marked contrast to the policies of some of the other major colonial powers, such as the Dutch and the Portugese, who prefered to keep the people of their colonies in the dark, fully dependent, and thoroughly exploited. Although the British did visit many atrocities on the people they ruled in India, they were comparatively mild.

Finally, it was not really until the end of the 19th century that the Bengalis began to recover some of their self-esteem in the face of British colonialism and with that strengthening recovery they were drawn back to the roots of their own traditions with new respect. This recovery was no doubt aided by the growing sense of nationalism and heightened national identity that was the result of the events and aftermath of the "mutiny" of 1857 (the great Indian rebellion). Initially, the Indians, not just the Bengalis, were deeply impressed by British power, culture, intellectual life, and religion. This initial impression of the British also provoked at the same time something of a sense of shame and embarrassment in the Indians of some generations, embarrassment occasioned by viewing, through distorting lenses provided by the British, their own culture, intellectual history and achievements, and religious beliefs and practices, and comparing them with those of the British or of Europe at large. Over time, however, as the Indian population had more time to observe the British *ubermensch* in action, suspicion grew into fulfledged disillusionment with the "enlightened" British and their plans for India. With the mutiny in 1857, it became clear that British rule was really a threat to the Hindu way of life as well as to that of the Muslims with whom Hindus had lived more or less peacefully for many centuries. The Muslims had after all adapted to and flourished in India and among its native populations since the 12th century. The result of this growing disillusionment with and critical outlook towards all things British was a desire among the younger generations of the second half of the 19th century to return to the roots of their own culture and traditions, to rediscover themselves in the beliefs and practices of their ancestors.

Perhaps there is no better example of this process of changing attitudes, first admiration and then rejection, towards British culture and religion than can be found in the life of Raja Rammohun Roy (1772?-1833 C.E.) who lived through the early period of Indian engagement with British rule and culture. Rammohun as a young man became deeply influenced by the criticisms leveled at Hindu religion and culture by the Christian missionaries of the time. He became convinced that the worship of stone and metal images that was so much a part of the practice of Hindu piety was indeed "idolatry" and moreover that it was a rank misunderstanding of the original, "pure," revelatory insights of the ancient Hindu sages found in the Vedas and the Upaniṣads. Even at the age of sixteen he wrote a tract critical of the Hindu tradition called *The Idolatrous System of the Hindus* which managed to anger many conservative members of Hindu society and effectively ruin his relationship with his high caste *brahmin* father.[3] He believed and argued that the ancient texts taught a monotheistic faith in "the existence of one supreme God—a God endowed with a distinct personality, moral attributes worthy of His nature and an intelligence befitting the Governor of the universe."[4] By making such arguments he drew upon himself the ire of the Hindu population of his father's generation, but attracted the support and sympathy of many in his own and younger generations. When, however, he turned his attention to Christianity, he found signs of a similar corruption by idolatry in Christian belief and practice, a critique of which he expressed in his book *The Precepts of Jesus a Sufficient Guide to Peace and Happiness* (1820), which contains a selection of passages from the Gospels with his own critical introduction. As Stein says, "While he praised the morality of Jesus, he rejected his divinity and his miracles. Moreover, he took exception to all the abstruse and supernatural presentations of his teachings, decrying them as superstition or mythological nonsense."[5] To discover the true religion of the Hindus, Rammohun returned to the roots of the tradition, the ancient texts. This became the model for the later generations of Vaiṣṇavas of the Caitanya tradition, though the supreme god that they found there was not the abstract, impersonal absolute of Rammohun that was beyond speech and intellect, but the lover god Kṛṣṇa who was regarded as very much embodied and, as a result, very close and approachable.

Among the Caitanyite writers who participated in the Vaiṣṇava renaissance were Śrī Haridāsa Goswami (1867-1946) whose reworking of the life of Caitanya in two massive volumes, one for the Navadvīpa portion and one for the Jagannātha Purī portion of his life, was called the *Śrī Caitanya-bhārata* (1906) because it was enormous in size like the great Indian epic, the *Mahābhārata*. Shishirkumar Ghosh's (1840-1911) *Beautiful Life of Nimai (Śrī Caitanya)* (*Amiyā Nimāi Carita*, 1904) extended to six volumes in Bengali and two large volumes when an abidged version was finally published in En-

[3]William Bysshe Stein, *Two Brahman Sources of Emerson and Thoreau*, v.

[4]ibid., vi-vii.

[5]ibid., ix. Rammohun's position was admired and supported by the Unitarians of New England, a reaction that paved the way for Rammohun's later influence, through his translations, on such American savants as Emerson and Thoreau.

glish (1922). Vipinavihārī Goswami (1850-1919) wrote his lengthy *The Delight of the Ten Roots* (*Daśa-mūla-rasam*, 1898) which presents, in Bengali verse with Sanskrit citations from numerous texts, the entire theology of the Caitanya tradition on the basis of ten fundamental principles.[6] To these names should be added those of the great traditional pundits Śrī Śyāmalāla Goswami and Śrī Prāṇagopāla Goswami who published great numbers of works belonging to Caitanya Vaiṣṇavism around the turn of the 20th century and in that century's twenties and thirties respectively.

Śrī Surendranātha Goswami, the father of Śrī Kanupriya Goswami, the author of the text translated here, is accredited with some thirty-two works ranging from poetry, plays, and other literary productions to essays on science, philosophy and, of course, *bhakti*. Towards the end of the period, the historian Dr. Radhagovinda Nath produced his massive five-volume presentation of the philosophy of Caitanya Vaiṣṇavism and completed his multivolume editions of the major biographies of Caitanya with his notes and commentaries. Prolific writers and scholars like Rasikamohana Vidyābhūṣaṇa and Sundarananda Vidyavinoda produced numerous works on various subjects relating to the history and philosophy of Caitanya Vaiṣṇavism. Bimanbihari Majumdar's work, though appearing well towards the end of this period or even after it had ended, should also be included in this company. His seminal study of the materials available for constructing the life of Śrī Caitanya is now a classic in Caitanyite studies. The field is almost too vast to describe, and much of the literary output remains unknown or has been lost.

Along with the production and publication of new works on Caitanya Vaiṣṇavism in Bengali and Sanskrit, the period witnessed the repeated, almost periodic, publication of the major scriptural source

[6]The ten roots are: (1) The statements of accepted scripture are the main sources of evidence for knowledge about the divine, (2) Hari, who is Kṛṣṇa, is the highest truth in the universe, (3) he possesses all powers, (4) he is an ocean of divine savors (rasas), (5) all living beings are his separated parts, (6) because of being a marginal power (*taṭastha-śakti*), all living beings in their bound state are imprisioned by material nature, (7) because of being a marginal power, all living beings in their liberated state are freed from material nature, (8) the living beings and material nature are simultaneously different from and not different from Śrī Hari, (9) pure *bhakti* is the means to blessedness for the living beings, and (10) pure love for Kṛṣṇa is the goal for all living beings. These are taken from the work of one of Vipinavihārī Goswami's disciples, Bhaktivinoda Ṭhākura and confirmed in *Bāghnāpāḍā-sampradāya o Vaiṣṇava Sāhitya*, 529-31. More will be said about these in the section of Caitanyite theology.

texts of Caitanya Vaiṣṇavism, beginning in the 1880s with the publications of the works of the Vṛndāvana Gosvāmins with major commentaries and Bengali translations by Rāmanārāyaṇa Vidyāratna at Barahampura in the Murshidabad District of Bengal. That body of publications was reissued in several newer editions by Rāmanārāyaṇa's son, Rāmadeva Miśra, even into the 1930s. The canon was again published by Nityasvarūpa Brahmacārī from Vrindaban in Devanagari script in the early years of the 20th Century and again in the 1930s and 1940s by Haridāsa Dāsa Bābājī from Navadvīpa in Bengali script with Bengali translations. In the 1940s, 1950s, and 1960s, Kṛṣṇadāsa Bābājī began the process all over again publishing the whole canon and then some in Devanagari script with Hindi translations while simultaneously Puridāsa Mahāśaya published the canon with verse indices and annotations on variant readings and manuscript sources in Bengali script. Finally, Haridasa Sastri published the whole canon again in the 1970s and 1980s, also in Devanagari script with Hindi translations and largely based on the previous editions of Kṛṣṇadāsa Bābā whom he, as a young man, had assisted in the earlier publication work. When I say canon here, I do not mean to imply that Caitanya Vaiṣṇavism has a fixed canon of scriptural texts. Nevertheless, there are seminal works that are considered paradigmatic expressions of the theology and practices of the tradition. That set of works, though not officially codified, is what I am refering here to as the canon. No doubt the repeated publication and therefore easy availability of the original scriptural texts of the Caitanya tradition in all of these editions contributed greatly to the renaissance of Vaiṣṇava literature in the first half of the 20th century.

Though he entered the field rather late, his first book entitled *The True Nature and Religion of the Living Being* (*Jīver Svarūpa o Svadharma*) came out in 1934, Śrī Kanupriya Goswami became even in this field of literati one of the most respected writers of the writer/theologians of the Caitanyite renaissance. The short work presented in translation here is based on a series of lectures he gave towards the end of his life and gives only a brief introduction to aspects of the thought of this master of his tradition. Nevertheless, many of the main themes of his larger body of work can be found briefly expressed in this short text.

A Short Biography of the Author

Śrī Kanupriya Goswami was born in north Kolkata in 1891 on the street that is now known as Vivekananda Road. His father's name was Surendranath Goswami and his mother's name was Vindhyavasini Devi. He was born into an old, respected Vaiṣṇava family that traces its ancestry back to some of the famous companions and followers of Śrī Caitanya.[7] Kanupriya was a member of the eleventh generation from Kānu Ṭhākura (16th-17th centuries) who was the grandson of Sadāśiva Kavirāja, a direct companion of Śrī Caitanya. Sadāśiva Kavirāja and his son and grandson are mentioned in several of the old hagiographies of Śrī Caitanya, and a short Sanskrit hymn praising Śrī Caitanya in fifteen verses survives in Sadāśiva's name.[8] His son was Puruṣottama Dāsa, another leader and writer of the early movement,[9] and Puruṣottama's son was Kānu Ṭhākura, another important member of the early Caitanya movement and a composer of numerous Bengali songs.[10] For instance, in the last of the biographies of Śrī Caitanya, the *Immortal Acts of Śrī Caitanya* (*Śrīcaitanya-caritāmṛta*) (completed in around 1612) by Kṛṣṇadāsa Kavirāja we find this:

> Śrī Sadāśiva Kavirāja was a very great being.
> And Śrī Puruṣottama Dāsa was his son.
> From birth he[11] was intent on serving at Nityānanda's feet.
> He ceaselessly enacted childhood sports with Kṛṣṇa.
> His son was the great soul Śrī Kānu Ṭhākura.

[7]See the second appendix for a discussion of Kanupriya Goswami's family by Rasikamohana Vidyābhūṣaṇa.

[8]The hymn is entitled the "Fourteen on the Unusual Son of Śacī (Caitanya)" (*Śrī Śrī Śacīnandana-vilakṣaṇa-caturdaśakam*) and is printed in *Śrī Śrī Caitanyacandrodaye Viśiṣṭa Tārakātraya* by Sundarananda Vidyavinoda, 26-48. It is written using verbs in the present tense indicating that it was written during the lifetime of Caitanya.

[9]Puruṣottama is best known for his compendium of important verses from the *Bhāgavata Purāṇa* strung together with his connecting statements and comments. It is called the *Collection of the Essential Principles of Bhakti for Hari* (*Śrī Hari-bhakti-tattva-sāra-saṅgraha*).

[10]Kānu Ṭhākura's songs are found scattered throughout the numerous collections of Vaiṣṇava songs that were created in the 17th and 18th centuries.

[11]Puruṣottama Dāsa.

In his body resided the ambrosia of love of Kṛṣṇa.[12]

Although Kanupriya was thus born in such a distinguished family in the Vaiṣṇava community, it was the quality and depth of his writing that brought him the greatest recognition and respect. It comes as something of a surprise to learn then that he had no formal education.[13] He never attended any school or college. His nephew, Kishoraray Goswami, whose short essay on Kanupriya's life is half hagiography, points to this fact as miraculous evidence of Kanupriya Goswami's high level of religious attainment in his previous life. Though it may be true that Kanupriya never went to school formally and was to a large degree self-taught, it is hard to believe that his father did not either teach him himself or hire a tutor for him when he was a young boy. Kanupriya's knowledge of the scriptures of the Caitanya tradition, especially the *Bhāgavata Purāṇa*, the *Bhagavad-gītā*, and the writings of the Gosvāmins of Vṛndāvana, was indeed enormous and his writing style in Bengali was complex, sophisticated, and grammatically correct.

His fame became established with the appearance of his first book, the *True Nature and Function of the Living Being* in 1934. It had been published serially in a popular Vaiṣṇava journal, *Śrī Śyāmasundara Patrikā* (*The Journal of Śyāmasundara* [Dark-beautiful Kṛṣṇa]), edited by another well known Vaiṣṇava savant and writer of the renaissance, Śrī Prāṇagopāla Goswami of Navadvīpa. His cogent and logical presentation of some of the fundamental beliefs about the nature of human life, on the backdrop of the universal drama of the cycle of life, and about the purpose of human life in cultivating its truer inner nature in relationship with the divine was warmly received by a populace that was troubled by the political unrest

---

[12]Kṛṣṇadāsa Kavirāja, *Śrī Caitanya-caritāmṛta*, 1.11.38-40:

শ্রীসদাশিব কবিরাজ বড় মহাশয়|
শ্রীপুরুষোত্তমদাস তাঁহার তনয়||
আজন্ম নিমগ্ন নিত্যানন্দের চরণে|
নিরন্তর বাল্য লীলা করে কৃষ্ণ সনে||
তাঁর পুত্র মহাশয় শ্রীকানু ঠাকুর|
যাঁর দেহে রহে কৃষ্ণ প্রেমামৃতপুর||

[13]Kishoraray Goswami, *Śrī Nāmāśraye jīvana theke nitya jīvane Jaya Śrī Śrī Gaurarāyahari*, 6.

and uncertainty of the struggle for independence, and unsettled by modern philosophies, theories, and ideologies like historical materialism, evolution, and nihilism. It was his second book, however, that really brought him into prominence. His second book was entitled the *Thought-jewel of the Holy Name* (*Śrī Nāma-cintāmaṇi*) (1943) was an even greater success than his first. It was an elaborate apologetics on the power of the divine name, an important aspect of Caitanya Vaiṣṇava theology, again presented in a cogent and logical way with numerous examples and analogies drawn from the ordinary, familiar lives of his Bengali audience. As a result of the success of that book, Kanupriya Goswami was given the title of "Teacher of the Science of the Divine Name" by other Vaiṣṇava writers and groups of the time. The rest of Kanupriya's books were in some way centered around his book on the holy name. Two more volumes of the *Thought-jewel* came out eventually and two other books, *A Small Piece of the Mystery of Bhakti* and *Spotlight on the Mystery of Passionate Bhakti*, both rather large in size, both of which the author introduces as texts meant to be read as introductions to his main work on the divine name. Thus, Kanupriya produced six major texts in Bengali with numerous citations from the Caitanya Vaiṣṇava scriptures and a series of essays edited by his nephews that were based on his lectures delivered at various times and in various places. In the course of all these books and lectures, Kanupriya Goswami presents a reasonably well-argued and scripturally authenticated theology of the Caitanya tradition. Taken all together, in fact, his books present a relatively complete treatment of the worldview, philosophical orientation, and practices of modern Caitanya Vaiṣṇavism.

Though Kanupriya Goswami never formally became a renunciant, he lived a life of simple renunciation, austerity, and religious practice. He never married and instead devoted his full attention to the service of the sacred image that he worshiped throughout his life, an ancient painting of Śrī Caitanya inherited from his father. The image's name is Śrī Gaurarāya, another name for Śrī Caitanya, and is an image of Śrī Caitanya in the pose of and holding the flute of Śrī Kṛṣṇa. It is thus Caitanya but identified as Śrī Kṛṣṇa. For all intents and purposes Śrī Gaurarāya was Kanupriya's family. His life was largely devoted to the daily worship and service of Śrī Gaurarāya, the study of the sacred texts of his tradition, private worship/practice (*bhajana*) and the writing of books and giving of lectures and speeches on holidays and special occasions. He passed away in 1975.

Śrī Gaurarāya

On a visit to Navadvīpa in the early 1970s, I had the good fortune of meeting Śrī Kanupriya Goswami a few years before his passing. We sat and chatted for a few minutes on his veranda and that was when I first learned of his published books. He was very impressive to behold, the very image of saintliness and gentility. He wore a clean, white, cotton *dhoti* and *kurta* with an uppercloth or cotton shawl wrapped around his shoulders. His right hand was planted in a cotton bead-bag in which he kept *japa* beads which always seemed to be gently tapping together in constant motion. His complexion was a very light brown and his finely chiseled face was quite handsome. His head was abundantly covered with bright, snowy white hair and his expression at once very peaceful and benevolent. He seemed to me at the time to be the perfect gentleman-saint. I do not recall the subjects of our discussion, but I recall being encouraged to study the languages and the texts of the Caitanya tradition and to make them available in English for readers in the West. When we were finished he sent me to the shop of one of his disciples in the local market place (Rajabazaar) where I was able to pick up many of his Bengali books.

Theology in the Modern Caitanya Vaiṣṇava Context

What does theology mean when applied to the works of writers like Śrī Kanupriya Goswami in the context of the modern world? Obviously, theology does not mean the academic or systematic study of theology. Writers like Kanupriya were never trained nor did they study in any academic institution or environment. As far as I know there are no institutions in existence that do for the Caitanya tradition what seminaries and yeshivas do for the Christian and Jewish traditions. For writers like him theology was a part of their religious practice. One of the forms of practice that is prominent among followers of the Caitanya tradition, and indeed of many of the *bhakti* traditions of North India, is Kṛṣṇa-kathā, participating in discourses on, discussions, narrations, textual recitations, and elucidations of the mythical story and character of Kṛṣṇa. It is a form of oral and aural meditation and the source of deep emotional and sometimes ecstatic responses in the audience. Such experiences are called *rasa* or *bhakti-rasa* and are much sought after in the tradition. This practice naturally extends to all of Kṛṣṇa's descents or *avatāras*. Thus, discourses on Śrī Caitanya, who is believed to be a special descent of Kṛṣṇa, are also included in the practice of Kṛṣṇa-kathā.

One might expect amateur theologians like Kanupriya Goswami to lack the philosophical sophistication of their counterparts in the West who were trained in the monasteries and great universities of Europe and the *madrasas* of Northen Africa and the Middle East. Just as the great Christian, Jewish, and Muslim theologians drew heavily upon Greek (Plato, Aristotle, etc.) and Roman philosophers (Plotinus, etc.), Hindu theologians had a rich inheritance of traditional Sanskrit learning and philosophical reflection to draw upon. Thus, when discussing epistemology and when framing valid syllogisms, writers like Kanupriya could draw upon the discussions of the schools of the ancient logicians (Naiyāyikas) and Vedāntins (those who dealt most directly with the Upaniṣadic texts), as he does, for instance, in the opening sections of his book, *A Small Piece of the Mystery of Bhakti.*[14] When discussing and applying hermeneutics to various verses of the *Upaniṣads* and the *Bhāgavata Purāṇa* such writers could also turn to techniques developed in the early school of Hindu philosophy called Mīmāṃsā to aid in the interpretation of Vedic texts. When discussing aesthetics, there was the rich tradition of Sanskrit aesthetics stretching back a thousand and a half years to draw on, especially relating to the aesthetic experience (*rasa*, aesthetic rapture). It is not even necessary for Kanupriya to be aware of the ultimate sources of or histories of the ideas and methods he uses to be able to apply them properly to the problems at hand. Three thousand years of unbroken and self-reflexive tradition come to the aid of writers like Kanupriya Goswami much like that extra pair of arms so often included in the iconic images of Viṣṇu.

Kanupriya Goswami follows certain conventions in presenting his theology. Perhaps the most noticeable is that of rigorous citation of scriptural sources or supporting texts for just about everything he says. This is considered the highest form of theological discourse in the Caitanya tradition. Thus, Kanupriya Goswami's works look like long garlands of verses which he has strung together in particular ways and orders in order to make the points he wants to make. The present work is a fine example of that sort of procedure. The primary sources for his citations are naturally the texts considered authoritative for the Caitanya tradition. This amounts primarily to the *Bhāgavata Purāṇa*, the *Bhagavad-gītā*, and the *Caitanya-caritāmṛtra* of Kṛṣṇadāsa Kavirāja (16th-17th cents. C.E.). Occasionally, other highly respected texts are referred to: the *Sandarbhas* of Śrī Jīva Gosvāmin or a commentary on the *Bhāgavata* or perhaps even an Upaniṣadic passage or two. One of the delightful traits of Kanupriya's writing arises from the way he sometimes surprises one with the citations he uses. There are certain well trodden paths through the dense forest of Caitanya Vaiṣṇava doctrine and scripture. Once one is familiar with those commonly taken paths one can almost predict which verses and passages will be cited next. Kanupriya Goswami often manages to avoid those well-beaten trails and blazes his own new trails through the dense woods. Though he

[14]Kanupriya Goswami, *A Small Piece of the Mystery of Bhakti* (*Śrī Śrī Bhakti Rahasya Kaṇikā*), 1-4.

was "untutored" in the usual sense of having a secular education, his knowledge of the Vaiṣṇava texts seems to have been enormous. His books, therefore, have a quality of newness or freshness about them when viewed against the backdrop of other Caitanya Vaiṣṇava writings in Bengali in the Twentieth Century.

Kanupriya Goswami seems to have in many respects excelled in what some scholars of religion have called the religious or theological imagination. According to Mary Farrell Bednarowski, a scholar of modern American religions:

> I define the theological imagination as a creative human capacity—and an inclination—to formulate meaning systems, models of the universe, by which men and women are able to orient and interpret their lives. Broadly, the task of the theological imagination is twofold: to articulate an understanding of our circumstances as human persons in the world, including our relationship to whatever power orders the world, and to formulate the proper response to these circumstances. The constructs—the meaning systems—that emerge from the creative work of the theological imagination must have the capacity to touch the heart as well as to compel the intellect and to suggest ways of being in the world.[15]

This nicely characterizes Kanupriya's work and its reception in his projected audience, which was made up of educated, socially conservative or traditional Bengali men and women. He was in high demand as a speaker and lecturer during his later days.

In the case of Kanupriya Goswami and others like him who write within strongly traditional systems, the meaning systems with which they work are inherited from the earlier writers of those traditions, that is in Kanupriya's case, primarily the Gosvāmins of Vṛndāvana (16th cent.) and a select group of interpreters of the tradition who lived between then and Kanupriya's time. Thus, in the case of Kanupriya Goswami and other Caitanya Vaiṣṇava writers in the twentieth century, we must focus on what may be called the "dialectic" of the theological imagination, that is, those conversations

[15]Mary Farrell Bednarowski, *New Religions: the Theological Imagination in America*, 1. (Bloomington: Indiana University Press, 1989)

or dialogues between them as members of the modern world and as heirs to the theological imaginations of the previous generations of their tradition. The belief that the meaning system of a given tradition does not change is, of course, an illusion that can only be maintained by various interpretive strategies or by not examining it very closely. This illusion is fostered by that same procedure that is so highly regarded in traditional forms of religious discourse, the periodic and faithful reciting of scriptural sources as evidence for one's views. The presence of scriptural citations gives the reader the impression that the system has remained the same as it has always been when in actuality it has been altered, sometimes subtly and sometimes quite dramatically. Thus, the theological imagination finds its most creative play in the reinterpretation for modern audiences of those citations from scripture.

To give an example, Śrī Kanupriya plays with the concept of *nirguṇa*, which means "without quality." Quality-less or thread-less is the way certain Hindu traditions describe the distinctive nature of the absolute. These are generally non-dualistic schools in which the absolute is regarded as beyond all plurality, variegation, partiality, change and differentiation. To have quality or "threads" is to be changeable and divided between substrate or qualified and quality. This also implies, however, that the quality-less absolute is impersonal, inactive, undifferentiated, unevolving. Such a conception of the absolute is also recognized in Caitanya Vaiṣṇavism as Brahman, but it is considered the lowest or least defined manifestation of absolute deity. Deity may be manifest as just consciousness (awareness) and eternal being without any manifestation of its divine traits or powers. This unqualified manifestation of deity is behind the quality-less absolute of the non-dualistic schools and is usually what is meant by *nirguṇa*. In these non-dualistic schools, along with the idea that the absolute is without quality goes the idea that any manifestation of deity that has qualities or powers is a lower, less elevated manifestation of the absolute. Kanupriya Goswami, however, reverses this order and to do so takes "without quality," not as absence of any quality whatsoever, but only as absence of the three material qualites or threads: transparency or clarity (*sattva*), translucence (*rajas*), and opaqueness (*tamas*). One ancient and important line of Hindu thinking called Sāṅkhya teaches all things in the world are made of various combinations of these three qualitites or threads and thus for something to be beyond the world, transcendent, it must be free of these threads. So instead of absolute quality-ness Kanupriya takes *nirguṇa* to mean freedom from the material qualities, but not absent of quality per se. The absolute may still have qualities, qualities not connected in any way to the three qualities that make up the material or mundane world. Thus, the absolute may indeed be endowed with powers and traits, may still be personal and yet still be absolute. With this understanding in mind, I have often translated *nirguṇa* as threadless, that is, not composed of the three threads, that are thought, in various mixtures or weaves, to make up the manifest things of this world.

Kanupriya Goswami's work contains a number of creative flourishes like the one described above and it is this quality of his reflection on traditional Caitanya Vaiṣṇava theology that made his writing and speaking engagements so popular during his active days and that makes his work in general an interesting study for those who want to try to understand modern, mainstream Caitanya Vaiṣṇavism.

The Theologies of Caitanya Vaiṣṇavism

There is no one, commonly accepted, systematic theology in Caitanya Vaiṣṇavism. Theology has tended to vary with almost every writer on the subject. Moreoever, Caitanya Vaiṣṇavism has not founded any schools or institutions devoted to the study and development of a comprehensive and systematic theology. Still, though there are many different systems of theology, there is nevertheless an overlapping of much theological terminology and ideology in them. The only way to survey reliably the various systems of Caitanya Vaiṣṇava theology is to "do the numbers," so to speak, that is, to count up from one, discussing for each number the system or systems of theology to which it corresponds. Some numbers indeed point to several theological systems and some numbers may have no theological systemization associated with it. Numbering important ideas, elements, or categories of things is an ancient practice dating back to Vedic times (2nd millennium BCE) in India. Since then just about every philosophical school or religious tradition at some point has tried to summarize its views by numbering all the important or essential elements of its philosophy or belief system.

In this respect, Caitanya Vaiṣṇavism is no different. The word "theology" in this discussion refers primarily to a discussion or description of the nature of deity or deities in a specific religious tradition. Other related topics often included in theological discussions in the West—such as epistemology, cosmogony, cosmology, ethics, eschatology, soteriology, theodicy, and so forth—are also present, in various ways and to varying degrees, sometimes explicitly and sometimes implicitly, in these theologies.

Let us begin, then, with the number one. One points to the most fundamental belief in Caitanya Vaiṣṇavism, that there is but one absolute truth, one without a second,[16] and that absolute truth, though possessing numerous names, is known most commonly as Kṛṣṇa.[17] Kṛṣṇa is regarded as the supreme person, but a person unlike any other we ordinarily think of as persons. Persons are normally thought of as individuals, that is, indivisible. Kṛṣṇa, however, is the supreme dividual;[18] that is, he is infinitely divisible. One might say that his greatest divisibilty is what makes him the supreme being. All other beings, persons and things, divine and ordinary are in various diverse ways his partial manifestations. All are included, even us.[19] Moreover, he can divide himself into all the other gods and all the other beings and yet still remain full and complete in himself.[20]

---

[16] *Bhāgavata Purāṇa*, 1.2.11: वदन्ति तत्तत्त्वविदस्तत्त्वं यज्ज्ञानमद्वयम्, "Those who know it call the truth that which is non-dual consciousness."

[17] *Bhāg.*, 1.3.28: कृष्णस्तु भगवान् स्वयम्, "But, Kṛṣṇa is the supreme person (Bhagavān) himself." And, *Brahma-saṃhitā*, 5.1:

> ईश्वर: परम: कृष्ण: सच्चिदानन्दविग्रह:।
> अनादिरादिर्गोविन्द: सर्वकारणकारणम्॥

"The supreme controller is Kṛṣṇa whose form is being, consciousness, and bliss. He is beginningless, the beginning, Govinda, the cause of all causes."

[18] The idea of a "dividual" is one that I owe to Dr. McKim Marriott's interesting anthropological work on Indian society.

[19] *Brahma-saṃhitā*, 5.57:

> यस्यैकनि:श्वसितकालमवलम्ब्य
> जीवन्ति लोमविलजा जगदण्डनाथा:।
> विष्णुर्महान् स इह यस्य कलाविशेषो
> गोविन्दमादिपुरुषं तमहं भजामि॥

"The lords of the universes which are born from the pores of his bodily hair live only as long as one breath of Great Viṣṇu and yet he is but a part of that Govinda [Kṛṣṇa]. I honor him, Govinda, the original person."

[20] From an invocation found in the Upaniṣads, especially the famous invocation of

The idea of a composite person goes back to very ancient times in India. One can see it in the thousand-headed giant called Puruṣa of the Ṛg Vedic creation myth (10.90). Those thousand heads, and eyes and feet are all beings viewed as part of one super-being. Perhaps, it is also prefigured in the pronounced tendency, in the Ṛg Vedic hymns, of praising, in almost the exact same words, one deity at a time, one deity after another, implying thereby that they are all ultimately indistinguishable or the same, a tendency for which Max Muller coined the term henotheism.[21] The composite person combines with the deeply rooted tendency in India to create hierarchies. Only what emerges are rather peculiar hierarchies, hierarchies in which the fullest being, the being that is the most divisible and complex, that is, from another perspective, the most inclusive, stands at the top. That person, according to Caitanya Vaiṣṇavism, is Śrī Kṛṣṇa. Other traditions may fill that place with some other being: Śiva, or Śakti (the Goddess), or Brahman. The being that can suffer no further division, the "atom," so to speak, is at the bottom of the hierarchy. It is the least complete being, the most fragmentary, the in-dividual, the being that can do only very limited things, the being that only gains meaningful significance by participating (*bhakti* as participation) in a more complete being. This leads occasionally to some curious and clumsy language. Kṛṣṇa's various forms are sometimes classified as full (*pūrṇa*), fuller (*pūrṇatara*), and fullest (*pūrṇatama*) in a kind of calculus of qualities that finds

---

the *Īśopaniṣad:*

> ॐ पूर्णमदः पूर्णमिदं पूर्णात्पूर्णमुदच्यते।
> पूर्णस्य पूर्णमादाय पूर्णमेवावशिष्यते॥

> "That world is full; this world is full.
> From the full the full arises.
> Removing the full from the full,
> The full itself remains."

[21]Another influential hymn of the Ṛg Veda envisions one supreme deity as described by different poets in different ways and with different names. In the *Asya Vāmasya Hymn* (Ṛg, 1.164) it is said:

> इन्द्रं मित्रं वरुणमग्निमाहुरथो दिव्यः स सुपर्णो गरुत्मान्।
> एकं सद्विप्रा बहुदा वदन्त्यग्निं यमं मातरिश्वानाहुः॥

"They call him Indra, Mitra, Varuṇa, Agni. Then he is the bird of the heavens possessing wings. Being one, poets describe him in many ways. They call him Agni, Yama, and Mātariśvān.

the Kṛṣṇa of Vraja, as opposed to the Kṛṣṇa of Mathurā or Dvārakā, at the top of the fullness scale.[22] The justification for talking about fullness and its gradations is perhaps to be found in the idea that the distinction between the various grades is a matter of manifestation, not of absence. All the qualities are fully present in all three forms, but some of those qualities, though present, are not manifested or actualized in the full and fuller forms. The form in which all qualities are manifested is the fullest form.

The other numbers of theological significance in Caitanya Vaiṣṇavism involve for the most part an unpacking of this all-inclusive number one, the infinitely divisible and inexhaustible one which contains all others. The idea of two, for instance, is a recognition of the one as fundamentally divisible into power (*śakti*) and the possessor of power (*śaktimān*). Here, too, gender is introduced since in India power, *śakti*, is understood as a feminine attribute because the grammatical gender of the word *śakti* is feminine. The possessor of power is male and the power is female. Thus, the two are often in this tradition visualized as Kṛṣṇa and his female consort or lover Rādhikā. Without his power, Kṛṣṇa would be incapacitated, ineffectual. It is the power that gives him not only his godly might, but also distinguishes him as a personal being with personal traits known technically in the tradition as Bhagavān, the fortunate one or supreme person, from the other widely accepted conception of the absolute, impersonal Brahman. Both are understood to be one

---

[22]Rūpa Gosvāmin, *Bhakti-rasāmṛta-sindhu* (2.1.220-3):

नित्यगुणो वनमाली यदपि शिखामणिरखिलनेतृणाम्।
भक्तापेक्षिकमस्य त्रिविधत्वं लिख्यते तदपि॥
हरिः पूर्णतमः पूर्णतरः पूर्ण इति त्रिधा।
श्रेष्ठमध्यादिभिः शब्दैर्नाट्ये यः परिपठ्यते॥
प्रकाशिताअखिलगुणः स्मृतः पूर्णतमो बुधैः।
असर्वव्यञ्जकः पूर्णतरः पूर्णो ऽल्पदर्शकः॥
कृष्णस्य पूर्णतमता व्यक्ताभूद्गोकुलान्तरे।
पूर्णता पूर्णतरता द्वारकामथुरादिषु॥

"Though forest-garlanded Kṛṣṇa, whose qualities are eternal, is the crown-jewel of heros, his threefold nature, which depends on his different *bhaktas*, is written about. Hari [Kṛṣṇa] is threefold: fullest, fuller, and full, which corresponds to the words 'best,' 'middling,' and so forth in the field of drama. The one in whom all qualities are manifest is recollected as the fullest by the wise. The one in whom all qualities are not revealed is fuller and the full is the one in whom only a few are shown. Kṛṣṇa's fullest state is manifested in Gokula [Vraja] and his full and fuller states in Dvārakā and Mathurā, respectively."

and the same absolute truth, but Brahman is a vision of the absolute in which the power, though fully present, is either not grasped by the perceiver, because of some inadequacy in the perceiver, or is not manifested or expressed in the absolute.[23] Thus, it is the manifestation or expression of that power that reveals itself in the absolute personal dimensions and traits. The expression of that power makes impersonal Brahman into personal Bhagavān.[24]

On the other hand, the power does not, cannot exist apart from its possessor for without the guidance, control and grounding of that possessor it would be chaotic, uncontrolled, and dangerous, incapable of creating an ordered cosmos. Thus, the two are intimately connected with each other, indeed inseparable, and it is this

---

[23]Śrī Jīva Gosvāmin, *Bhagavat-sandarbha*, para 2: तदेकमेवाखण्डानन्दस्वरूपं तत्त्वं थुत्कृतपारमेष्ठ्यादिकानन्दसमुदयानां परमहंसानां साधनवशात्तादात्म्यमापन्ने सत्यामपि तदीयस्वरूपशक्तिवैचित्र्यां तद्ग्रहणासामर्थ्ये चेतसि यथा सामान्यतो लक्षितं तथैव स्फुरद्वा तद्वदेवाविविक्तशक्तिशक्तिमत्ताभेदतया प्रतिपाद्यमानं वा ब्रह्मेति शब्द्यते, "That one truth whose essence is unbroken bliss, appearing as characterized in a generic way in minds that are incapable of grasping the variegatedness of its essential power (*svarūpa-śakti*), though such variegatedness indeed exists, those minds belonging to *parama-haṃsas* ("the highest geese," that is, those aspirants who have mastered the distinction between the permanent and the impermanent) who through their practice have achieved oneness with that truth and who have rejected the [lesser] pleasures of the demiurge and others, or, that truth being resorted to by them in that way without clearly discerning the difference between the power and the possessor of power, is called Brahman." To put it briefly and succinctly, Brahman is the absolute truth as experienced by those whose minds are not capable of experiencing the variegatedness of that truth's essential power or in which the difference between the power and the possessor of power in that truth is not expressed or manifest.

[24]ibid., अथ तदेकं तत्त्वं स्वरूपभूतयैव शक्त्या कमपि विशेषं धर्तुं परासामपि शक्तीनां मूलाश्रयरूपं तदनुभवानन्दसन्दोहान्तर्भाविततादृशब्रह्मानन्दानां भागवतपरमहंसानां तथानुभवैकसाधकतमतदीयस्वरूपानन्दशक्तिविशेषात्मकभक्तिभावितेष्वन्तर्बहिरपीन्द्रियेषु परिस्फुरद्वा तद्वदेव विविक्ततादृशशक्तिशक्तिमत्ताभेदेन प्रतिपाद्यमानं वा भगवानिति शब्द्यते।, "Thus, to assume some distinction through its essential power, that one truth, which is the fundamental support of the higher powers, either appears in the internal and external senses, that have been infused with *bhakti*, a particular power consisting of his essential joy and the single most effective means of causing perception of him, those senses belonging to the *parama-haṃsas* who are his votaries and for whom the joy of Brahman has been subsumed into the joy of perceiving him, or, that truth is resorted to in that way with a clearly distinguished differentiation between that sort of power and the possessor of power. It is then called Bhagavān." In other words, that one truth is called Bhagavān when it appears with distinction in the senses of *bhaktas* (votaries) for whom the joy of Brahman has been subsumed in the joy of perceiving Bhagavān or when it is approached in such a way that the difference between power and possessor of power is clearly distinguished.

that points to the relationship characteristic of the Vedantic expression of this school, the relationship of difference-in-non-difference (*bhedābheda*). So under this perspective, the absolute turns out to be a dual-deity, a male and female deity, sometimes imagined in tight embrace, each having a separate realm of influence, and thus separable from the other and yet inseparable from the other as well. It is this peculiar relationship of separable inseparability or inseparable separability that is described by one of the leading theologians of the school as "unthinkable (*acintya*) difference and non-difference.[25]

The number three points to some interesting features of the absolute as Caitanya Vaiṣṇavas conceive of it. The three major focii of service, worship and contemplation in the tradition are the divine loving couple (the *yugala-kiśora*) already discussed above as the dual-godhead, the power and possessor of power, or Śrī Rādhā and Kṛṣṇa, and the special manifestation of deity embodied in the founder of the tradition, Śrī Caitanya or Śrī Gaurāṅga (the golden-limbed one). If the first two already represent the whole of godhead where does this third one come from? Śrī Gaurāṅga represents the first two joined in one form. This understanding of the nature of the founder of the tradition arose from theological reflections on him by some of his early and close followers who grappled with understanding his actions, utterings, and ecstacies. An important verse encapsulates this view very nicely:

> The transformed love of Rādhā and Kṛṣṇa is the pleasure-giving power. Because of it, though they are one they appeared previously on earth in different bodies. Now, those two have become one and appeared as Caitanya. I bow down to that essential form of Kṛṣṇa decorated with the feelings and colorings of Rādhā.[26]

---

[25]Śrī Jīva Gosvāmin, *Sarva-saṃvādinī*, p 22 (Puridāsa ed.) on para. 6 (p. 18) of the *Bhagavat-sandarbha* (Śāstrī ed.): तस्मात्स्वरूपादभिन्नत्वेन चिन्तयितुमशक्यत्वाद्भेद:, भिन्नत्वेन चिन्तयितुमशक्यत्वादभेदश्च प्रतीयत इति शक्तिशक्तिमतोर्भेदाभेदावेवाङ्गीकृतौ, तौ चाचिन्त्याविति।, "Therefore, difference is recognized because of being unable to conceive of its [power's] being non-different from the essential nature, and non-difference is recognized because of being unable to conceive of it as different from the essential nature. Thus, difference and non-difference of power and its possessor are both accepted, and those together are inconceivable."

[26]Kṛṣṇadāsa Kavirāja, *Caitanya-caritāmṛta*, verse 5:

Śrī Caitanya represents, then, the two, Rādhā and Kṛṣṇa, joined together in love, without negating or sublating either of them, without their being lost in the oneness of their union. Thus, the theological perspective has shifted dramatically in the move from two theological categories to three. In the twofold system the focus is primarily metaphysical, that is, concerned with answering the question: what aspects of the divine are there? In the threefold system it becomes fundamentally relational or perhaps better, aesthetic, that is, concerned with answering the question: how are those aspects of the divine actively related to each other? Apart from speaking to a concern for the nature of the relationship between power and its possessor, since we are all in some way part of that divine reality, it registers a concern for understanding our own parts, however small, in the divine unfoldment or play. So Śrī Caitanya represents the love, technically called *preman*, that draws and holds the power and the possessor of power together. All other beings are similarly bound up in this divine love. the divine embrace, in various ways.

Śrī Caitanya is thus regarded as revealing aspects of that divine love that have never been revealed before, or at least not for a very long time. Though that love has many forms and expressions the highest or most elevated expression is considered erotic or romantic love. That is the kind that exists between Kṛṣṇa and his power Rādhā and that is the kind Śrī Caitanya revealed the inner workings of, according to his close companions. One of those close companions, Śrī Rūpa Gosvāmin, expresses this in an important verse:

> May he who descended out of compassion in the Age of Kali in order to offer the good fortune of his own *bhakti*, comprised of incandescent pleasure (*ujjvala-rasa*),[27] which

---

> राधाकृष्णप्रणयविकृतिर्ह्लादिनी शक्तिरस्माद्
> एकात्मानावपि भुवि पुरा देहभेदं गतौ तौ।
> चैतन्याख्यं प्रकटमधुना तद्द्वयं चैक्यमाप्तं
> राधाभावद्युतिसुबलितं नौमि कृष्णस्वरूपम्॥

Another way of reading this verse separates Rādhā from Kṛṣṇa in the first compound word of the first quarter. Thus one gets: "Rādhā is the transformed love of Kṛṣṇa, the pleasure-giving power, from which, though they are one ... ." This verse is said to be from the notebook of Svarūpa Dāmodara, one of Śrī Caitanya's intimate companions during the last period of his life at Purī in Orissa.

[27] The "enflaming relish." This is one of the many names of the erotic form of divine love when tasted or relished in the context of literary or artistic expressions

> had not been offered for a long time—may that Hari, who is illuminated by beautiful rays of gold, the Son of Śacī, always appear in the caves of your hearts.[28]

Śrī Caitanya is regarded as the embodiment of the love of Rādhā and Kṛṣṇa for each other. The tradition recognizes three areas of discovery in this loving relationship the details of which were revealed during the descent or *avatāra* of Śrī Caitanya. Those three areas of revelation are presented in another verse attributed to Caitanya's close companion, Svarūpa Dāmodara, and again cited in the *Immortal Acts of Śrī Caitanya* (*Caitanya-caritāmṛta*) of Kṛṣṇadāsa Kavirāja:

> What is the nature of the greatness of Śrī Rādhā's love? Or, what is my astonishing sweetness, which she tastes, like? Or, what is the joy she feels from perceiving me like? Out of an intense desire to know these things, the moon Hari, putting on her feelings, was born in the ocean of the womb of Śacī.[29]

Rādhā, as the personal embodiment of his power (*śakti*), or more specifically of his essential or internal power (*svarūpa-śakti*), or even more specifically of his pleasure-giving power (*hlādinī-śakti*) which is the core of that power, is considered the finest example or model of love for Kṛṣṇa, the possessor of power. Understanding the nature of her love for Kṛṣṇa is considered extremely important and

---

or as part of religious practice or cultivation. *Madhura-rasa* or "the sweet relish" is another name for the same.

[28]Śrī Rūpa Gosvāmin, *Vidagdha-mādhava*, verse 2:

> अनर्पितचरीं चिरात्करुणयावतीर्णो कलौ
> समर्पितुमुन्नतोज्ज्वलरसां स्वभक्तिश्रियम्।
> हरिः पुरटसुन्दरद्युतिकदम्बसन्दीपितः
> सदा हृदयकन्दरे स्फुरतु वः शचीनन्दनः॥

[29]Cc., 1.1.6:

> श्रीराधायाः प्रणयमहिमा कीदृशो वानयैवा-
> स्वाद्यो येनाद्भुतमधुरिमा कीदृशो वा मदीयः।
> सौख्यं चास्या मदनभवतः कीदृशं वेति लोभाद्
> तद्भावाढ्यः समजनि शचीगर्भसिन्धौ हरीन्दुः॥

uplifting by those in the tradition. But love is a two-way street and as such the question soon arises: what is it about Kṛṣṇa that draws Rādhā's love to him so intensely? Kṛṣṇa's attractiveness or sweetness is known only to those who know him best. Not even he can know this about himself. Thus, he seeks to see himself through the eyes of the one who knows him and loves him the best, Rādhā. The final inquiry into the nature of Rādhā's love concerns the joy or pleasure she experiences because of it and that, too, captures Kṛṣṇa's interest. Thus, Śrī Caitanya joined the loving couple (Rādha and Kṛṣṇa) in the pantheon, making it a triad, as a result of the three wishes or desires of Kṛṣṇa.

Śrī Caitanya is primarily understood, then, by the tradition he founded or rather that crystallized around him as a descent of Kṛṣṇa himself trying to discover what his own power and greatest lover-devotee Rādhā experiences loving him. To do this he borrows or assumes her feelings and her colorings or physical beauty. Here again we find that quality of "dividuality" that was noted in the discussion of the theology of one. Apparently, the feelings and colorings and probably other traits are detachable and can be taken or borrowed. As we shall see when we discuss the theology of fives what remains of a person after some of those traits are borrowed can continue on and play a role in the theology as well. This vision of Śrī Caitanya was developed in part out of reflection on the complex and subtle nuances of erotic love found in Sanskrit aesthetics and literature, out of ambient Tantric ideas in those days about the gendered nature of reality and the absolute, and out of inferences based on observations of the ecstatic trances and utterings of Śrī Caitanya himself.

This is one of the theologies of three found in the Caitanya tradition. Another is offered by the author of this book, Śrī Kanupriya Goswami. It is the theology of another three: Bhagavān, the supreme person; *bhakta*, the "part-taker" or participant (sometimes called the devotee, all living beings possessing this potential); and *bhakti* or the power or state of participation. These three form a single entity: the one who possesses parts (*bhaga-vat*), the part (*bhakta*), and the relationship between them that glues them together (*bhakti*). All of these words may all have come from the same Sanskrit root $\sqrt{bhaj}$ meaning "to divide, to distribute, to participate, to share." This triad presents in a sense a complete picture of reality. There is the whole, represented by Bhagavān (part or share possessor), and the parts (*bhaga* or *bhakta*), represented by the *bhakta*, and the relationship between them. The parts are separable but not separate. The metaphor usually supplied in this case is that of the fire and its sparks. The fire is the source of and indeed is composed of many tiny sparks. The sparks and fire are the same stuff, differing only in the degree of power and light each has. The relationship of participation or *bhakti* is most fully manifest in love or *preman*. *Preman* is considered the fullest expression of *bhakti*. It is defined as the essence of the consciousness-ehancing power inseparably joined with the essence of the pleasure-giving power.[30] This theology is thus fully relational and highlights an intimacy, indeed an interpenetration between deity and its tiny parts or aspects. What interferes with this relationship, it turns out, is forgetfulness (*vismaraṇa*) on the part of the parts, the forgetfulness, that is, of the part's participation in the whole. The process of restoring this relationship is a process of anamnesis, remembering. The relationship is regarded as eternal and unaltered, regardless of whether it is remembered or not. This theology will be more fully unpacked by the author of this book with special emphasis on how the process of anamnesis is initiated (association with the holy) according to the Caitanya Vaiṣṇava tradition.

In Caitanya Vaiṣṇavism there are theologies of four, five, six, seven, eight, nine, and ten, but full discussions of those should perhaps be reserved for another occasion. Since the theology of the author of this book is a theology of three, as briefly outlined above, this might be a good place to discontinue our discussion of Caitanyite theology. To continue would increase unnecessarily the size and ponderousness of this introduction. Let us instead give just a brief summary of some of the other theologies of number.

A theology of four calls attention to the relationship between Śrī Kṛṣṇa (the possessor of power) and his three powers (aspects of the one power mentioned earlier): the internal power (*antaraṅga-śakti*, his intimate realm), the external power (*bahiraṅga-śakti*, the phenomenal realm), and the liminal or marginal power (*taṭastha-śakti*, the living beings).[31]

A theology of five discusses the five *tattvas*, truths or aspects

[30] ह्लादिनीसारसमवेतसंवित्साररूपेति, Baladeva, *Siddhāntaratnaḥ*, 1.40.

[31] This is based on a hint given in the *Svetāśvatara Upaniṣad* (6.8):

(*pañca-tattva*), of Caitanya's descent and their relationships: Mahāprabhu Śrī Kṛṣṇacaitanya (Kṛṣṇa as his own *bhakta*), Nityānanda Prabhu (the essential form of the *bhakta*), Advaita Prabhu (descent as a *bhakta*), Gadādhara Paṇḍita (the power of the *bhakta*) and Śrīvāsa (the *bhakta*).[32]

Another theology of five focuses on a discussion of the five *rasas* or emotional experiences enjoyed in the five relationships that the tradition believes are possible between the *bhakta* and Śrī Kṛṣṇa.[33]

परास्य शक्तिर्विविधैव श्रूयते।
स्वाभाविकी ज्ञानबलक्रिया

"The higher power of this one (the supreme person) is heard to be manifold. It is inherent [i.e., natural to him] and features knowledge, strength, and activity."

Another passage from the *Viṣṇu Purāṇa* (6.7.61) also describes a threefold division of power:

विष्णुशक्तिः परा प्रोक्ता क्षेत्रज्ञाख्या तथापरा।
अविद्याकर्मसंज्ञान्या तृतीया शक्तिरिष्यते॥

"The power of Viṣṇu is said to be the "higher," another called the knower of the field and yet a third power, called ignorance and action, is acknowledged."

This is summarized by Jīva Gosvāmin in his *Bhagavat-sandarbha* (para. 16): शक्तिश्च सा त्रिधा—अन्तरङ्गा बहिरङ्गा तटस्था च, "And that power is threefold: internal, external, and marginal."

[32]From a verse found in the *Caitanya-caritāmṛta* of Kṛṣṇadāsa Kavirāja (1.1.14):

पञ्चतत्त्वात्मकं कृष्णं भक्तरूपस्वरूपकम्।
भक्तावतारं भक्ताख्यं नमामि भक्तशक्तिकम्॥

"I bow to Kṛṣṇa who has five aspects: him as his own *bhakta*, the essence or true form of the *bhakta*, the descent of the *bhakta*, the *bhakta* and the power of the *bhakta*." This in turn is based on a passage from Kavikarṇapūra's (16th century) *Gaura-gaṇoddeśa-dīpikā* (*Light on the Identification of the Followers of Gaura*), 6:

यद्वत्पुरा कृष्णचन्द्रः पञ्चतत्त्वात्मकोऽपि सन्।
यातः प्रकटतां तद्वद्गौरः प्रकटतामियात्॥

"As previously the moonlike Kṛṣṇa, though composed of five principles, appeared, so does Gaura (Caitanya) now appear." Dr. Radhagovinda Nath in his Bengali commentary on this verse in his edition of the *Immortal Acts of Caitanya* (*Caitanya-caritāmṛta*), writes: "Śrī Kṛṣṇa, in addition to his own true form, manifests himself by the power of his desire in four other forms: his *vilāsa* or sport form, his descent (*avatāra*) form, his *bhakta* form, and his power (*śakti*) form."

[33]Based on a verse from the *Bhakti-rasāmṛta-sindhu* (*Ocean of the Nectar of the Rasas of Bhakti*) by Rūpa Gosvāmin:

शुद्धा प्रीतिस्तथा सख्यं वात्सल्यं प्रियतेत्यसौ।
स्वपरार्थ्यैव सा मुख्या पुनः पञ्चविधा भवेत्॥

"That [kṛṣṇa-rati] is simple [contemplative appreciation], affection [a servant's loyalty and love], friendship, parental love, and erotic love. Though self-promoting or other-promoting, that main [form of rati] is again fivefold."

A different theology of five has been developed by an important later (17th cent.) teacher of the tradition, Rādhādāmodara, in a work called the *Vedānta-syamantaka* (*Jewel of Vedic Conclusion*). The five categories of theological reflection in that text are: God, the living being, nature, time, and action.[34] Śrī Jīva Gosvāmin gives a theology of six in the *Saṭ-sandarbha* (*Six Treatises*) in which he devotes a separare treatise to each of the six following topics: fundamental principles or truths (*tattva*, i.e. the means gaining valid knowledge, the scriptural sources of the tradition, etc.); the supreme person (*bhagavat*); the Highest Self (*paramātman*, the supreme person in relation to the manifest world and its living beings); Kṛṣṇa (the highest object of worship); *bhakti* (the process of worship); and finally divine love (*prīti*, the ultimate goal or end of worship).

A theology of seven is suggested by the first verse of a set of eight teaching verses that are considered in the Caitanya tradition to have been composed by Śrī Caitanya himself. These teaching verses are called collectively the *Śikṣāṣṭaka* or the *Octave of Instruction*. They appear scattered throughout the collection of Vaiṣṇava poetry assembled by Rūpa Gosvāmin called the *Padyāvalī* (*Garland of Verses*). In the case of each of the verses the author is identified as Śrī Bhagavān, which was Rūpa's way of referring to Śrī Caitanya. The verse that is the source of this theological septet is the twenty-second verse of Rūpa's collection:

> Cleansing the mirror of the mind,
> Extinguishing the great forest fire
> Of mundane existence, spreading
> Moonlight on the white lotus, highest good,
> Bringing to life the wife of knowledge,
> Increasing the ocean of bliss,
> Causing one to taste full ambrosia
> At every step, bathing the whole self,
> This singing in praise of Kṛṣṇa
> Is supremely victorious![35]

---

[34]Summarized in the following statement (chap. 2): अथ प्रमेयाणि निर्णीयन्ते। तानि च पञ्चधा ईश्वरजीवप्रकृतिकालकर्मभेदात्।, "Now the objects of valid knowledge are determined and they are five: God, the living being, nature, time and action." Edited and translated into Hindi by Bālakṛṣṇa Gosvāmī. See the bibliography.

[35]Śrī Caitanya, *Śikṣāṣṭaka* 1; Rūpa Gosvāmin, comp., *Padāvalī*, 22:

The seven adjectives in the verse of "singing in praise of Kṛṣṇa" (*Śrī Kṛṣṇa-saṅkīrtana*) have been considered by members of the tradition as significant indications of important theological teachings, specially in relationship to the central practice of public performance of singing songs in praise of Kṛṣṇa. Even the order in which the adjectives are placed is considered significant. The first has to do with the belief that the singing in praise brings about the purification of the mind of the practitioners. The mind is compared with a dirty or dusty mirror and the singing cleanses that mirror allowing the participant to perceive things more clearly. The second provides an image of what the participant will perceive once his mind-mirror becomes cleaner. The world is like a raging forest fire which is being extinguished by the same force that is cleaning the participant's mind, the singing in praise of Kṛṣṇa. In other words, the practitioner's suffering in worldly existence is expected to decline. The third adjective provides the metaphor of the spreading of the cooling rays of the moon, causing a white lotus, which stands for our highest good, to blossom. To put it differently, the singing in praise causes our fortunes to change and our welfare to improve.

The fourth adjective gives us the image of bringing back to life the wife of knowledge or wisdom. Here knowledge or wisdom is envisioned as a wife (or a husband, I suppose) suggesting that one's knowledge is intimately connected and always with one. Its moribund state is reversed by the singing in praise. In other words, one gains some special kind of knowledge or awareness by participating in the practice. Next, the ocean of joy or bliss is increased. That is to say, the singing in praise of Kṛṣṇa not only brings about one's own joy, but also that of others, those who hear (whether one is human or animal or plant, as we shall see). This leads to one's tasting the fullness of ambrosia at every moment. Here, ambrosia is important for it means more than joy. It also mean immortality (*amṛta*). One thus gains immortality by participation in singing in praise. Finally, the whole self is bathed or cleansed. Cleansed from what? From one's own past *karma*, or the fruit of one's past actions, whether

---

चेतोदर्पणमार्जनं भवमहादावाग्निनिर्वापनं
श्रेय:कैरवचन्द्रिकावितरणं विद्यावधूजीवनम्।
आनन्दाम्बुधिवर्धनं प्रतिपदं पूर्णामृतास्वादनं
सर्वात्मस्नपनं परं विजयते श्रीकृष्णसंकीर्तनम्॥

good or bad, which drive the process of reincarnation. One thus becomes free, liberated, and no longer has to take another birth. Thus, we see that in these seven statements we have an overview of the whole process of overcoming our bondage and forgetfulness of Kṛṣṇa and of finding our way into his presence. Along with that a view of the nature of reality and our place in it as understood by the Caitanya tradition is communicated to us. This is theology intimately tied to practice.

A theological octet is suggested by Caitanya's eight verses taken as a whole. Though they appear separately and scattered throughout Rūpa's collection of verses, they were gathered together in the twentieth chapter of Kṛṣṇadāsa Kavirāja's *Immortal Acts of Caitanya* (*Caitanya-caritāmṛta*), apparently in the order that they appeared in in Rūpa's work. Together they build upon the seven teachings contained in the first verse and add a touching emotional and experiential dimension to the process of awakening to one's relationship with Kṛṣṇa. The first verse features the power and centrality of the singing in praise of Kṛṣṇa (*Śrī Kṛṣṇa-saṅkīrtana*) in the Caitanya tradition and dwells on the gradual transformation of the participant into a liberated being. The second verse identifies the source of the power of that practice in the power of the holy name:

> All of your own powers are placed
> In your many names; nor is there
> Any certain time to remember them.
> Though so great is your compassion, o Lord,
> My misfortune is also great,
> Since I feel no passion for them.[36]

This verse gives the fundamental teaching of the holy name, that it is non-different (*abhinna*) from the holy named, possessing all his powers.[37] Nor are there any restrictions on when it may be repeated or sung, unlike with other *mantras* or Vedic chants and

---

[36]Śrī Caitanya, *Śikṣāṣṭaka*, 2:

> नाम्नामकारि बहुधा निजसर्वशक्ति-
> स्तत्रार्पिता नियमित: स्मरणे न काल:।
> एतादृशी तव कृपा भगवन्ममापि
> दुर्दैवमीदृशमिहाजनि नानुराग:॥

[37]The verse usually cited as evidence of this is said to be from the *Padma Purāṇa*:

hymns the repetition or recitation of which is regulated by many rules. Caitanya in the role of the *bhakta* laments his misfortune at not being able to appreciate the great gift of the holy name. This is meant to represent an early stage in the cultivation of divine love (*preman*) as well as an example of the kind of self-examination and criticism that is necessary for effective practice.[38]

The next instruction concerns the proper attitude with which one should approach the practice of singing in praise of Kṛṣṇa. This instruction may be taken either as advice for the neophyte or as an expression of a sense of humility that develops over the course of the practice aimed at cultivating *bhakti*. The verse may be translated:

> By one who regards himself as
> More humble than a blade of grass
> And more tolerant than a tree,
> A giver of respect who expects none,
> Hari is always to be praised.[39]

Arrogance and hubris are regarded as impediments to spiritual cultivation in the Caitanya tradition. On the other hand, humility is considered evidence of advancement in the cultivation of *bhakti*.

> नामचिन्तामणिः कृष्णश्चैतन्यरसविग्रहः।
> पूर्णः शुद्धो नित्यमुक्तोऽभिन्नत्वान्नामनामिनोः॥
>
> "Kṛṣṇa," the embodiment of
> The enjoyment of consciousness,
> Is a thought-jewel, full, pure, ever free,
> Since name and possessor of name.
> Are not different from each other.

A "thought-jewel" (*cintāmaṇi*) is a mythic jewel by which all one's desires are fulfilled, something like a touch-stone.

[38]According to the Caitanya tradition, *bhakti* or *preman* cannot be produced or created. They are eternal, uncreated, and uncaused. One can only prepare oneself to receive them when they are infused into or planted in one. Cultivation here means something like preparing the ground to receive the seed of *bhakti*. When it comes it is a gift. In this sense, it is much like the idea of *śakti-pāta*, the descent of power, in the Kaśmīri Śaivite tradition. There are a number of similarities between the traditions.

[39]ibid., 3:

> तृणादपि सुनिचेन
> तरोरिव सहिष्णुना।
> अमानिना मानदेन
> कीर्तनीयः सदा हरिः॥

The next instruction reveals a change of concerns in the practitioner as a result of engagement in the cultivation of *bhakti* through singing in praise. The common values and attachments drop away and are replaced by a burning desire for *bhakti*. Voiced in the common ideology of the Hindu belief in rebirth, the verse points perhaps beyond it:

> Not wealth, not servants, nor fair poetry
> Do I desire, o lord of the world;
> Just let there be for me, birth after birth,
> Uncaused *bhakti* towards you, my lord.[40]

The verse implies the overcoming of all mundane desires, since even the desire for liberation from the repeating cycle of birth and death in the world is transcended. Uncaused *bhakti* means unmotivated *bhakti*. If the motivations of wealth and servants or progeny do not attract one, what motivation will drive one to *bhakti* besides the desire for *bhakti* itself?

The fifth instruction teaches what the tradition considers to be the eternal and natural position and relationship of the living being with respect to Kṛṣṇa. The word used in this verse is *kiṅkara* which means an insignificant servant or slave. This instruction is another attack on the hubris with which we usually conduct our lives. The verse reads:

> O Son of Nanda, I am your servant,
> Fallen into this vexatious
> Ocean of mundane existence;
> Please consider me like the dust
> Clinging to your lotus-like feet.[41]

To place oneself at someone's feet in India means to place oneself in a position of subordination, submission, or surrender towards that

[40]ibid., 4:

> न धनं न जनं सुन्दरीं कवितां वा जगदिश कामये।
> मम जन्मनि जन्मनीश्वरे भवताद्भक्तिरहैतुकी त्वयि॥

[41]ibid., 5:

> अयि नन्दतनुज किङ्करं पतितं मां विषमे भवाम्बुधौ।
> कृपया तव पादपङ्कजस्थितधूलिसदृशं विचिन्तय॥

person, the feet representing the lowest part of a person. It also suggests intimacy, because to be "at someone's feet" is to be close to that person.

The next instruction is an instruction through exemplification. It expresses the intense longing said to arise in the heart of the *bhakta* at a certain point in their development and also describes some of the outward signs of advancement in the cultivation of *bhakti*, results of the powerful emotional responses it invokes:

> My eyes with flowing streams of tears,
> My face with speech blocked by stammers,
> My body covered with goosebumps,
> When will those be so when I say your name?[42] (6)

The physical symptoms described here are part of a group called the *sāttvika-bhāvas* or states or manifestations of intense inner emotion. The classic list, drawn from the world of dramaturgy, includes eight of them: stupefaction, perspiration, horripilation, cracking of the voice (or stuttering), shuddering, changing bodily color, and fainting.[43] Besides the canonical eight there are others as well such as rolling around on the ground and honking. These are believed to be outward signs of powerful inner emotional turmoil.

The seventh instruction also models a state of mind that arises at an advanced stage in the cultivation of *bhakti*. It might be compared with that famous condition in Christian mysticism called the "dark night of the soul," described in St. John of the Cross's 16th century poem of that name. In Caitanya Vaiṣṇavism, it is referred to as *viraha*, or love-in-separation, and is experienced as an intense feeling of emptiness in the absence of the object of one's love, Kṛṣṇa. In Caitanya Vaiṣṇavism, however, it is not regarded as a "crisis" in one's spiritual development or a test in any sense. Instead, it is considered clear evidence of the depth and power of one's love for

---

42

> नयनं गलदश्रुधारया वदनं गद्गदुद्धया गिरा।
> पुलकैर्निचितं वपुः कदा तव नामग्रहणे भविष्यति॥

43 Rūpa Gosvāmin, *Bhakti-rasāmṛta-sindhu*, 2.3.16:

> ते स्तम्भस्वेदरोमाञ्चाः स्वरभेदोऽथ वेपथुः।
> वैवर्ण्यमश्रु प्रलय इत्यष्टौ सात्त्विकाः स्मृताः॥

Kṛṣṇa. It is thought to reflect Rādhā's deep feeling of separation from Kṛṣṇa when she is separated or about to be separated from him. Caitanya's verse is:

> A moment for me has become an age,
> My eyes have become the rainy season,
> My whole universe has become empty,
> In my separation from Govinda.[44]

The final instruction exemplifies the state of total self-surrender, the sort that many would consider pathological today. Nevertheless, there is a kind of rustic beauty in it, in the complete surrender of one's own will and desires for the pleasure of another. Perhaps the survival of the species has depended on it in our evolutionary past. Caitanya's verse expresses it this way:

> Let him squeeze me tightly as his servant;
> Or, let him strike at my heart through absence;
> Let that lascivious boy do
> Whatever it is he wants to.
> He is still the lord of my life
> And not anyone else.[45]

The adjectives modifying "me" in this verse are in the grammatical feminine gender indicating that the speaker is to be understood as a woman. This sense of the feminine as the most exalted lover of Kṛṣṇa concludes the teachings thought to be Caitanya's own. This naturally refers to the cowherd women or *gopīs* who are for Caitanya and his tradition the greatest and deepest lovers of Kṛṣṇa. They are the finest models of that love. Along with the metaphysical teachings in them, these eight verses closely track the practical side of the

---

[44]ibid.,

> युगायितं निमेषेन चक्षुषा प्रावृषायितम्।
> शून्यायितं जगत् सर्वं गोविन्दविरहेण मे॥

[45]ibid.:

> आश्लिष्य पादरतां पिनष्टु मां
> अदर्शनान्मर्महतां करोतु वा।
> यथा तथा वा विदधातु लम्पटो
> मत्प्राणनाथस्तु स एव नापरः॥

tradition, that is, the main methods the tradition used to cultivate its sense of intimacy with the divine, or, Kṛṣṇa (the singing in praise of Kṛṣṇa, etc.). This suggests, especially through this last verse, that the goal of cultivation was the practitioner's transformation into a female lover of Kṛṣṇa. Caitanya models this expectation by speaking in the voice of a cowherd woman for whom Kṛṣṇa is the one and only lord whether he chooses to embrace her or to leave her aside for another. The tradition later worked this expectation out by inventing the persona or identity of the *mañjarī*, or "flower-bud," for the practitioner to adopt in his meditations and visualizations. We will get a glimpse of this identity in action in the fifth chapter of Kanupriya's work.[46]

There is a theology of nine that is discussed in a work by an 18th century Caitanya Vaiṣṇava teacher, Baladeva Vidyābhūṣaṇa (d. 1768?), called the *Prameya-ratnāvalī* (*Necklace of Settled Truths*). Those truths are: Viṣṇu (Kṛṣṇa) is the highest, he is the subject of the teachings of all scriptures, the world is real, difference is real, the living beings are servants of Kṛṣṇa, there is a hierarchy among

[46]Another theology of eight can be drawn from a poem on the holy name by Śrī Rūpa Gosvāmin called the *Kṛṣṇanāmāṣṭaka*, or *Eight Verses on the Name of Kṛṣṇa*. That text was used as the basis of Kanupriya Goswami's major work on the theology of the holy name, *Śrī Nāma Cintāmaṇi* (*Thought-jewel of the Holy Name*). Since I intend to translate that work separately, I will give a short synopsis of the theology of the holy name found in those verses:

1. The holy name is more elevated than the Vedas.
2. Even if uttered without respect and only a little, it destroys all one's powerful sufferings.
3. Like the sun, even its reflection destroys the darkness of ignorance.
4. It destroys one's already fructifying *karma* (*prārabdha-karman*) unlike the direct experience of Brahman which does not.
5. The holy name has many forms and natures according to the many manifestations of the lord.
6. Between the holy name and the holy named the former is more compassionate because one who has committed offenses to the latter is freed from them by repeating the former.
7. The holy name is destroyer of the sufferings of the surrendered, is of the nature of condensed joy, and is completely non-different from the holy named.
8. The holy name enlivens the finest music and is sweeter than the sweetest things.

them (the living beings), liberation is the attainment of Kṛṣṇa's presence, its cause is his flawless worship, and the sources of knowledge of this are perception, inference, and verbal testimony.[47] A similar, though probably spurious, book called the *Nava-ratna* (*The Nine Gems*) is registered in the name of Harirāma Vyāsa who was a well known writer of Braj-bhasha songs on the subject of Kṛṣṇa's Vṛndāvana sports. Some of his songs are preserved in the songbooks of the Rādhāvallabha tradition. The same nine categories as in Baladeva's work are given.[48]

Another theology of nine organizes and encapsulates the practical aspects of Caitanya Vaiṣṇava practice. It describes nine steps or stages on the road to divine love (*preman*) and comes from a couple of verses of Rūpa Gosvāmin found in his *Ocean of the Nectar of Devotion* (*Bhakti-rasāmṛta-sindhu*).[49] Though these verses describe the successive stages in the development of divine love, they point beyond the practical to deep philosophical and theological issues that have broad applications.[50] One could, as has been done in many cases with the other numerical groups, write a whole book exploring the implications of these nine. Here I will just give a brief account of them with some hints about possible directions in which a deeper discussion might head. One quick note before we begin. It may be that Rūpa Gosvāmin in framing these nine stages of *bhakti-yoga* had the eight-limbed yoga (*aṣṭāṅga-yoga*) in mind. There seems to be a

---

[47] Baladeva Vidyābhūṣaṇa, *Prameyaratnāvalī* (1.8):

श्रीमध्वः प्राह विष्णुं परतममखिलाम्नायवेद्यञ्च विश्वम्
सत्यं भेदञ्च जीवान् हरिचरणजुषस्तारतम्यञ्च तेषाम्।
मोक्षं विष्ण्वङ्घ्रिलाभं तदमलभजनं तस्य हेतुं प्रमाणम्
प्रत्यक्षादित्रयञ्चेत्युपदिशति हरिः कृष्णचैतन्यचन्द्रः॥

As the verse attests, these nine objects of theological knowledge were developed under the influence of the South Indian Vaiṣṇava teacher Madhva (12th cent. CE).

[48] The text is included in the edition of Baladeva's *Prameya-ratnāvalī* by Haridāsa Śāstrī. See the bibliography.

[49] Rūpa Gosvāmin, *Bhakti-rasāmṛta-sindhu*, 1.4.15-16.

[50] That this way of viewing the manifestation of *bhakti* is considered theologically important is demonstrated by the number of the tradition's books that take these nine steps either as their organizing principle or as the organizing principle of major sections of them. The earliest such work is that of Viśvanātha Cakravartin (1650-1725?) called *The Rain Cloud of Sweetness* (*Mādhurya-kādambinī*). An example of a modern book in which these nine stages play a major role is the *Wishing Vine of Bhakti* (*Bhakti-kalpa-latā*) by one of the abbots (*mahāntas*) of the renunciant community at Rādhākuṇḍa (Vraja, UP, India), Kuñjabihārī Dāsa Bābājī (1976).

correspondence between some of the stages and counterparts in the yoga system, especially in the higher stages. First, let's hear Rūpa's verses:

> In the beginning there is faith,
> Then association with holy ones;
> Then one learns methods of worship;
> Cessation of harmful habits follows;
> Then comes steadiness and after that taste;
> Next develops attachment, then feeling;
> Finally divine love appears.
> Such should be the practitioner's progress.[51]

The very first stage raises the question of faith, confidence, or trust, (*śraddhā*), in the teachings of the tradition and plunges us into deep philosophical waters. What is it? Where does it come from? How does one get it? Rūpa is mostly silent on these questions. His nephew Śrī Jīva, however, posits a condition prior to faith in which one benefits from association with good or holy people (*sādhu*) and hears from them the words of the sacred texts. From contact with these arises faith. This entire book by Kanupriya Goswami is about this very power of association with holy people to engender the proper kind of faith in someone, a faith suitable for entering onto the path leading towards *bhakti*. It is a discussion immensely important to the Caitanya tradition. The next stage, however, is again association with holy ones. This later association, according to Śrī Jīva, has a different purpose, however. It is now pursued in order to learn the methods of practicing worship, which constitutes the third stage. From regular practice comes the gradual destruction or cessation of the misconceptions, inauspicious habits, and obstacles referred to as *anarthas* or unwanted or harmful things.[52] Once

---

[51]ibid.:

> अदौ शद्धा ततः साधुसङ्गोऽथ भजनक्रिया।
> ततोऽनर्थनिवृत्तिः स्यात्ततो निष्ठा रुचिस्ततः॥
> अथासक्तिस्ततो भावस्ततः प्रेमाभ्युदञ्चति।
> साधकानामयं प्रेम्नः प्रादुर्भावे भवेत्क्रमः॥

[52]The Rain Cloud of Sweetness (*Mādhurya-kādambinī*) of Viśvanātha Cakravartin mentions four types of *anartha*: those arising from misbehavior or bad actions, those arising from good behavior or good actions (attachment to the pleasures resulting

those are diminished one gains a steadiness or a state of unwavering regularity in practice called *niṣṭhā*.

Taste (*ruci*) means desire. At a certain point in one's spiritual development desires for other things subside and one comes to desire *bhakti*) strongly. Though it is not without calculation, it is still considered a positive sign of advancement towards the goal of manifesting *bhakti*. Here, on the stage of taste, it is understood that desire is directed primarily at the activity of worship or *bhajana*. On the next stage, the stage of attachment (*āsakti*), however, the same desire evolves into attachment to the object of worship, that is, to the one who is being worshiped, Kṛṣṇa. On this stage it is thought that ignorance, which is the root of sin, comes to an end and one's mind becomes firmly fixed on the forms, qualities, and sports of Kṛṣṇa. From the stages of faith to attachment one is engaged in *bhakti* as practice or means (*sādhana*). After attachment one reaches *bhakti* as goal or achievement (*sādhya*). One might consider the stages of taste and attachment as reflecting the early dawning light or influence of *bhakti* which rises like the sun in the next stage.

The last two stages represent progressive stages of accomplishment. Feeling (*bhāva*) and divine love (*preman*) are *bhakti*. The gradual illumination that begins with "taste" (*ruci*) and becomes brighter with attaction becomes fully luminous with the rise of *bhakti* in the heart of the *bhakta*. In naming this stage "feeling" or *bhāva* Rūpa is nodding to the tradition of Sanskrit literary criticism in which real feelings are called *bhāvas*. *Bhakti* itself has often been described in that tradition as *bhāva* by numerous of its leading writers.[53] The specific feeling referred to here is love of Kṛṣṇa (*kṛṣṇa-rati*). In the foundational text of Sanskrit dramaturgy, the *Treatise on Drama* (*Nāṭya-śāstra*), the feelings are distinguished from the aesthetic experiences that resemble them, the *rasas*. So here the feeling love for Kṛṣṇa is also distinguished from the relishing of that feeling which is called divine love (*preman*). Love for Kṛṣṇa softens the *bhakta*'s heart; divine love completely melts it. Thus, we have Rūpa Gosvāmin's nine stages in the unfolding or arising of divine love. Each of those stages has a theological underpinning that reveals the richness of Caitanyite theological reflection.

---

from past good actions), those arising from *bhakti* (the desire for fame, respect, or money because of one's demonstration of *bhakti*), and those arising from offences.

[53] Ānandavardhana, Mammaṭa, Jagannātha, to name just a few.

Another theology of nine was inherited by the Caitanya tradition from earlier Vaiṣṇava texts and writers. This is the theology of the nine forms or limbs of *bhakti* (*navavidha-bhakti*). It is based on a pair of verses from the *Bhāgavata Purāṇa* and was used as an organizing principle in the *bhakti* text by Vopadeva (13th cent. C.E.), *The Pearl* (*Muktāphala*). The verse from the *Bhāgavata* is:

> Hearing and telling of Viṣṇu
> Remembering him, bowing at his feet,
> Honoring his image, praising,
> Servitude, friendship, offering oneself.
> If *bhakti* of these nine types is
> Offered by a person to Lord Viṣṇu,
> Then truly I regard such a person
> The best educated of all.[54]

Here there appears to be a gradual progression of the forms of *bhakti* from the least intimate form (hearing of Viṣṇu) to the most intimate form (offering of oneself entirely to Viṣṇu). These nine forms of *bhakti* are described in this passage as a kind of education in which the student becomes transformed from a forgetful, lost, ignorant living being wandering through repeating cycles of birth and death to an intimate companion of Viṣṇu (Kṛṣṇa). The final form, offering oneself, is reminiscent of the kind of *bhakti* practiced by the cowherd girls, considered the most intimate of Kṛṣṇa's *bhaktas*.

A theology of ten is found in a more recent tradition of theological reflection that is traceable to a 19th century Caitanya Vaiṣṇava writer, Vipinavihāri Gosvāmī (1850-1919?). Gosvāmī wrote a massive work in Bengali, with citations of numerous Sanskrit verses from a variety of proof texts, called the *Daśa-mūla-rasa* (*The Juice [Essence, Flavor, Joy] of the Ten Roots*) which was published in 1904. The ten roots are according to a brief summary of the text: determination of the sources of knowledge, the truth of Śrī Kṛṣṇa, his possession of all powers, the truth of *rasa* or sacred rapture, the

---

[54]*Bhāg.*, 7.5.23-4:

> श्रवणं कीर्तनं विष्णोः स्मरणं पादसेवनं।
> अर्चनं वन्दनं दास्यं सख्यमात्मनिवेदनम्॥
> इति पुंसार्पिता विष्णौ भक्तिश्चेन्नवलक्षणा।
> क्रियेत भगवत्यद्धा तन्मन्येऽधीतमुत्तमम्॥

living being, the difference between the living being and God, the living being as a separated portion (*vibhinnāṃśa*) of God, the cause of the distinction between the living being and God, the definition of *bhakti* as practice, and the various kinds of *rasa*.[55]

Apart from these there are several other numbered theologies that I will not discuss here. There is a theology of eleven elements involving the ten offences to the holy name plus an eleventh added by Sanātana Gosvāmin (inattentiveness).[56] There is a theology of fourteen developed by Viśvanātha Cakravartin which shares many elements of Rūpa Gosvāmin's theology of nine, but adds a few new stages. A theology of twenty has been constructed out of the first twenty forms or limbs of *bhakti* described by Rūpa Gosvāmin in his *Ocean of the Nectar of Devotion* (*Bhakti-rasāmṛta-sindhu*). Those first twenty beginning with "finding shelter at the feet of a guru" (*guru-pādāśraya*), are regarded as the "doorway" into the world of *bhakti*. Moreover, all sixty-four limbs of *bhakti* discussed in Rūpa's texts might be regarded as a theology of sixty-four. Rūpa himself, however, singles out the last five as having special power in facilitating the birth of feeling. He says:

> There is little need for faith in these five,
> Which have a hard-to-comprehend
> And amazing power such that
> Even small connection with them
> Produces feeling in the good-hearted.[57]

Those five are: serving the sacred images, tasting the meaning of the *Bhāgavata*, associating with *bhaktas* who have similar affections for

---

[55]Kānanavihārī Gosvāmī, *Bāghnāpāṛā-sampradāya o Baiṣṇava Sāhitya*, 530. I have never seen this text personally.

[56]The ten offences to the holy name have become more important in modern Caitanya Vaiṣṇava theology, especially for writers like Kanupriya Goswami. They are referred to numerous times in this book and many more times in his other books. As such, they come to represent a kind of negative theological summary or list of "don'ts" that is influential in modern Caitanya Vaiṣṇavism. The ten offences are listed later in this book in a footnote on page 73.

[57]Rūpa Gosvāmin, *Bhakti-rasāmṛta-sindhu*, 1.2.238:

> दुरूहाद्भुतवीर्येऽस्मिन् श्रद्धा दूरेऽस्तु पञ्चके।
> यत्र स्वल्पोऽपि सम्बन्धः सद्धियां भावजन्मने

Kṛṣṇa, singing the holy names, and residing in the land of Mathurā (where Kṛṣṇa is thought to have lived/to live).[58]

Perhaps the most fascinating, most mysterious, and most profound of all the theologies mentioned here is the theology of zero, the theology of absence or *abhāva*. This theology, though hinted at in various passages of the vast Caitanya literature, has yet to be fully recognized, recovered, and discussed. This is certainly not the place for that. If, perhaps, this author is lucky he will get an opportunity in another work to pull together the scattered and multihued threads of this vision of ultimate reality and weave them into a coherent theological/philosophical tapestry.

Suffice it to say that each theology discussed here is, within its own limitations and from the perspective of its authors, complete. Rather than expressing differing or conflicting views, they are more representative of different ways of slicing up the same theological pie. These differing divisions bring out diverse aspects of the realm of Caitanya Vaiṣṇava theology, belief, and practice, and suggest different ways of understanding what the tradition regards as the fundamental nature of the self-revelation of the divine in the life of Śrī Caitanya and his immediate followers. Moreover, understanding the theologies of the numbers in their proper historical and social contexts provides a multifaceted and multivalent picture of Caitanya Vaiṣṇava theological reflection as it developed, expanded, and transformed over time.

The Tripartite Theology of Kanupriya Goswami

The simplified tripartite theology presented here by Śrī Kanupriya Gosvāmī is, as far as I know, unprecedented, though certainly anticipated by many of the previous Caitanya Vaiṣṇava texts and theologies. It is a very straightforward, deeply relational theology: God (Bhagavān), worshipper (*bhakta*), and the love that binds them together (*bhakti*). Everything except the essentials is stripped away. No mention is made of cosmology, cosmogony, teleology, eschatology, theodicy, soteriology, and so forth. All forms of God are included in Bhagavān; all relationships with God are represented in *bhakti*; and all living beings are included in the category of *bhakta*,

[58]ibid., 1.2.225-237 and 1.2.239-243.

though they may be either actualized or potential. The envisioned unity of the referrents of the three terms is reinforced by the common root, $\sqrt{bhaj}$, of the terms themselves. In turn, their distinctions from each other are indicated by the different forms and semantic registers of the words that refer to them: *bhagavān*, *bhakta*, and *bhakti*.

The point of this simplified theology is to focus attention on the process of socialization, or the passing on of the special memes connected with the Caitanya Vaiṣṇava forms of worship and practice, or, as it (socialization) is called in the text, *saṅga*. *Saṅga* at its simplest means "moving with" or "traveling together," or, "coming together." It means being in the company of someone or a group of someones for a period of time. On the face of it, this seems like a mutual or egalitarian arrangement. But as envisioned by Kanupriya Goswami and as many have experienced in actuality, it is often onesided and hierarchical. This is not meant in a negative way. The *bhakta* is the main or most important element in the society that moves together. Inside the *bhakta* reside both the power that is *bhakti* and Bhagavān himself. In the company of the *bhakta* ordinary persons are exposed to and "infected," as it were, with the power and presence of the divine and, according to Goswami, are profoundly influenced and possibly even transformed. This is the main channel, according to Caitanya Vaiṣṇavism, through which *bhakti* is spread. It cannot be gotten through reading or thinking, though those are useful aids and reinforcements, but through rubbing shoulders, so to speak, with those who already have it. Goswami provides several arguments for this based on the Caitanyite literature and on several examples also drawn from the same literature.

The Power and Provenance of Saṅga

As mentioned before there are many ways of describing this transmission of *bhakti*. Memetics is one way of thinking about such things that is popular today. The idea of the meme was first suggested by Richard Dawkins in his classic work on evolutionary biology called *The Selfish Gene.*[59] Susan Blackmore, Daniell Dennett, and others have picked up the term and developed it in their own ways.[60] Memes are units of imitation that are passed from one mind to another. A meme might be a song, a story, or something as simple as a phrase or even manner of pronunciation. Memes also extend to non-verbal behavior.[61] Thus, facial expressions, manners of dress, personal rites and practices might also be passed from one person to another.[62] The phenomenon of *bhakti* is a memeplex (a complex of memes) that is passed from *bhakta* to non-*bhakta* as a result of *saṅga* in Caitanya Vaiṣṇavism. The result is that the non-*bhakta* is often transformed into a *bhakta*, which means he or she takes on the memeplex of *bhakti*, if the *saṅga* is long enough and occurs under the right conditions.

From a memetic perspective Kanupriya Goswami's book can be viewed as an effort of stewardship meant to improve the reproductive efficiency of the memeplex that is the Caitanya Vaiṣṇava form of *bhakti* by praising and to a large extent mythologizing *saṅga* or association with great saints, the *mahat.*[63] Merely praising *saṅga* is not enough, however. One has also to suggest why it is such an effective means of becoming infected with *bhakti* and why *bhakti* is such a good thing to become infected with.

Goswami first distinguishes between different types of faith (*śrad-*

---

[59]Richard Dawkins, *The Selfish Gene.* Chapter Eleven. Oxford: Oxford University Press, 1976.

[60]Susan Blackmore, *The Meme Machine* (Oxford: Oxford University Press, 1999) and Daniel Dennett, *Breaking the Spell* (Penguin Books, 2006).

[61]See Dawkins' amusing account of the habit of one of his students when thinking deeply over a question. Her habit or meme was traced back to her parents who got it from their teacher, Wittgenstein. Foreword, vii, in *The Meme Machine* by Susan Blackmore.

[62]Dawkins says: "Examples of memes are tunes, ideas, catch-phrases, clothes, fashions, ways of making pots or of building arches. Just as genes propagate themselves in the gene pool by leaping from body to body via sperm or eggs, so memes propagate themselves in the meme pool by leaping from brain to brain via a process which, in the broad sense, can be called imitation," (*The Selfish Gene*, 192).

[63]Mythologizing is not meant in a negative sense here. Those who have studied the roles of mythology in religious communities know that myths tell the most fundamental and meaningful stories that a community possesses. The myths of a community give that community its sense of identity and place in the world. Calling a story a myth is not commenting on whether it is historical or fictional. Calling a story a myth is claiming it as an essential narrative that provides the members of a community with meaning and direction.

dhā). Faith is of many kinds and each has its range of operation and efficacy. Only faith of the non-qualified or threadless variety, however, is capable of preparing the ground for the appearance of non-qualified, threadless or unmixed *bhakti*. What exactly faith means in this context is a little unclear. Since it is required as the basis of some form of action, it appears to be primarily an inclination or impetus to undertake a certain kind of action and a confidence that that kind of action will issue in the result desired. Is faith in this sense a meme? One might argue that the expressions of faith, the various actions that are encouraged as a result of faith, are memes. Those can easily be copied or imitated from the appropriate model, the accomplished *bhakta*, or "great one" (*mahat*). But can a frame of mind or attitude be a meme?

An answer is suggested by a commonly held view of how religious practice or cultivation works. As early as Śaṅkara (650-700 CE) imitation was regarded as one of the surest means of cultivating a religious or enlightened mind set. In commenting on an important verse in the Second Chapter of the *Bhagavad-gītā*, Śaṅkara recognizes the efficacy of imitating the traits of an enlightened person as a way to becoming similarly enlightened oneself. In that passage of the *Gītā* Arjuna asks Kṛṣṇa:

> What is the description of one steady in wisdom, Keśava? Of one situated in *samādhi* (trance)? How would one of steady knowledge speak, sit, and move about?[64]

In response Kṛṣṇa says:

> When one gives up all the desires, Pārtha, that are situated in the heart and is satisfied with the self in the self alone, then that one is called steady in wisdom.[65]

---

[64]Bg., 2.54:

> स्थितप्रज्ञस्य का भाषा
> समाधिस्तस्य केशव।
> स्थितधी: किं प्रभाषेत
> किमासीत व्रजेत किम्॥

[65]Bg., 2.55:

> प्रजाति यदा कामान्सर्वान्पार्थ मनोगतान्।

In his commentary on the latter verse Śaṅkara writes:

> From the verse beginning with *prajahāti* (2.55) to the end of the chapter, the characteristics of and means of becoming one steady in wisdom (*sthita-prajña*) are taught to both those who from the very beginning have renounced actions and are devoted to the application of knowledge and those who have reached that stage through the application of action. Everywhere in texts on the highest self the characteristics of the one who has reached success are taught as the means leading to that success because they are accomplished with effort. And those things that are accomplished with effort, the means to success, become the characteristics of the successful.[66]

In the Caitanya tradition one of the founding fathers of the tradition's theology, Sanātana Gosvāmī, expresses the same idea in his auto-commentary on his *Great Ambrosia of Those Who Love the Lord* (*Bṛhad-bhāgavatāmṛta*). In verse 167 of the Third Chapter of the second part of the text, he says:

> Take to singing the holy names with as much intensity of feeling as the crying of *cātaka* birds in the rainy season without clouds or of female ruddy geese sleeping apart from their husbands in the night.[67]

In his commentary on this verse, Sanātana explains the logic behind this recommendation in the following way:

आत्मन्येवात्मना तुष्टः स्थितप्रज्ञस्तदोच्यते॥

[66]Śaṅkara's comm. on Bg., 2.55: यो ह्यादित एव संन्यस्य कर्माणि ज्ञानयोगनिष्ठायां प्रवृत्तो यश्च कर्मयोगेन तयोः स्थितप्रज्ञस्य प्रजहातीत्यारभ्याध्यायपरिसमाप्तिपर्यन्तं स्थितप्रज्ञलक्षणं साधनं चोपदिश्यते। सर्वत्रैव ह्यध्यात्मशास्त्रे कृतार्थलक्षणानि यानि तान्येव साधनान्युपदिश्यते यत्नसाध्यत्वाद्। यानि यत्नसाध्यानि साधनानि लक्षणानि भवन्ति।

[67]Sanātana Gosvāmin, *Bṛhad-bhāgavatāmṛta*, 2.3.167:

नाम्नास्तु सङ्कीर्तनमार्तिभारान्
मेघं विना प्रावृषि चातकानाम्।
रात्रौ वियोगात्स्वपते रथाङ्गी-
वर्गस्य चाक्रोशनवत् प्रतीहि॥

Cātaka birds are mythological birds that live only on the rain that falls from the sky. Both birds represent intensity of suffering in the absence of what they love the most.

> The characteristic of the accomplished become the practice of the practitioner.[68]

Thus, by taking on or imitating (enacting?) the traits of someone who has achieved divine love, or in the former case of one who is steady in wisdom (*sthitaprajña*), one eventually becomes someone who has divine love or is steady in wisdom. If one sings the names of Kṛṣṇa as if one loved him immensely one will someday love him immensely. Fake it 'til you make it.

Thus, though a state of mind or attitude may not itself be a meme or memeplex, the effects, outward signs, and actions associated with that state of mind might be imitated in such a way as to produce that state of mind.[69]

In many respects, the Vaiṣṇava notion of *śraddhā* is very similar to the Mahāyāna Buddhist idea of *bodhicitta*, which can mean a wish to become awakened, a mind set on *bodhi* or awakening. The wish itself requires a certain amount of knowledge and realization and so does the threadless type of faith that leads to *bhakti*. *Bhakti* and *bodhi* must be distinguished from other potential goals as specially desirable or preferable and that requires some knowledge. One might, however, argue that the belief on which faith or *bodhi* is based, that there exists something like *bhakti* or *bodhi* and that it is surpassingly desirable, is a meme which can be successfully transmitted from mind to mind through the process of *saṅga*.

Some might object to my referring to *bhakti* as a meme or memeplex since the idea of memes comes out of the field of the evolution of culture. Evolution as conceived in this field and in its parent field, evolutionary biology, is blind, that is to say, not guided. What determines whether a meme is successful or not is simply whether it is able to get itself replicated or not. The memeplex of Caitanyite *bhakti* has been around for over five hundred years, and one might argue it existed before in other memes and memeplexes connected with prior traditions centered on the worship of Kṛṣṇa. Whole strands of prior Kṛṣṇa memeplexes were incorporated into

---

[68]Sanātana, *Bṛhad-bhāgavatāmṛta-ṭīkā*, 2.3.167: सिद्धस्य लक्षणं यत्स्यात्साधनं साधकस्य तदिति न्यायात्

[69]The field of Sanskrit aesthetics has some important insights into and reflections on how this works in the evocation of aesthetic rapture or *rasa*. See my *The Rasa Theory of Rūpa Gosvāmī* (forthcoming) and the introduction to my translation of Rūpa Gosvāmī's *Blazing Sapphire* (*Ujjvala-nīlamaṇi*, vol. 1, forthcoming) for more details.

the Caitanyite memeplex. That is a good indication of the success and vitality of the Kṛṣṇa memeplex. Nevertheless, treating *bhakti* as a memeplex means in the minds of many that there is no intentionality involved. One neither intends to "catch" the *bhakti* memeplex nor does anyone intend to spread it. This might come as a surprise to some, but this is very close to the way the Caitanya tradition itself, under the influence of the *Bhāgavata Purāṇa*, understands and describes the way one picks up *bhakti*. The relevant word used is *yadṛcchayā*, "by chance," in the relevent text from the *Purāṇa*.[70] In other words, acquiring *bhakti* is something of a happenstance, a mystery.

Bhakti replicates itself with the help of certain "tricks" as Blackmore calls them. Those tricks are themselves memes that improve or increase the rate or ease with which another memeplex is replicated.

Conventions Observed in this Translation

There are number of conventions followed in this translation that should be mentioned here. I have used the standard form of transliteration for Sanskrit for words and passages in Sanskrit and also for words and passages in Bengali. This means that sometimes there is an extra "a" at the end of the Bengali words that is not pronounced in spoken Bengali. Those who know Bengali will not be surprized by this. The "a" is actually there in the Bengali script, but it is not pronounced or in some cases it is pronounced like an "o." Sanskrit citations in the main text are done in transliteration while those in the footnotes are done in the Devanāgarī script. Bengali texts cited in the footnote are done in Bengali script.

The translations of the Sanskrit verses cited in the text in general follow the Bengali translations of those verses of Kanupriya Goswami which are more often interpretations than they are strict, word-for-word translations. Without doing it this way, sometimes

---

[70] *Bhāg.*, 11.20.8:

यदृच्छया मत्कथादौ जातश्रद्धस्तु यः पुमान्।
न निर्विण्णो नातिसक्तो भक्तियोगोऽस्य सिद्धिदः॥

But to the person who by chance develops faith in my stories and such, being neither too detached nor overly attached, the discipline of *bhakti* brings success.

the connections Goswami makes between the points he is arguing and the verses he cites as evidence for those points would not be as clear. Moreover, his translations are indeed plausible interpretations of the verses, even if they do add some things that are not in the original.

I have not followed the usual custom of translating the word *guṇa* as "quality" when it refers to the three *guṇa* of material nature (*prakṛti*). *Guṇa* also means "thread" and that meaning makes more sense to me when it is used in connection with the creation of the world. One can imagine for instance mother nature "weaving" the world together like some great tapestry out of the three "threads" with their different natures. In addition, threads can be thought of as joining together to make ropes which connect the *guṇa* with the idea, often emphasized in discussing material nature and cyclic existence, of bondage and being bound by ropes to the world. This leads to some odd expressions, I will admit: "threaded" or "threadless" faith and *bhakti*, for instance. Nevertheless, I think translating *guṇa* in this way brings out some aspects of the original text and worldview that are lost by following the recent conventions in translation. One might point out that one of the finest translators of the *Bhagavad-gītā*, Franklin Edgerton, used the word "strand" to translate the word *guṇa* almost ninety years ago. Thus, this is not a particularly new or revolutionary idea.

Along the same lines, I have not translated the individual names of the *guṇa* as is usually done with the words goodness (*sattva*), passion (*rajas*), and darkness or ignorance (*tamas*). Instead, taking a hint from the *Bhagavad-gītā*, I have chosen the words: transparent, translucent, and opague. *Rajas*, for instance, really means "dust" and may not be connected at all with the root $\sqrt{raj}$ which means "passion." Dust suggests a cloudiness or lack of clarity, but not a complete lack of it. This gives us a hint that we are dealing with a progression of some sort in these three words. On the one end is clarity or the near clarity I call transparency which is given the name *sattva*. *Sattva* means "being in itself" and suggests clarity by implying a minimum of distortion, a condition in which there is little more than "being itself" present, minimal additives or adulterants to distort or obscure the thing in itself. Cloudiness is introduced by the next condition, the dusty condition, in which something is partially clouded, distorted, or obscured as in a dust storm. Thus, the word I use for this is translucent which suggests a partial covering and a partial uncovering. Here, the thing is only partially obscured. Finally comes *tamas* the opaque or opacity. In this condition being is completely covered, completely obscured.

In the *Gītā* an example is given that may well apply to how the *guṇa* were understood at the time. In verse 38 of Chapter Three we find:

> As a fire is covered by smoke, and as a mirror is covered by dirt, and as a foetus is covered by the womb, so is this [knowledge] covered by it [desire].[71]

The first of these, a fire covered by smoke, exemplifies transparency (*sattva*). The second, a mirror covered with dirt, represents translucency (*rajas*), and the foetus covered by the womb represents opacity (*tamas*). All together they represent the various ways in which material nature, according to our author, covers the true self and causes the living being to forget its true nature. The living being clothed in a set of clothes made by nature out of the three threads forgets itself and Kṛṣṇa.

This translation has been many years in the works. Kanupriya Goswami is difficult to translate. His language is very rich and at times quite complex. One of his sentences can stretch on for half a page or more. In Bengali this works, but it does not work so well in English. Of all his works, however, this work is perhaps his easiest. That may be because it was recorded and edited by his nephew Gauraray Goswami, rather than written down himself. My work on it started out in part because I was interested in its subject matter and in part because I wanted to gain experience and improve my ability as a translator in order to try to tackle his more difficult and longer works, his classics *The True Nature and Function of the Living Being* (*Jīver Svarūpa o Svadharma*) and *The Thought-jewel of the Holy Name* (*Śrī Śrī Nāma Cintāmaṇi*). Let us see if it worked!

I have many people to thank beginning first of all with my wife Betsy who read through the manuscript and made many valuable

---

[71] Bg., 3.38:

> धूमेनाव्रियते वह्निर्यथाऽऽदर्शो मलेन च।
> यथोल्बेनावृतो गर्भस्तथा तेनेदमावृतम्॥

suggestions and corrections. The book would not read half as well without her help. I also wish to thank my friend and *guru-bhai*, Joseph Knapp, who took an interest in this book and encouraged me for years to try and finish it. He also read through many of the drafts and made many valuable corrections and improvements. Apart from that I must recognize the kindness and support of my daughter Jahnavi who also helped with this and other projects in various ways, but who mostly was just kind to her odd-ball father during this long process. Finally, thanks to my former colleages and current friends at Truman State University: Lloyd Pflueger, Mike Ashcraft, Derek Daschke, Jennifer Jesse, Ding-wha Hsieh, and Mark Appold who read through an early version of this introduction and gave me many useful comments and suggestions.

Works Cited

Bednarowski, Mary Farrell. *New Religions: the Theological Imagination in America.* Bloomington: Indiana University Press, 1989.

Kanupriya Goswami. *A Small Piece of the Mystery of Bhakti* (*Śrī Śrī Bhakti Rahasya Kaṇikā*). Kalikātā: Śrī Gokulānanda Gosvāmī, Gaurābda 473 [1958].

Stein, William Bysshe. *Two Brahman Sources of Emerson and Thoreau.* Gainesville, Fla.: Scholar's Facsimiles & Reprints, 1967.

Bengali Editor's Introduction

I consider the primary cause of the appearance of the present book before the eyes of the people of the world to be the auspicious will and unbounded compassion of Śrī Śrī Gaurarāyahari[1] And, for his special grace on this fallen soul, I wish before all else to offer my humble respect at his lotus-like feet—the reservoir of all his blessings.

I think there is a special need on the part of this humble soul to offer a few very brief comments on the history and purpose of editing and publishing this book.

The speaker of all the materials of this book is my most honorable [uncle] Śrīmat Kānupriya Goswami—who has written many works full of fundamental research and the determinations of the holy texts, books such as *The True Nature and Function of the Living Being* (*Jīver Svarūpa o Svadharma*), *The Thought-jewel of the Holy Name* (*Śrī Nāma-cintāmaṇi*), *A Small Particle of the Secret of Bhakti* (*Śrī Bhakti-rahasya-kaṇikā*), and so forth. All are well known to many good folk in the Vaiṣṇava world and are studied and highly respected by them. It seems hardly necessary to point out futile it is for an insignificant person like me to introduce someone like him.

I will only humbly present, in the next few pages, what little needs to be said concerning the beginnings and history of the materials I have collected together and edited into these essays, now

[1]This is the name of the sacred image worshiped by the author, Śrī Kanupriya Goswami, and his nephew, Gaurarāya Dāsa Goswami, the collector and editor of this collection of his uncle's lectures.

issued in the form of a book. All these materials are collected from his lectures on Hari.

At present[2] most revered Goswami Prabhu has lived in his *āśrama*-house near the bank of the Ganges in the holy abode of Navadvīpa and has remained wholeheartedly engaged in the daily service of his sacred image Śrī Gaurarāyahari, year after year for twenty years. This many people know. People from the surrounding area also know about the regular lectures that he gives in the courtyard of his *āśrama*-house in observance of every special holy day, before audiences of *sādhus* and good folk.

His lectures focus on methods and goals drawn from the teachings of the Gauḍīya Vaiṣṇava tradition, and especially emphasize the principles and greatness of the holy names. Local people also know how many of them, hearing those lectures, feel themselves greatly edified and filled with an indescribable joy. I have myself on many occasions been fortunate enough to be present in that *āśrama* when he delivered those lectures. Realizing the special usefulness of all those priceless lectures in bestowing superb guidance for travellers on the path of the highest goal and in pointing out the means of obtaining the greatest peace in the midst of the inhospitable conditions of the present time, I always carefully keep notes on all the topics I have heard. It is not possible, however, to keep any written account of all the lectures that Śrīmat Goswami Prabhu has given to date. Whether or not someone else from among his circle of listeners has made any efforts in this matter, I don't know. All those lectures are very sweet and are enlivened by the force of his own deep feelings. With their fine conclusions on many matters that are very difficult to understand and their analysis of considerations and arguments that is quite appropriate for the present age, they are most useful and enjoyable for a broader general public. But since there is no suitable arrangement to make them available, they will remain engraved in the memories of a few bright people for a while and then in the end disappear beyond time's veil into the unknown. I find this to be a truly painful and lamentable matter.

For the present world which is scorched by the torments of the

[2]This book was published in 1970. So the editor of the Bengali text wrote this introduction in 1969 or 1970. At that time, Śrī Kanupriya Goswami was still alive. The translator of this work also met Kanupriya Goswami several years later in 1974 at his house in Navadvīpa.

Age of Kali, all of his lectures are like a great, powerful medicine, which has issued from his heart through the inspiration of Śrī Gaura. They seem as if they have appeared almost on their own. If one were able to put all those lectures into the form of an essay and publish it as a book, it would have a less fleeting existence. This was how I thought about it, at least within my own deliberations. How others may think of it or accept it, I have no way of knowing. On this matter, everyone has his own independent way of thinking.

That is the reason for this effort on the part of someone as low and ignorant as me who is unqualified in every way. Yet, I feel the inspiration of a greater portion of the grace of Śrī Gaurahari, who is the friend of the lowly, on this poor soul. The first fruit of this insignificant person's labors is the publication of the present essay as a book.

In my editing of the lectures into an essay, I have tried as much as possible to leave unchanged the words he used in particular places. Nevertheless, in the process of making them into an essay, it is not unexpected that some errors, inadvertent mistakes, and such may have been introduced through my own inexperience. If the intelligent readers of the audience will please point out any failings like that, I will, with thanks, endeavor to correct it. If there is any need to inquire further about some subject or inform me about something, please write to the publisher's address.

The present essay is a much altered, enlarged, and corrected version of an essay that was published previously under the title "The Roots of the Birth of *Bhakti* for Kṛṣṇa is Association with Holy Men" (*Kṛṣṇabhakti Janmamūla—Haya Sādhusaṅga*) in various issues (14-2-69 to 14-8-69) of the journal, *Himādri*. In the publication of that essay, because of its many flaws like printing mistakes, exclusions, the changing around of words and sentences, it became practically incomprehensible. Also since the essay was published in parts, absorbing its full meaning was difficult. For all these reasons and especially because of being implored on the necessity of its being reprinted in the form of a book by several sympathetic readers, the corrected essay is published as the present book under the name *On Associating with Great Ones* (*Mahat-saṅga Prasaṅga*).

There is another announcement. If this present book infuses a little enthusiasm into the community of its good and intelligent readers, if they perceive it as useful, and if as a result they express an interest I will be encouraged in this work. I will write this kind of essay using the brief notes of his other lectures which I have collected and publish them gradually as a series of the name "A Garland of Works on Talks About the Lord" (*Śrībhāgavatī-vāṇī Granthamālā*). Nourishing this hope, the present work, as an introduction, has been selected as the first blossom of that garland. After this, the only provisions on the path of fulfilling this great undertaking for someone insignificant like me is the causeless grace of Śrī Gaurahari, the blessings and good wishes of his *bhaktas* and, of course, the grace of Śrī Guru; this is for me my only source of strength.

Finally, there is this announcement: the entire responsibility for the work of printing this book along with the burden of correcting its proofs was undertaken with special enthusiasm by the retired librarian of the municiple corporation of Calcutta, Śrī Ahīndranārāyaṇa Śarmā Caudhurī. Without his help the publication of this book would not have been possible. Therefore, feeling deeply indebted to him I pray for the complete prosperity and favorability of his worship at the feet of Śrī Gaura.

Begging for the grace of the *bhaktas*,
the humble editor (Śrī Gaurarayadas Goswami)
Śrī Dolapūrṇimā, 1376 (1970), Śrī Caitanyābda 484

Part I

On Associating with Great Ones

Chapter One

I praise him, the Lord, Śrī Kṛṣṇacaitanya, whose grace makes even a lame person cross over a mountain and a mute person recite the Vedas.[1]

Among all embodied beings, the fleeting human body is very rarely attained. Even then, meeting someone who is dear to Vaikuṇṭha is even rarer still.[2]

At the beginning of this essay on the auspicious topic of the great benefit and influence of contact with those few, very rare great souls, a bit of clarity is needed concerning the causes of the conditions of misery, consisting of bondage to the cycle of rebirth and redeath that is produced by the adverse actions of embodied living beings who are beginninglessly[3] turned away from Hari. In the *Gītā*

---

[1]Cc., 1.3.1:

पङ्गुं लङ्घयते शैलं मूकमावर्तयेच्छ्रुतम्।
यत्कृपा तमहं वन्दे कृष्णचैतन्यमीश्वरम्।

[2]Bhāg., 11.2.29:

दुर्लभो मानुषो देहो देहिनां क्षणभङ्गुरः।
तत्रापि दुर्लभं मन्ये वैकुण्ठप्रियदर्शनं॥

[3]The word is *anādi*, "without beginning." The idea of the living being's beginningless sojourn in the cycle of rebirth is usually taken to mean not that the causes of that bondage are eternal, but that they are lost in the mists of time and cannot ever be known with certainty. Perhaps, too, it is a way of saying, with the Buddha, that the question of how bondage came about is not an edifying one. The only important question is how to become free.

the Lord himself says:

> Transparency (*sattva*), translucency (*rajas*), and opacity (*tamas*), the [three] threads (*guṇa*) born out of Nature (Prakṛti), bind the imperishable, embodied being to the body, Great-armed one.[4]

Although by true nature a changeless, eternal, and deathless self, the living being, beginninglessly turned away from Kṛṣṇa, is, through its own adverse works, united by *māyā*[5] with a body made of the three threads (*guṇa*) and as a result of that it wanders through the jungle of cyclic material existence on the two feet of birth and death. From time without beginning it wanders so. Therefore, becoming freed from connection with those three threads, transparency and so forth, is the way for all living beings to be saved from fear, anxiety, unhappiness, and lamentation and to reach immortality. That is taught in the *Gītā*, too:

> Passing beyond these three threads that spring from the body, the embodied being is freed from birth, death, old age, and misery and becomes immortal.[6]

If one is to overcome those three threads, one needs at the root of that endeavor the appropriate faith (*śraddhā*), since at the root of all of the endeavors of living beings the presence of the appropriate type of faith is necessary. The natural faith of the living being who is bound by the three threads is in accordance with the different

---

[4]Bg., 14.5:

सत्त्वं रजस्तम इति गुणाः प्रकृतिसम्भवाः।
निबध्नति महाबाहो देहे देहिनमव्ययम्॥

[5]*Māyā* is sometimes thought of as the Lord's power of illusion or ignorance. In Caitanya Vaiṣṇavism it is regarded not as an illusion, but as one of the three real powers of Kṛṣṇa, the external or *bahiraṅga-śakti*. It is the power through which the external or material world, which is thought to be real, is created. *Māyā* secondarily does involve illusion or ignorance in that it causes the embodied living being to think it is part of the material world it creates and to act accordingly.

[6]Bg., 14.20:

गुणानेतानतीत्य त्रीन् देही देहसमुद्भवान्।
जन्ममृत्युजरादुःखैर्विमुक्तो ऽमृतमश्नुते।

threads among the three, transparency and so forth, and thus is of three types. By that thread-induced faith the living being strives for a thread-bound object. As [stated in the *Gītā*]:

> Threefold is the faith of embodied beings born of their natures: transparent, translucent, and opaque. Hear of that from me.[7]

Therefore, the faith that is needed as the basis of efforts to overcome the three threads should itself be free of the threads or thread-less (*nirguṇa*). Striving for a thread-less object is not produced by the natural, thread-bound faith of the living beings. The Lord himself says that by means of a particular kind of faith one strives for a particular kind of object:

> Faith in matters of the higher self (knowledge, yoga, austerity, etc.) is from transparency; faith in the rites (that bring one to heaven and so forth) is from thread of translucency; and faith in matters contrary to piety (or the law) is from the thread of opacity. However, faith in my service is free of the threads.[8]

Therefore at the root of an attempt to cultivate pure *bhakti*,[9] free from all the material threads and having the form of worship of the Lord, one must have a thread-free faith relating to the Lord. By means of a faith different from that, a faith influenced by the material threads, it is not possible to strive to cultivate thread-free

---

[7]Bg., 17.2:

> त्रिविधा भवति श्रद्धा देहिनां सा स्वभावजा।
> सात्त्विकी राजसी चैव तामसी चेति तां शृणु॥

[8]Bhāg. 11.25.27:

> सात्त्विक्याध्यात्मिकी श्रद्धा कर्मश्रद्धा तु राजसी।
> तामस्यधर्मे या श्रद्धा मत्सेवायां तु निर्गुणा॥

[9]*Bhakti* is a difficult word to translate. The usual translation, "devotion," is rather inadequate. The other translations, "participation" or "worship," are somewhat better, but still not entirely satisfactory. Since this text gradually unfolds the meaning of the term, as understood in the Caitanya tradition, as it proceeds, I have decided to leave it untranslated.

bhakti. For this reason, when one obtains by some stroke of tremendous good luck thread-free faith, one will be able to engage in the cultivation of *bhakti* for the Lord. And by that *bhakti* one will easily become freed from the ropes made of the three material threads.

For this reason, the Lord himself has pointed out the way that is the best and the easiest for the living beings among all the other ways of becoming freed from the ropes of *māyā*'s three threads:

> This divine *māyā* of mine, composed of the threads, is very difficult to cross beyond. Those who surrender to me cross beyond this *māyā.*[10]

Thus, the best way to cross over the difficult-to-cross, three-threaded *māyā* is *bhakti* defined as surrender to the Lord alone. For the living being, who is a minute particle of consciousness under the control of *māyā*, taking shelter at the feet of the Lord, who is unlimited consciousness in control of *māyā*, is the natural path to overcoming *māyā.* Nevertheless, as long as at the root of that endeavor, thread-free faith in matters relating to the Lord, has not been infused into one, even if the Lord himself instructs one to adopt pure *bhakti* characterized by surrender, no living being can take it up, not without that thread-free faith. Therefore it is seen that after giving instructions on topics of rites, knowledge, yoga, austerity, and so forth, as his last order and highest instruction, the Lord himself, offering freedom from fear to living beings who are wandering about restlessly on the path of mundance existence in repeated birth and death, calls out to them with great emphasis to give up all other practices and simply surrender to him:

> Give up all other duties (*dharmas*) and surrender to me alone. I will free you from all sins. Do not grieve.[11]

---

[10]Bg., 7.14:

> दैवी ह्येषा गुणमयी मम माया दुरत्यया।
> मामेव ये प्रपद्यन्ते मायामेतां तरन्ति ते॥

[11]Bg., 18.66:

> सर्वधर्मान् परित्यज्य मामेकं शरणं व्रज।
> अहं त्वां सर्वपापेभ्यो मोक्षयिष्यामि मा शुचः॥

To respond to that call, however, one needs thread-free faith related to the Lord. Without that no one can respond to that accentuated call. Therefore, those engaged in rites, those cultivating knowledge, those practicing yoga, and so forth, each according to his or her own respective thread-influenced faiths—whatever subject they are engaged in—they remain endowed with faith in that subject. The reason for this is that without being connected with thread-free faith, even the Lord's own invitation to take shelter with the Lord who is beyond all the threads is useless—as long as along with that call one is not infused with thread-free faith relating to the Lord.

In order to reveal this secret to all living beings befuddled by *māyā* with her three threads the Lord himself said:

> Those situated in translucency, transparency, and opacity worship the gods and so forth, headed by Indra who dwell in translucency, transparency, and opacity. In such a manner, they do not worship me.[12]

Therefore, one is able to understand this: the appearance or non-appearance in a living being, who is under the control of *māyā*, of engagement in thread-free *bhakti* for the Lord, which is the very best way to gain freedom from worldly existence, has but one cause—the connection or lack of connection with a suitable thread-free faith in the Lord.

The sublime event that is at the root of thread-free faith relating to the Lord, or in other words, the one and only way to obtain *bhakti* for the Lord, is association with and service of the great *bhaktas*[13] of the Lord.

> By contact with the saintly arise discussions, like medicines for the heart and ear, that reveal my prowess. By enjoying those, faith [ie., *bhakti* as practice preceded by

---

[12]Bhāg. 11.21.32:

> रजःसत्त्वतमोनिष्ठा रजःसत्त्वतमोजुषः।
> उपासते इन्द्रमुख्यान् देवादीन्न तथैव माम्॥

[13]As with the word *bhakti*, the word *bhakta* is hard to translate. It basically means "one who has *bhakti* for the Lord."

> faith], attraction [ie., *bhakti* as feeling (*bhāva*)] , and *bhakti* [ie., *bhakti* as love (*preman*)] towards [me], who am the path to final freedom, quickly develop, one after another.[14]

Now I will begin to discuss, as far as I am able, the nature and greatness of those rare great ones, the lovers of the Lord, who are the only means to attain that very difficult-to-attain *bhakti*.

Bhakti is primarily of two types: threaded and unthreaded. For the embodied living being who is in the state of being threaded or bound by the threads of transparency and so forth, deceit or ignorance must exist. Therefore, as long as that deceit continues, people in general are inclined, in accordance with the threads and their operations, to engage in efforts to achieve thread-bound enjoyment and also liberation. In the *Caitanya-caritāmṛta* this point has been made:

> That deceit that I call the opacity of ignorance
> Is the desire for piety, wealth, sense enjoyment, and liberation.
> Among those the primary deceit is the desire for liberation.
> Because of that *bhakti* for Kṛṣṇa disappears.[15]

The natural inclination towards the thread-free Lord or towards *bhakti* for him in the form of service and so forth is unable to appear. Therefore, in the thread-bound condition allowances are made in all the scriptures for enjoyment and liberation, that is, the "group of

---

[14]Bhāg. 3.25.24:

> सतां प्रसङ्गान्मम वीर्यसंविदो
> भवन्ति हृत्कर्णरसायणाः कथाः।
> तज्जोषणादाश्वपवर्गवर्त्मनि
> श्रद्धा रतिर्भक्तिरनुक्रमिष्यति॥

[15]Kṛṣṇadāsa Kavirāja, *Caitanya-caritāmṛta* (Cc), 1.1.50:

> অজ্ঞানতমের নাম কহি যে কৈতব
> ধর্ম, অর্থ, কাম, মোক্ষ-বাঞ্ছা এই সব
> তার মধ্যে মোক্ষ-বাঞ্ছা কৈতব প্রধান
> যাহা হৈতে কৃষ্ণভক্তি হয় অন্তর্ধান

four" (*caturvarga*) made up of striving for piety, wealth, sense enjoyment, and liberation, so that one might gain the greatest benefit possible in accordance with the threads. For that a natural, thread-bound faith is useful for people in general.

Now, let's briefly consider this subject a bit more. In the material world generally speaking the "group of four," also known as the "four goals of human life" (*puruṣārthas*), are piety, wealth, and sensual pleasure within the category of enjoyment and, beyond those, liberation. They are all related to the material threads. At the root of all the actions of living beings is a faith born of their natures. By the translucent and the opaque faiths, according to their natures, an interest in enjoyment arises and by the transparent or luminous faith an interest in liberation arises. But, *bhakti* is essentially thread-free. In a living being touched by the threads, because of the absence of thread-free faith connected with the Lord, an interest in or inclination towards thread-free behavior connected with the Lord or pure *bhakti* does not arise.

In the *Gītā* this is said with respect to the inclination towards material or thread-bound things arisng from thread-induced faith:

> The transparent or illumined worship the gods, the translucent worship supernatural spirits [*yakṣas* and *rakṣas*, semi-divine beings] and the others, the opaque or unillumined people, worship the dead, the ghosts.[16]

Though the faiths of the three threads are discussed in this place in the *Gītā*, thread-free faith is not mentioned. The thread-free faith in the form of service to the Lord has been discussed in the previously cited verse from the *Bhāgavata Purāṇa* (3.25.24).

Now the thing to know is that in order for practices like rites, cultivation of knowledge, *yoga*, and penance and so forth, which are undertaken out of thread-induced faiths,—in order for such practices to succeed, connection with *bhakti* is completely necessary. For this reason the *bhakti* that is connected with the performance of all those thread-bound practices so that they are brought to life and

---

[16]Bg., 17.4:

> यजन्ते सात्त्विका देवान् यक्षरक्षांसि राजसाः।
> प्रेतान् भूतगणांश्चान्ये यजन्ते तामसा जनाः॥

made successful is known by the name "threaded *bhakti*" (*saguṇa-bhakti*). The *bhakti* that is pure, free of the intention of achieveing one's own happiness, and has the sole objective of serving the Lord free of desire is known as thread-free *bhakti* (*nirguṇa-bhakti*). Śrī Rūpa in his *Ocean of the Nectar of Bhakti* (*Bhakti-rasāmṛta-sindhu*) has described it in this way:

> All efforts or exertions of the body, mind, and speech for Kṛṣṇa if they are not antagonistic but completely favorable [towards him] are called *bhakti*. And if that *bhakti* is not clouded by any other sort of desire or the quest for knowledge or for ritual success or something like that, and thus is completely unmixed then it is called the highest *bhakti*.[17]

When this supreme or pure *bhakti* arises, not even the slightest desire for any thing else awakens in the *bhakta*'s heart except for the desire to meet the Lord in order to serve him.

That a connection with and the assistance of *bhakti* is necessary for the success and invigoration of all the other forms of practice is understood from the scriptures:

> As all living beings thrive in the shelter of their mothers, so do all successes (*siddhi*) thrive by resting themselves on *bhakti*.[18]

Therefore the author of the *Caitanya-caritāmṛta* has expressed that same idea in his book in many places:

> Without *bhakti* no form of practice
> Is able to produce any result
> *Bhakti* bestows all results,
> Independent and powerful.[19]

---

[17] Rūpa Gosvāmin, *Bhakti-rasāmṛta-sindhu* (Brs)., 1.1.11:

> अन्याभिलाषिताशून्यं ज्ञानकर्माद्यनावृतं।
> आनुकूल्येन कृष्णानुशीलनं भक्तिरुत्तमा॥

[18] Gopāla Bhaṭṭa, *Hari-bhakti-vilāsa*, 11.569:

> जीवन्ति जन्तवः सर्वे यथा मातरमाश्रिताः।
> तथा भक्तिं समाश्रित्य सर्वा जीवन्ति सिद्धयः॥

[19] Cc., 2.24.65:

"Rituals, *yoga*, and cultivation of knowledge look to the face of *bhakti*." Therefore, if any performance of the group of four human activities is done without *bhakti*, it will not produce results. For this there is much evidence in the scriptures. Though *bhakti* is manifested in both forms, thread-bound and unthreaded, in actuality they are both the same *bhakti*. It is just like a mother who has two conditions, one as a servant of Kṛṣṇa and the other as the protector of her children. The servant of Kṛṣṇa form is her bright and shining, pure condition. And again in the process of caring for her children, her caring for them requires her to do unclean things sometimes and thus she is seen in an impure form through contact with the impure. In that way too even *bhakti*, though by nature pure, appears as unthreaded or threaded because of being pure or impure in accordance with whether the intention of its possessor is "for Kṛṣṇa" or "for myself." When connected with the threads it does not bring about the manifestation of its main result which is unthreaded *prema-bhakti*. Rather, being by nature like a desire-fulfilling tree, in its threaded form it joins itself with the various means and practices to achieve the desires of the living beings such as enjoyment, liberation, and the supernatural powers, and thus only bestows its secondary results: it invigorates those various means or practices.

On the other hand, if that unthreaded source of faith in the Lord, self-manifesting *bhakti* or *bhāgavata-dharma* (the characteristic traits of a lover of Bhagavān, the Lord), is not infused into the living being itself by its own grace through the medium of association with unmotivated great ones, then it cannot be attained even with the thousands of practices like rituals, cultivation of knowledge and so forth that are touched by the threads. Therefore, that most beneficial *kṛṣṇa-bhakti*, which is beyond all human effort, is very rarely attained.

> Through the path of knowledge, liberation is easily attained, as are enjoyments like heaven and so forth through sacrifices and other pious acts. But this [self-revealing] *bhakti* to Hari is very hard to attain even with thousands of those sorts of threaded practices.[20]

ভক্তি বিনা কোনো সাধন দিতে নারে ফল
সর্ব ফল দেয় ভক্তি স্বতন্ত্র প্রবল

[20] Brs., 1.1.36:

Therefore, it has been determined that the main result of *bhakti* to the Lord is the appearance of love for the Supreme Lord Śrī Kṛṣṇa and its secondary or subsidiary result is success in the group of four (*caturvarga*) human endeavors. This is known from the scriptures:

> Whatever results are attainable through sacrificial rites, penance, knowledge, renunciation, the eightfold *yoga* system, charity, and even other beneficial practices my *bhakta* quickly attains through *bhakti* to me. My *bhakta* attains even heaven, liberation, and my own abode, if somehow, though my *bhakta* does not desire them [for himself], he has even a little desire for them because they may be favorable to his worship [of me].[21]

This unthreaded or pure *bhakti* is also called perfected-by-nature, the highest, singular, unmixed, unadulterated, and so forth. There is only one way for it to be planted in the heart of a living being—the finest association with and mercy of the great *bhaktas*, that is, of the saintly ones, and of the discussions of Hari that arise from that. That sort of association is called "uncaused" (*ahaituka*), which is to say that it is not attained as a result of one's own ability, wealth, or effort.

> Some people through some special good fortune attained by chance or, in other words, by association with and the grace of a *bhakta* of the Lord, have developed faith in discussions of the Lord's names, qualities, forms, and sports and are not overly detached from rituals and their results, thinking them illusory like those desiring liberation do, nor are they, on the other hand, overly attached to them like those who desire enjoyment from them. For

---

ज्ञानतः सुलभा मुक्तिर्भुक्तिर्यज्ञादिपुण्यतः।
सेयं साधनसाहस्रैर्हरिभक्तिः सुदुर्लभा॥

[21]Bhāg., 11.20.32-33:

यत्कर्मभिर्यत्तपसा ज्ञानवैराग्यतश्च यत्।
योगेन दानधर्मेण श्रेयोभिरितरैरपि॥
सर्वं मद्भक्तियोगेन मद्भक्तो लभते ऽञ्जसा।
स्वर्गापवर्गं मद्धाम कथञ्चिद्यदि वाञ्छति॥

> such people *bhakti* brings about success [that is, it bestows love (*preman*)].[22]

One can give the following example here. It is like how in the ordinary world one can acquire, in exchange for an adequate amount of money, silver, gold, ordinary jewels and precious stones at a shop. But one cannot acquire the truly rare jewels like the Kaustubha, Syamantaka, or Kohinor there. Even if one can pay an adequate amount of money, those rare jewels cannot be bought. Those priceless gems are things rightfully enjoyed by emperors and kings of kings. Only through such an emperor's dear friends and by their grace is one able to acquire those kinds of jewels. Pure *bhakti* is like a great jewel, too. Apart from the compassion of one of the Lord's dear friends there is no other way to obtain that jewel.

The difference between *bhakti* in its threaded and unthreaded forms can be understood from Kapila's teaching to his mother Devahūti. First he talks about threaded *bhakti*:

> *Bhakti-yoga* is understood to be of many types by its different paths, noble lady. Its state is variegated by the manner of the threads and nature of the human beings [who practice it].[23]

Then thread-free *bhakti* is described. Just as the pure stream of the Gaṅgā, the purifier of the fallen, arises from its source in Gomukhī and flows down in a thousand streams and purifies everything and everyone who touches it, so too do the streams of pure *bhakti*, originate from the eternal companions of the Lord in his eternal abode, appear in this universe produced by *māyā* through the

---

[22]Bhāg., 11.20.8:

> यदृच्छया मत्कथादौ जातश्रद्धस्तु यः पुमान्।
> न निर्विण्णो नातिसक्तो भक्तियोगोऽस्य सिद्धिदः॥

Śrī Jīva glosses the phrase *yadṛcchayā*, "by chance," in this verse by saying "somehow by the appearance of some good fortune born of the completely independent grace of and association with a *bhakta* of the Lord," केनापि परमस्वतन्त्रभगवद्भक्तसङ्गत-त्कृपाजातमङ्गलोदयेन, in the *Bhakti-sandarbha* of Śrī Jīva.

[23]Bhāg., 3.29.7:

> भक्तियोगो बहुविधो मार्गैर्भाविनि भाव्यते।
> स्वभावगुणमार्गेण पुंसां भावो विभिद्यते॥

lineal successions of the great ones, and infuse the hearts of living beings with pure *bhakti* whose source is faith connected with those who love the Lord.

> Just as the Gaṅgā flows in a stream of pure water without ceasation down to the sea, the mind moves without interruption, through the mere hearing of my qualities, to me who am in the hearts of all. Thus is exemplified the characteristic of thread-free *bhakti-yoga*, *bhakti* for the Supreme Person which is not clouded by knowledge, rituals, and so forth and which is not performed for any other purpose.[24]

The definition of the highest type of *bhakti* that is given in the *Nārada's Five Nights* (*Nārada-pañcarātra*) is not in any way different from the definition of pure or the highest *bhakti* described by Rūpa Gosvāmin in his verse beginning "Free of desire for anything else ... " (*anyābhilāsitāśūnyam*).[25] For instance:

> That service of Hṛṣīkeśa (Kṛṣṇa) by means of the senses that is free of all qualifications [free of all desires for personal enjoyment in this world and the next] and that, being linked only with the desire to please Kṛṣṇa alone, is pure [unclouded by knowledge, rites, and so forth], is the highest *bhakti*.[26]

Therefore, that highest or purest *bhakti* which is the very core of the power of consciousness (*saṃvit*) intimately united with the

---

[24]Bhāg., 3.29.11-12:

> मद्गुणश्रुतिमात्रेण मयि सर्वगुहाशये।
> मनोगतिरविच्छिन्ना यथा गङ्गाम्भसो ऽम्बुधौ॥
> लक्षणं भक्तियोगस्य निर्गुणस्य ह्युदाहृतम्।
> अहैतुक्यव्यवहिता या भक्तिः पुरुषोत्तमे॥

[25]That is, Brs., 1.1.11 which was cited previously.

[26]*Nārada-pañcarātra* cited at Brs., 1.1.12:

> सर्वोपाधिविनिर्मुक्तं तत्परत्वेन निर्मलं।
> हृषीकेण हृषीकेशसेवनं भक्तिरुत्तमा॥

core of the power of pleasure (*hlādinī*) within the essential powers (*svarūpa-śakti*)[27] cannot be any part of this deadened world of *māyā*. That self-manifesting characteristic (*dharma*) of the lover of the Lord in the form of waves of *bhakti*, in order to enlarge the ultimate good fortune of living beings, who are bound beginninglessly to this world, flows in one stream from Śrī Kṛṣṇa to Brahmā, from Brahmā to Nārada and from Nārada to Vyāsa, Śuka and so forth, and also in another stream in the lineage from Saṅkarṣaṇa to the Catuḥsana, to Sāṅkhyāyana, Parāśara, Maitreya, Vidura and so forth. Then, both streams uniting into one in Śuka's words, and gushing up like a fountain of the highest ambrosia in the presence of thousands and thousands of seers, *brāhmaṇa*-seers, king-seers, great seers, god-seers, and seers of Brahman in the assembly occasioned by King Parīkṣit's sitting down in his fast unto death, the one united stream ceaselessly flows in this phenomenal world through channels in the form of the successions of pure *bhaktas*. The simultaneous conjunction of these two causes—(1) the most elevated contact with the successions in the form of unmotivated association with the great ones, and (2) hearing discussions of Hari, like streams of the Gaṅgā, from the mouths of those saintly ones—infuses pure *bhakti* into the hearts of living beings. This subject was mentioned previously in the verse beginning: "By contact with the saintly arise discussions ... " (*satāṃ prasaṅgān mama vīryasaṃvidaḥ*).[28]

The living being is beginninglessly turned away from Hari and struck low by *māyā* through the beguilement of ignorance; it has forgotten its true self-nature and confuses itself with the lumpen body. As a result of that, it becomes blinded by illusions in the form of the subtle traces or residual desires (*vāsanā*) for material objects. Therefore, when the living being is in that state of identification with matter, its own essential and innate condition as a servant of Kṛṣṇa is not revealed. Just as at the touch of the morning's rays of light, a lotus flower gradually begins to blossom in the light of day, so does the lotus of a living being's heart, in which, after the beginningless darkness of ignorance is destroyed by contact with

[27]The phrase that defines *bhakti* in the Caitanya tradition is: *hlādinī-sāra-samaveta-saṃvit-sāra-rūpā*, "the essence or core of [the power of] consciousness intimately united with the essence or core of [the power of] pleasure." See Baladeva, for instance, *Siddhānta-ratna*, para. 38. [Trans.]

[28]*Bhāg.*, 3.25.24

the great ones, a sense of being a servant of Kṛṣṇa, or of turning back toward Kṛṣṇa, awakens. It is said: *matsmṛtiḥ sādhusevayā,*[29] "from contact with and service of the saintly, a living being's recollection of me (Kṛṣṇa), lost for an eternity, is awakened." In this way a living being who has turned towards Kṛṣṇa is transformed into a pure living being. In that state, pure *bhakti* in the form of stories about Kṛṣṇa arising from contact with the great is passed into the pure heart of the living being and finally, like nectar suffusing a lotus flower, the heart of the living being is infused with the honey of divine love (*preman*), which is the only thing enjoyed by the bumblebee Kṛṣṇa.

A small pot that is upside-down in a rainstorm is at first, by the force of the rain, turned rightside up and then along with that is filled by the rain showers. But when water falls on the pot when it is upside-down, though the dirt on the outside is surely cleansed away, it is not filled with water.[30] In a similar way when one has contact with stories about Kṛṣṇa in some other fashion, not through contact with the saintly, the exterior impurities of the heart are indeed removed. But one only gets the secondary results of that in the form of the group of four [goals, that is, piety, wealth, sense enjoyment, and liberation]. As a result of contact with the saintly, however, like a pot being straightened up by the rain, the operations of the heart of the living being are changed from being beginninglessly turned away from the Lord to being turned towards the Lord, and in the succeeding showers of pure *bhakti* in the form of stories about Kṛṣṇa from the mouths of the saintly, the vessel of the heart, beginning with faith and so forth, becomes filled with the water of thread-free *bhakti.* The destruction of the border-line (*taṭastha*) living being's identification with matter and the living being's becoming identified with the Lord's essential power (*svarūpa-śakti*) through pure *bhakti* is the benefit of all benefits—the highest attainment of all attainments. This can only occur from the happenstance conjunction of two causes simultaneously—the instrumental cause of contact with the saintly and the material cause of stories about Kṛṣṇa [heard in that company].

---

[29] Bhāg., 11.11.45.

[30] In a rain storm, small, upside-down pots are often turned over by the force of the falling rain. However, when one simply pours water onto a small, upside-down pot it does not turn over. This is the difference intended by this analogy.

Practically speaking, apart from the conjunction of contact with the saintly and the *bhakti-yoga* of hearing and praising that comes from that, there is no other way to attain *bhakti*. This is because I am the only shelter of the saintly.[31]

[31] Bhāg., 11.11.48:

प्रायेण भक्तियोगेन सत्सङ्गेन विनोद्धव।
नोपायो विद्यते सम्यक्प्रायणं सतामहम्॥

Chapter Two

"Association with the saintly is the source of the birth of *bhakti* for Kṛṣṇa." (*kṛṣṇabhakti-janmamūla haya sādhusaṅga*).[1] By this statement, association with the saintly (*sādhu-saṅga*) is said to be the root of the birth of *bhakti* for Kṛṣṇa. Therefore, it is first necessary to discuss to some degree the nature of the saintly or great ones, that is, to ascertain their essential defining characteristics.

In the case of the knower, knowledge and the thing known, by the conjunction of those three with each other, each of the three is known. In the presence of one of them the presence of the other two is unavoidable. In the same way the *bhakta*, *bhakti*, and Bhagavān (the Lord) have an unbreakable connection with each other. Therefore, wherever the *bhakta* is, there is *bhakti* in the form of discussions about Hari. And wherever *bhakti* is, there Bhagavān is certain to be present too. Therefore, there is an inseparable connection between these three. These three are one and one is these three. And the co-existence of these three together is known in the world as *bhāgavata-dharma*, the way of the Lord.

Though discussions of Hari or talks about the names, the forms, the qualities, and the sports of Bhagavān are not different from him, there is in a special sense a principle of eternal non-difference between the holy name and the holy named. It is like a chickpea inside its skin. Though from the outside with the skin on, it appears to be one, inside the skin the existence of two peas is well known. In the same way in the covering of the skin of truth (*tattva*) the holy

---

[1] Cc., 2.22.48:

কৃষ্ণভক্তি-জন্মমূল হয় সাধুসঙ্গ|

named and the holy name are non-different. Even so, freed from their covering they each exist separately. For the two peas in their skin there is no way to determine whose function it is to bud and so forth and thus those functions are perceived as simultaneously accomplished by both. In the same way the functions of endless creation and so forth are understood to be accomplished from both the natures of the holy named and holy name together.

Therefore, Brahman or Kṛṣṇa and the *praṇava* or the name of Kṛṣṇa that are mentioned in *śruti*[2]—the Named and the Name—to both of those is non-different agency assigned. [Concerning] Brahman and the conveyor of Brahman, the *praṇava* (*oṃ*): since the two are principles that are not different from each other, what all of the *śruti* texts say about Brahman in passages like: *sarvaṃ khalvidaṃ brahma*,[3] "all this is Brahman," they also say about the conveyor of Brahman in passages like *omitīdaṃ sarvam*,[4] "om is all this," and *omityetadakṣaramidaṃ sarvam*,[5] "the syllable *om* is all this." In relationship to this non-difference, an even clearer statement exists in *śruti*:

> This syllable [*oṃ*][6] is Brahman; this syllable is the highest. Knowing this syllable, whatever one desires one achieves.[7]

The Brahman, or the principle of non-dual knowledge (*advaya-jñāna-tattva*), mentioned in *śruti* is manifested in two ways: it is either with or without qualification. Brahman with qualification is Śrī Kṛṣṇa, concealed in indirect language.[8] Brahman without qualification is Śrī Kṛṣṇa's bodily glow. Therefore, he is the foundation

---

[2]*Śruti* refers to the ancient texts that are believed to be revelations in the Hindu tradition. Those are the four Vedas, the Brāhmaṇas, the Āraṇyakas, and the Upaniṣads. All else is *smṛti*, "remembered" texts or tradition.

[3]Chānd. U., 3.14.1.

[4]Tait. U., 1.7.

[5]Māṇḍukya U., 1.

[6]*akṣara*, also "imperishable."

[7]Kāṭhaka U., 2.16:

> एतद्ध्येवाक्षरं ब्रह्म एतद्ध्येवाक्षरं परम्।
> एतद्ध्येवाक्षरं ज्ञात्वा यो यदिच्छति तस्य तत्॥

[8]*Śruti* (*Gopāla-tāpanī* ?): कृष्णो ब्रह्मैव शाश्वतम्, "Kṛṣṇa is eternal Brahman itself."

or resting place of Brahman. In the *Gītā*, we have Śrī Kṛṣṇa's own statement on the matter: *brahmaṇo hi pratiṣṭhāham*, "I am the foundation or ground of Brahman without qualification."

Therefore, when Brahman, the subject of speech, and the speech that conveys it, the *praṇava* or *oṃkāra*, are said to be non-different, then, too, the subject of speech, the Named, Śrī Kṛṣṇa, and the speech that conveys him, the Name Kṛṣṇa or the holy name, should also be understood as non-different. Bhagavān and Bhagavān's name are non-different as has been made well-known in all sacred texts. Take for instance the *Padma Purāṇa*: *abhinnatvān nāma-nāmino*, "because of the non-difference of the Name and the Named." There is a detailed discussion of this subject in the first section of my *Thought-jewel of the Holy Name* (*Nāma-cintāmaṇi*).

Again, since Brahman is the unqualified manifestation of Śrī Kṛṣṇa, the *praṇava* which conveys Brahman is the unqualified manifestation of Śrī Kṛṣṇa's name or, put in another way, the *praṇava*'s qualified manifestation is Śrī Kṛṣṇa's name, the name of Bhagavān. This, too, is understood on the evidence of the sacred texts. Just as from the *praṇava* the manifestation of the creation and of the Vedas and such is said to arise, so too from the eighteen-syllable mantra of Kṛṣṇa's names,[9] the entire creation along with the Vedas and the rest are said to arise. In the *Gopāla-tāpanī Upaniṣad* and other *śruti* texts that is presented in a more detailed manner.

Therefore, from our deliberations on this subject so far, this much can be established: when the three, *bhakta*, *bhakti*, and *Bhagavān* are found together in one place, then by referring to it as "association with the saintly," one means the meeting together in one place of the three: the *bhakta*, *bhakti*, and *Bhagavān* in his non-different nature as the holy name and the holy named. "Talks about Hari" (*hari-kathā*) from the lips of a *bhakta* means discourses about the names, forms, qualities, and sports of Hari. Moreover, since the names are mentioned first, the names are then understood to be the most important of them all, the very whole [of which the others are parts]. In addition, when the whole, the holy name, is present, its limbs or parts in the form of the nine types of *bhakti*, headed by hearing, praising, and so forth, and *bhakti*'s result, divine love (*preman*), are also present along with it. This is the essential def-

[9]The Gopāla-mantra.

inition of "the great" [in the phrase "association with the great," *mahat-saṅga*]. In other words, by contact with the "raiser of the dead" in the form of the grace of the "great" in the combination of all those elements, the finest spiritual nature is awakened in the living being suffering under *māyā*. When that happens, pure *bhakti*, as discussion of Hari from the mouths of the saintly, is infused into the heart of the purified living being. In the gradual arising of that unthreaded (*nirguṇa*) *bhakti*, it appears in the mind's states of unclean, clean, and fully clean as the *bhakti* of practice, the *bhakti* of feeling, and the *bhakti* of love. The living being (*jīva*) is transformed into a *bhakta* and attaining immortality is made eternally fortunate. This begins by the combination of being turned back towards Kṛṣṇa and of hearing the holy names from the mouths of the saintly, both of which result directly from association with the saintly. And then, as a result of those, the nine forms of *bhakti*, beginning with hearing and praising, appear and divine love arises gradually through the stages of faith and so forth. Since the holy name which is non-different from the holy named is present with the saintly, the holy name is worthy of being considered a material cause of pure *bhakti*. Therefore, in the *Caitanya-caritāmṛta* it is said: *sādhu-saṅga nāma vinā prema nāhi haya*:[10] "without association with the saintly and the holy name divine love does not arise." In other words, association with the saintly is the instrumental cause of divine love and the holy name is the material cause.

Next we have to discuss the "seed principle," that is, the primal cause of the root of the birth of *bhakti* for Kṛṣṇa. Just as the seed is the cause of the cause or the cause of the root of a tree, it is known from sacred text that the Named and the Name, in essence non-different from each other, are simultaneously the seed of the root of the creation. Therefore, the Named and the Name are found being described as the seed principle in the sacred texts. For instance [Kṛṣṇa says]:

> Know me to be the eternal seed of all beings, son of Pṛthā.[11]

---

[10]Cc., 3.3.253. The text found in Dr. Radhagovinda Nath's edition is slightly different: *sādhu-kṛpā nāma vine prema nāhi haya*, "Without the grace of a holy one and the holy name, divine love does not arise."

[11]Bg, 7.10:

Again, in reference to the holy name there is a statement: "seed of the tree of *dharma*."[12] Or, in the *Caritāmṛta*: *kṛṣṇa-nāma bīja tāhe nā haya aṅkara*,[13] "the seed of the holy name in him has not sprouted," and *bhakti-latā bīja*, "the seed of the vine of *bhakti*."

In the statement from *śruti*, *omitīdaṃ sarvam*,[14] "the *om* is all this," the indistinct name of Bhagavān is specified as the seed at the root of creation. Again in the *Brahma-saṃhitā*, in the verse *śabda-brahma-mayaṃ veṇuṃ vādayantaṃ mukhāmbuje*, "playing the flute made of sound-brahman with his lotus mouth ... ," the presence of the holy name and the holy named is established, through the flute, before the creation of the world by Brahmā. The holy name and the holy named, in their non-different essence, is established as the seed, as is the agency of the holy name in the creation of that world. In the previously mentioned *Gopāla-tāpanī Upaniṣad* Kṛṣṇa's name in the form of the eighteen-syllable *mantra* is described as the seed of the entirety of the universe of rebirth or as the cause of all and thus the supremacy of the name of Kṛṣṇa which is not different from Kṛṣṇa in the causation of the creation is introduced. Not only is it the cause or seed of the universe; the supremacy of the name of Kṛṣṇa as the seed at the root of the creation of the Vedas from the *gāyatrī*, of the *gāyatrī* from the *praṇava* has been proclaimed in the sacred texts. Though this requires a lengthy discussion, a little glimpse of this subject can be had from the following quote:

> *Praṇava*, the great word, is an image of God.
> From the *praṇava* arise all the Vedas and the world.[15]

Therefore, from the seed, Kṛṣṇa's name, which is non-different from Kṛṣṇa, appears the entire universe along with the sacred texts headed by the Vedas. Also, although association with the saintly is said to be the root of *bhakti*, the seed or first cause of that root is the presence of the holy name in a saintly person's heart and at

---

बीजं मां सर्वभूतानां विद्धि पार्थ सनातनम्।

[12] *Padyāvalī*, 19: बीजं धर्मद्रुमस्य

[13] Cc, 1.8.26.

[14] Tait. U., 1.7.

[15] Cc., 2.6.158:

প্রণব সে মহা-বাক্য ঈশ্বরের মূর্তি

প্রণব হৈতে সর্ব-বেদ জগতের উৎপত্তি

the beginning of all discussions about Hari heard from the lips of saintly persons.

Thus, this much is known from the essential definition of the saintly or the great person, that through associating with the saintly it is possible to attain simultaneously association with the *bhakta*, with *bhakti*, and with the Lord (in the indistinguishable forms of name and named) all together. Moreover, from the secondary definition, or the definition based on knowledge of the effects of a thing, it is known that from the discussion of and hearing about the names, forms, qualities, and sports of Hari through the words of the saintly ones pure *bhakti* is infused into the hearts of living beings.

"The living being's true identity is eternal servant of Kṛṣṇa."[16] In accordance with this statement of the *Caitanya-caritāmṛta* being a servant of Kṛṣṇa is the living being's eternal state of being, which, though eternally remaining in the hearts of living beings deluded by *māyā*, is not capable of manifestation because of their being beginninglessly turned away from him. By the influence of the association of the saintly the state of turning towards Kṛṣṇa arises. When that happens the backward conditions produced by ignorance: being an enjoyer (I am the enjoyer), being the agent (I am the doer), and being the master (I am the master) are erased from the hearts of the living beings and the pure awareness, "I am the servant of Kṛṣṇa, not of anyone else,"[17] arises. This is called being turned towards Kṛṣṇa. This is the living being's eternal, essential nature. From the association and grace of the great ones that long dormant state of being a servent of Kṛṣṇa is awakened. But, the appearance of pure *bhakti* in the heart of the living being is not part of its essential nature. That attribute is infused into it from contact with narratives about Hari received from the mouths of the great ones. Since pure *bhakti* which is a function of the essential or internal power (*svarūpa-śakti*) is not able to reside by itself in the living being which is part of the marginal power (*taṭastha-śakti*), the living being is not described as the eternal "*bhakta*" of Kṛṣṇa but as the eternal "servant" of Kṛṣṇa. Only when one's fullest sense of being a servant of Kṛṣṇa arises, can one, along with that, become a *bhakta* of Kṛṣṇa, too. Since apart from that, or without the grace and as-

[16]Cc, 2.20.101: জীবের স্বরূপ হয় কৃষ্ণের নিত্যদাস.

[17]*Padma Purāṇa*, 60.90: दासभूतो हरेरेव नान्यस्यैव कदाचन

sociation of the great ones, the conceits of being an agent either as a ritualist (*karmī*), a cultivator of knowledge (*jñānī*), or a practitioner of yoga (*yogī* or *yogin*) remain in all other living beings, the condition of being an eternal servant of Kṛṣṇa is not perceived.

In a living being who is a religious aspirant in whom pure *bhakti* has been infused, the nine forms of *bhakti* as practice, beginning with hearing and repeating, are also infused and as their result the appearance of divine love occurs progressively through the stages of faith and so forth. Therefore, for the saintly one the repeating (*kīrtana*) is of primary importance and for the aspirant the hearing (*śravaṇa*) of that is of primary importance. And again within the hearing and repeating, the holy name is the most important of all.

Therefore, the tremendous greatness of repeating the holy names (*nāma-saṅkīrtana*) which is the seed of all is clearly praised in the *Bhāgavata*:

> For embodied beings who are rotating around [on the wheel of cyclic existence] there is no higher gain, since from this [loud repetition of the holy names] one attains the highest peace and the cycle of repeated birth and death is destroyed.[18]

Now we will consider the external definition (*taṭastha-lakṣaṇa*) or the influence or power of association with the great ones. The external definition is knowledge by means of the effects of something. By means of the effects which the great *bhaktas* or saintly ones have, their unsurpassed greatness or power is known.

It is well known that all sacred rivers like the Ganges and so forth and sacred sites like Kurukṣetra, Kāśī, Puṣkara, and so forth are able to destroy the sins of selfish living beings, help them gather merit, and bestow on them the group of four or the human objectives even up to bringing them liberation. But in the process of destroying sins and bestowing merit and the four objectives, they [the sacred sites] themselves become polluted and desecrated by accepting pollutions left behind by the pilgrims. In that condition,

---

[18]Bhāg., 11.5.38:

न ह्यत: परमो लाभो देहिनां भ्राम्यतामिह।
यतो विन्देत परमां शान्तिं नश्यति संसृति:॥

on the arrival of saintly *bhaktas* and by the power of their touch, the polutions are removed and all of the holy places again become sacred. As a result of that, they are able to become purifiers again. One can thoroughly understand this subject from the faithful statement of King Yudhiṣṭhira to the great-spirited Vidura.

> Great *bhaktas* like you are themselves [as pure as] the holy places, lord. They make the sacred places sacred through [the presence] within them of the lord who holds the club [Viṣṇu]. [They only go to them to make the holy places holy. Otherwise, they have no need to wander around to the holy places.][19]

The meaning of the verse is: the *bhaktas* of the lord have no personal purpose to fulfill by wandering around to the holy places. Still they selflessly visit all the holy places which have become polluted by contact with materialistic, selfish people in order to purify them through the gift of their own purity. What greater statement can be made about the greatness of those saintly *bhaktas*?

Moreover, since visits of the saintly in order to obtain purification are very rare, rivers with pious waters like the Ganges and so forth and auspicious holy places like Puṣkara and so forth themselves go where honey-like discussions of Hari flow from the lips of the saintly. As it is said:

> There do the Gaṅgā, Yamunā, the Confluence, the Godāvarī, Sindhu, and Sarasvatī as well as meritorious holy sites reside where there are magnificent discussions about Acyuta [Kṛṣṇa].[20]

Now here one may wish to ask: "How is it possible for all of the rivers like the Ganges and all of the holy places such as Kurukṣetra

---

[19]Bhāg., 1.13.10:

> भवद्विधा भागवतास्तीर्थभूताः स्वयं विभो।
> तीर्थीकुर्वन्ति तीर्थानि स्वान्तःस्थेन गदाभृता॥

The bracketed part of the verse is interpretation added by Goswami.

[20]Source unidentified:

> तत्रैव गङ्गा यमुना च वेणी गोदावरी सिन्धुसरस्वतीश्च।
> पुण्यानि तीर्थानि वसन्ति तत्र यत्राच्युतोदारकथाप्रसङ्गः॥

to come into limited and small places like those where the discussions of Hari are flowing from the mouths of the saintly? And why is that not seen by others?" In reply it must be said that all of the rivers and holy places do not go to places where discussions of Hari are taking place in their bodies. They come in the form of the overseeing spirits [of those rivers and places] and by the influence of their powers of invisibility they are not visible to ordinary sight. The powers of invisibility of even the demi-gods is well known in the sacred texts.

From our previous discussion it has been established that discussions of Hari from the lips of the saintly, that is, discussions of Hari's names, forms, qualities, and sports, are all non-different from Hari. Nevertheless, since it is especially germane, we shall now discuss in greater detail only the complete non-difference between the holy named and the holy name from among those four. It is said:

> [The Lord himself, Śrī Kṛṣṇa, said to Nārada:] I do not live in Vaikuṇṭha nor in the hearts of the *yogins*. Wherever my *bhaktas* sing, there I am present, Nārada.[21]

The intended meaning of this verse is: Kṛṣṇa is the Supreme Person himself. He does not reside in his own form in Vaikuṇṭha. Instead, his expansions and partial forms reside there. He also does not reside in the hearts of the *yogins* because the hearts of all living beings are the residence of his partial form, the Paramātman or Highest Self. That is understood from his statement in the *Gītā*:

> I am the Self (*ātman*) situated in the hearts of all beings, Guḍākeśa [Arjuna].[22]

Even though Bhagavān resides in the form of his partial manifestation, the Highest Self (Paramātman), in the hearts of all living

---

[21] *Padma Purāṇa*, cited in the *Hari-bhakti-vilāsa*, 8.284:

नाहं वसामि वैकुण्ठे योगिनां हृदये न च।
मद्भक्ता यत्र गायन्ति तत्र तिष्ठामि नारद॥

[22] *Bhagavad-gītā*, 10.20:

अहमात्मा गुडाकेश सर्वभूताशयस्थितः।

beings, that is not visible to ordinary living beings who face outwards. *Yogins* who practice the eight-limbed yoga[23] are able to see him as their object of worship. As it is said:

> Some remember through concentration the person (*puruṣa*), measuring only the span between the thumb and forefinger, sitting in the space of their hearts in their own bodies. He has four arms holding a lotus, a discus, a conch shell, and a club.[24]

But from the previous statement: "wherever my *bhaktas* sing, there I am present, Nārada," it is made clear that he is present in his own form where his names are being sung by his *bhaktas* with *bhakti*. Since the named and the name are a non-different principle, there is no mention of his being present in his partial Highest Self form. Moreover, he is not present there to attain purification by destroying his own impurities like the presiding spirits of the holy places mentioned before. That is because, in him who is Bhagavān himself, full of the six opulences, faults like pollution and so forth cannot exist even in the least degree. Therefore, there is no question of his having to rid himself of pollution. Since the named and the name are not different, wherever the name is, the named in his own form is also understood to be present. Also from the statement of the *Caitanya-caritāmṛta*: "Kṛṣṇa's resting place is always in the heart of his *bhakta*,"[25] it is understood he is not only in the mouth of the *bhakta* as discussions of Hari. In the heart of the *bhakta* Kṛṣṇa always experiences the happiness of repose—in his own form.

---

[23]The eight-limbed yoga or *aṣṭāṅga-yoga* is the classical form of yoga called by some Rāja-yoga, the king of yogas. Its eight limbs or practices are: the self-restraints (*yama*), the observances (*niyama*), the sitting postures (*āsana*), breath control (*prāṇāyāma*), withdrawal of the mind from the senses (*pratyāhāra*), concentration (*dhāranā*), meditation (*dhyāna*), and trance or union with the object of meditation (*samādhi*). These are presented and discussed in the classic text on yoga, the *Yoga-sūtra* of Patañjali.

[24]*Bhāg.*, 2.2.8:

> केचित्स्वदेहान्तर्हृदयावकाशे प्रादेशमात्रं पुरुषं वसन्तम्।
> चतुर्भुजं कञ्जरथाङ्गशङ्खगदाधरं धारणया स्मरन्ति॥

[25]Cc., 1.1.30:

> ভক্তের হৃদয়ে কৃষ্ণের সতত বিশ্রাম|

One in whose heart flows a bubbling stream of *bhakti* in the form of discussions of Hari, whose heart-temple is pure, free of the dust and smoke of inclinations for the objects of the senses, and in whose heart, since it is free of all the hullabaloo of self interest and completely absent of desire, it is silent, quiet, and solitary and in whom, apart from being for Kṛṣṇa alone, there is not even a speck of self consideration—such a pure, cool, peaceful *bhakta*'s heart-temple is a place suitable for Kṛṣṇa's repose. Repose does not mean sleep. It means the experience of happiness alone without any effort or strain. The hearts of ritualists, pursuers of knowledge, and *yogins* are not places of repose for him. In place of his [Kṛṣṇa's] interest exists selfishness or self interest in the form of desire for sense enjoyment, liberation, and supernatural accomplishments (*siddhis*). In his form as the Highest Self-as-Witness (*sākṣī-paramātman*), when he resides in the hearts of all living beings, though he himself is unaffected, he has to perceive all their auspicious and inauspicious subconscious trace-desires that result from their past actions (*karma-vāsanā*) and their experiences of the results thereof. As it says in the *Gītā*:

> Because of being beginningless and without [material] thread, this Higher Self is imperishable. Though situated in the body, Kaunteya [Arjuna, son of Kuntī], he does nothing and is not affected.[26]

In the hearts of desire-filled living beings, which are always full of the bad odors of sensual impressions (*viṣaya-vāsanā*) and a cacophony of screams for self-interest, whether it be for liberation in the case of those who pursue knowledge or for supernatural powers in the case of *yogins* or for something else, he [the Lord] cannot find repose in his form as the unaffected, beginningless, thread-less Highest Self. Because of being free from the subconscious impressions of desire (*kāmanā-vāsanā*) and of having rejected all forms of self interest for the pleasure of Kṛṣṇa, the *bhakta*'s heart is clean, supremely beautiful, and secluded. Therefore, for the pleasure of

---

[26] *Bhagavad-gītā*, 13.31:

> अनादित्वान्निर्गुणत्वात्परमात्माऽयमव्ययः।
> शरीरस्थोऽपि कौन्तेय न करोति न लिप्यते॥

uninterrupted repose, Śrī Kṛṣṇa has chosen the heart-temple of the *bhakta*. Not only that, in the way that two *vīṇās* (the Indian lute), matching each other string by string, produce one melody—reveal a harmony—the heart strings of Śrī Kṛṣṇa become harmonious with the heart strings of his devotee and in both hearts one melody is sounded. He has said this with his own lips:

> The saintly are the heart for me and of the saintly I am the heart. They know nothing other than me nor do I know anything other than them in the least.[27]

When there is oneness in the hearts of the devotee and Bhagavān in this way, through the harmony of the melodies in each of their hearts, their hearts develop a oneness of intention. But, because of the foul odor of sensual inclinations in the hearts of ritualists, pursuers of knowledge, and *yogins* and the cacophony of their being intent on achieving their own other purposes, not only is there no question of their reaching a oneness of heart with him, their hearts are unfit to be places of repose for Bhagavān. One can understand from his own words that apart from *bhakti* Bhagavān cannot be attained directly by any other means such as rites, yoga, cultivation of knowledge, and so forth:

> Uddhava, yoga does not achieve me, nor does Sāṅkhya, nor Dharma, nor study of the Veda, nor austerity, nor renunciation the way that strong *bhakti* for me does.[28]

About the cause for this it is therefore said in the *Caitanya-caritāmṛta*:

> Kṛṣṇa's *bhakta* is desireless
> and therefore is at peace.

---

[27] *Bhāg.*, 9.4.68:

> साधवो हृदयं मह्यं साधूनां हृदयस्त्वहम्।
> मदन्यत्ते न जानन्ति नाहं तेभ्यो मनागपि॥

[28] *Bhāg.*, 11.14.20:

> न साधयति मां योगो न साङ्ख्यं धर्म उद्धव।
> न स्वाध्यायस्तपस्त्यागो यथा भक्तिर्ममोर्ज्जिता॥

> Wishers for enjoyment, liberation, and powers (*siddhis*)
> are all without peace.[29]

[29] Cc., 2.9.132:

> কৃষ্ণভক্ত নিষ্কাম অতএব শান্ত|
> ভুক্তি-মুক্তি-সিদ্ধিকামী সকলি অশান্ত||

Chapter Three

According to the hierarchy of *bhaktas'* longing to serve Kṛṣṇa, excellence reaches its highest point in Śrī Rādhikā. Therefore, Bhagavān's repose is its happiest in the heart of Śrī Rādhikā, the great queen of *bhakti* whose very essence is *mahābhāva.*[1] Rādhikā's heart is full of the experience of only the happiness of serving Kṛṣṇa. In her case there is no independent experience of any happiness. In her heart, in the state of intensely experiencing the joy of serving Kṛṣṇa, that enjoyment becomes expanded; and when that internal experience boils over and manifests itself externally in hundreds and thousands of streams, that one Rādhārāṇī takes the forms of millions of cowherd girls and gives Śrī Hari, who sports in the bower of the heart, the happiness of repose. Externally, too, she creates unlimited bowers for that purpose. This is the bower-service of the cowherd girls of Vraja and Kuñjavihārī's [Kṛṣṇa's] love-sports in secluded forest bowers. Just as it always shines in the hearts of the devotees, so is it also always performed externally as well. It never ceases in either place [in the hearts or externally] at any time. One drop from that ocean of the experience of service bursting forth, overflowing in a thousand streams, and inundating the heart of the *bhakta* is found in the following words of a *bhakta*:

> I feel as if my heart, bobbing in a river, is spread wide,
> and on it golden Gaurāṅga dances.[2]

---

[1] The greatest emotional condition of love.

[2] Source unidentified:

> মনে করি নদে জুড়ি হৃদয় বিছাই
> তাহার উপরে সোনার গৌরাঙ্গ নাচাই

Nothing can be greater in excellence than a saintly *bhakta* of Hari in whose heart is the permanent place of Bhagavān's repose and who has become thoroughly identified, as it were, with both *bhakti* and Bhagavān. And among them again there is no limit to the greatness of those who are wholeheartedly sheltered in Kṛṣṇa. Therefore, in the sacred texts, the superiority of the *bhakta* or Vaiṣṇava over the ritualist, the pursuer of knowledge, the *yogin* and so forth is proclaimed. And among the *bhaktas* the superiority of the wholehearted ones is acclaimed in particular. Take for instance:

> Better than thousands of performers of sacrificial rites is one who has mastered all the Vedānta and better than millions of masters of Vedānta is one *bhakta* of Viṣṇu. Out of thousands of Vaiṣṇavas one who is wholehearted (*ekāntin*) is superior. Those persons who are wholehearted go to the highest realm.[3]

In this way, out of a thousand *bhaktas* one who is single-purposed (*ekānta*) [or wholehearted] is established as the best of all in the *Gītā*, the Lord's own words. Pointing to himself he said: "one who thinks of me alone." By this statement the superiority of the single-ended *bhakta* of Kṛṣṇa is confirmed. For instance:

> The *yogin* is considered greater than performers of austerity and greater than pursuers of knowledge, too. The *yogin* is greater than ritualists as well. Therefore, become a *yogin*, Arjuna. And among all *yogins*, one who worships me with faith, his heart having flown to me, is in my opinion the best.[4]

---

[3] *Garuḍa Purāṇa*, cited in the *Hari-bhakti-vilāsa* at 10.117:

सत्रयाजिसहस्रेभ: सर्ववेदान्तपारग:।
सर्ववेदान्तवित्कोट्या विष्णुभक्तो विशिष्यते॥
वैष्णवानां सहस्रेभ्य एकान्त्येको विशिष्यते।
एकान्तिनस्तु पुरुषा गच्छन्ति परमं पदं॥

[4] *Bhagavad-gītā*, 6.46-7:

तपस्विभ्यो ऽधिको योगी ज्ञानिभ्यो ऽपि मतो ऽधिक:।
कर्मिभ्यश्चाधिको योगी तस्माद्योगी भवार्जुन॥
योगिनामपि सर्वेषां मद्गतेनान्तरात्मना।
श्रद्धवान् भजते यो मां स मे युक्ततमो मत:॥

In this verse *mad-gatena* means "in me"—in Śrī Kṛṣṇa—and *antar-ātmanā* means "with the whole mind." Together they mean "attached to me in all respects." By this, it is established that those whose minds or hearts are "made of Kṛṣṇa" (*kṛṣṇa-maya*), they are the wholehearted or single-purposed *bhaktas*.

In another place in the *Gītā*, the same idea is stated in this way:

> Those who fix their minds in me and being constantly joined [with me] worship me, they, possessing the highest faith, I consider the highest *yogins*.[5]

Single-purposed *bhakta*-saints are "made of Hari" and Hari, too, becomes made of those kinds of *bhaktas* and enjoys the pleasure of resting in their hearts. The *bhaktas*, too, do not care for any pleasure for themselves other than the pleasure of perceiving the pleasure of the Lord. In the hearts of both, there is but one life; that is the meaning here. In this kind of situation the experiences in the hearts of Hari-made *bhaktas* are echoed in the heart of the Lord and the experiences in the heart of the Lord are echoed in the hearts of the *bhaktas*.

The meaning of the previously cited verse: "The saintly are my heart and I am the heart of the saintly," is that the *bhakta* and the Lord share but one life. We are also able to understand this clearly in the following verse in the Lord's own words:

> I am equal towards all living beings; I have neither enemy nor favorite. But those who worship me with *bhakti*, they are in me and I am in them.[6]

Śrī Bhagavān, who is the resting place of the delight-giving power (*hlādinī-śakti*), though by nature pleasure himself experiences pleasure and causes his *bhaktas* to feel pleasure by means of his delight-giving power. As it is said:

---

[5]ibid., 12.2:

मय्यावेश्य मनो ये मां नित्ययुक्ता उपासते।
श्रद्धया परयोपेतास्ते मे युक्ततमा मताः॥

[6]ibid., 9.29:

समो ऽहं सर्वभूतेषु न मे द्वेष्यो ऽस्ति न प्रियः।
ये भजन्ति तु मां भक्त्या मयि ते तेषु चाप्यहम्॥

> Though Bhagavān is the very form of delight, that by which he delights and causes delight is the pleasure-giving power. (*hlādinī-śakti*).[7]

This delight when it resides in Bhagavān is called "power" (*śakti*) and when it is in the *bhakta* it is called *bhakti*. By *bhakti* we generally mean being fond of or loving the Lord and by *bhakta* we mean the one who has that fondness or love. When the *bhakti* in the heart of the *bhakta* makes the Lord its object or becomes focused on him, it goes to him and touches him and then the Lord's delight appears. That pleasure of the Lord comes back to the *bhakta* and in turn gives the *bhakta* pleasure or bestows the joy of service on the *bhakta*. As by the soft touch of the evening breeze the budding tuberose blossoms and spreads its own sweet aroma on the breast of the breeze, and the breeze turns around and returns carrying that fragrance in its heart, so, being touched by the *bhakti* in the heart of the *bhakta*, the sleeping delight in Bhagavān is awakened and gives him (Bhagavān) pleasure. Then it returns to the *bhakta* carrying the pleasure of serving the Lord. By the touch of the fragrance of that pleasure the heart of the *bhakta* becomes filled to overflowing. Therefore, how can there be anything equal or superior to the magnificence of a great *bhakta* in whom the three: *bhakta*, *bhakti*, and Bhagavān are united with each other and share one life with each other, absorbed in the experience of each other's delight?

Previously I said that even places of pilgrimage become purified by contact with great *bhaktas*. Among all of the gods Brahmā and Rudra are the best. The might of the *bhaktas* or *bhāgavatas* (lovers of the Lord) is even greater than that of Brahmā and Rudra. This is evidenced by what the king of the gods, Indra himself, said:

> In the Age of Kali, the rare name "*bhāgavata*" [lover of the Lord] is not attained.[8] It is higher than the estate of

---

[7] Śrī Jīva, *Bhagavat-sandarbha*, para. 117: ह्लादकरूपो ऽपि भगवान् यया ह्लादते ह्लादयति च सा ह्लादिनी

[8] [Author's note:] Apart from the present Age of Kali in which Gaura has appeared, in all the other Ages of Kali even the titles "*bhāgavata*" and "*bhakta*" are very rare. This is hardly worth mentioning. The reason is that even though the name of Hari is the religious observation for all Ages of Kali, the humans in all those ordinary Ages of Kali are not inclined to take to it. "The people in Kali will not honor that" (Bhāg., 12.3.44: यक्ष्यन्ति न तत्कलौ जनाः). For this reason, since they are without religious

> Brahmā and Rudra. This my guru [Bṛhaspati] told me.[9]

Therefore, what joy in the worlds of humans and gods can be compared with the greatness of association with the great *bhaktas*? Even the joys of liberation or of heaven cannot be compared with a small speck of their greatness. As it is said:

> We cannot compare even the briefest association of the companions of the Lord with going to heaven or even not being reborn again. What more [need be said about comparing this association] with the desired objectives of mortals?[10]

As a result of visiting the holy places and worshipping the gods one attains heaven and liberation. When that attainment of heaven and liberation cannot be compared to even the briefest association with the saintly then to what can the greatness of association with the saintly be compared? The excellence of *bhakti*, the *bhakta*, and Bhagavān is greater than that of even Brahma-loka which is the

---

cultivation, *bhaktas* and association with the saintly are rare. But, about the present Age of Kali in which Gaura has appeared, an independent characterization is found in the sacred texts. In this Age of Kali it is said that many people will become devotees of Nārāyaṇa or *bhaktas* of Hari. "In Kali, indeed, there will be many intent on Nārāyaṇa" (Bhāg., 11.5.38: कलौ खलु भविष्यन्ति नारायणपरायणा:)

Moreover, in this Kali, the age's religious observance of repetition of the holy name is willingly accepted by all people. This is by the grace of the Lord. Therefore, even though there is no shortage of saintly *bhaktas* in the present condition of Kali, because of an abundance of Kali-instigated offenses to the holy name, *bhakti* is seen to arise in very few cases at present. This is due to the holy name's displeasure.

In this age, since the holy name is accepted and since, provided offenses to the holy name do not persist, there is a good opportunity the highest form of love of all to appear, the people of the Age of Satya and the other ages beg to be born in this special Age of Kali in which Gaura appeared. This also is understood from a verse of the *Bhāgavata*: "O King, the living beings born in the Kṛta and the other ages wish to be born in Kali" (Bhāg., 11.5.38: कृतादिषु प्रजा राजन् कलाविच्छन्ति सम्भवम्).

[9]Cited in the *Hari-bhakti-vilāsa*, 10.65:

> कलौ भागवतं नाम दुर्लभं नैव लभ्यते।
> ब्रह्मरुद्रपदोत्कृष्टं गुरुणा कथितं मम।

[10]Bhāg., 1.18.13:

> तुलयाम लवेनापि न स्वरं नापुनर्भवं।
> भगवत्सङ्गिसङ्गस्य मर्त्यानां किमुताशिष:॥

highest plane of all. With what else can the highest reaches of the greatness of those three joined together in the person of the *bhakta* be compared? By its absence the great respectability of Brahmaloka itself becomes less than insignificant. That is revealed by the following verse:

> A place where there are no streams of delight from stories about Vaikuṇṭha, no saintly *bhāgavatas* who are sheltered by him, and no great festivals celebrating that Lord of Sacrifice, even if [that place] is the world of the chief of the gods [Brahmā], it is not fit for habitation.[11]

Where can one find anything that can be compared with the greatness of association with great, saintly *bhaktas* who incorporate in themselves *bhakti*, Bhagavān, and *bhakta*, gathered together in unity? Only the greatness of Bhagavān himself remains shining above all else. A clear indication that Bhagavān chooses that sort of *bhakta* as his own representative is understood from the following verse:

> One who has mastered the four Vedas is not dear to me, but a dog-cooker who is my *bhakta is* dear to me. Things [meant to be offered to me] should be offered to him and [things that should be received from me] should be received from him, and he is to be honored just like me.[12]

Therefore, for those who are the representatives of Bhagavān, where will one find anything to equal their greatness? Thus, his own single-aimed *bhaktas*, who are bound to him by their shared

---

[11] Bhāg., 4.19.23:

> न यत्र वैकुण्ठकथासुखापगा
> न यत्र साधवो भागवतस्तदाश्रया:।
> न यत्र यज्ञेशमखा महोत्सवा:
> सुरेशलोको ऽपि न वै स सेव्यताम्॥

[12] *Hari-bhakti-vilāsa*, 10.92:

> न मे प्रियश्चतुर्वेदी मद्भक्त: श्वपच: प्रिय:।
> तस्मै देयं ततो ग्राह्यं स च पूज्यो यथा ह्यहम्॥

heart and shared life-breath, are dearest to him. Śrī Bhagavān, therefore, said with his own lips concerning Uddhava, one of the best of that sort of *bhakta*:

> They are not as dear to me as you, [Uddhava,] not Brahmā nor Śaṅkara nor Saṅkarṣaṇa nor Śrī nor even me myself.[13]

How deep Bhagavān's pleasure is with his single-purposed *bhaktas* can be understood from that forceful statement which bursts forth from the inner core of his heart. Therefore, it is not just a matter of representation or of being dear, Bhagavān's own subjugation by the *bhakta* is a well-known subject, too.

Bhagavān, though independent, is dependent on the *bhakta*; though the overlord of all he is submissive to the *bhakta*; and though self-manifesting his appearance depends only on the *bhakti* of the *bhakta*; these facts he himself reveals with great delight in his own words:

> I am dependent on my *bhakta*, o twice-born, as if I were not independent at all. My heart is captured by my saintly *bhaktas*. I am fond of my *bhaktas*. I do not want myself without my saintly *bhaktas*, nor do I want unsurpassed affluence, o brāhmaṇa, without those for whom I am the highest goal. Those who give up their wives, homes, sons, elders, lives, this world and the next and seek shelter in me, how dare I reject them? Those saintly ones whose hearts are bound to me, who look upon all things as equal, bring me under their control through their *bhakti*, like chaste wives do chaste husbands.[14]

---

[13]Bhāg., 11.14.15:

> न तथा मे प्रियतम आत्मयोनिर्न शङ्करः।
> न च सङ्कर्षणो न श्रीर्नैवात्मा च यथ भवान्॥

[14]Bhāg., 9.4.63-6:

> अहं भक्ताधीनो ह्यस्वतन्त्र इव द्विज।
> साधुभिर्ग्रस्तहृदयो भक्तैर्भक्तजनप्रियः॥
> नाहमात्मानमाशासे मद्भक्तैः साधुभिर्विना।
> श्रियञ्चात्यन्तिकीं ब्रह्मन् येषां गतिरहं परा॥

The tremendous, heart-filling excitement of the pleasure that the Lord of All feels in being dependent on his *bhaktas* has been proclaimed in the following verse:

> Though ever liberated, I am bound to my *bhaktas* by the ropes of affection. Though unconquered, I am conquered by them; though uncontrollable, I am controlled by them. For one who, having given up affection for friends and family, loves me, I am his one and only and he is mine; nor do we two have any other friend (*suhṛt*).[15]

The meaning of the word "friend" (*su-hṛt*) is "one whose heart is beautiful" or "a companion who is always in accord with one." Therefore, the heart of the *bhakta* which is free of lust, free of impurities, peaceful, and dispassionate, is the only place of repose for Bhagavān.

ये दारागारपुत्राप्तप्राणान् वित्तमिमं परम्।
हित्वा मां शरणं याताः कथं तांस्त्यक्तुमुत्सहे॥
मयि निर्बद्धहृदयाः साधवः समदर्शनाः।
वशे कुर्वन्ति मां भक्त्या सत्स्त्रियः सत्पतिं यथा॥

[15]*Hari-bhakti-sudhodaya*:

सदा मुक्तोऽपि बद्धोऽस्मि भक्तेषु स्नेहरज्जुभिः।
अजितोऽपि जितोऽहं तैरवश्योऽपि वशीकृतः॥
त्यक्तबन्धुजनस्नेहो मयि यः कुरुते रतिं।
एकस्तस्यास्मि स च मे न चान्योऽस्त्यावयोः सुहृत्॥

Chapter Four

Though Bhagavān himself, Śrī Kṛṣṇa, reposing in the heart of the *bhakta*, as previously described, remains immersed in the experience of effortless happiness and though there there is none of the dust of desire and impulse nor the noise of self-interest, there is another kind of dust that he greatly treasures. That is the dust of the feet of the *bhakta* or *bhakta-pada-reṇu*. Therefore, since that kind of dust is not obtained by merely residing in the *bhakta's* heart, he also follows after them, while remaining in their hearts, wishing to rub himself with the dust of their feet. Just hearing about his submissiveness to his *bhaktas* strikes at the hearts of and awakens goose-flesh in the bodies of the *bhaktas*: "Our Lord is so subservient to his *bhakta*!"

Now, a question might arise: since Bhagavān eternally rests in the heart of the *bhakta*, in order to attain the dust of the feet of the *bhakta* he must leave that place and come outside. How can he rest in one form and at one time both in the *bhakta's* heart and follow after the *bhakta*, too? In reply it must be said that Bhagavān is the possessor of all powers—he is the seat of all, inconceivable, contradictory and uncontradictory powers. Just as *śruti* says: "Seated he travels far; lying down he moves everywhere."[1] Since all difficult-to-accomplish, contradictory characteristics coexist in him simultaneously, he is Bhagavān—he is the regulator of all—the possessor of all powers. This inconceivable possession of all powers demonstrates the Bhagavān-ness of Bhagavān [the godhood of God]. Therefore, although he relaxes and lies down in the heart of the *bhakta*, following after a *bhakta* out of a desire for the dust of

[1] *Kaṭha Upaniṣad*, 1.2.21: आसीनो दूरं व्रजति, शयानो याति सर्वत:

the feet of the *bhakta* is not at all impossible for him. That is because while remaining in one form he is able to manifest many forms[2] and while remaining in one place he is able to go everywhere—through his possession of inconceivable power. What more can be said? Śrī Bhagavān wants to decorate his body with the dust of the feet of that sort of [pure-hearted] *bhakta*. He is more infatuated with desire for the dust of the *bhakta's* feet than he is with desire for the Sāmantaka, Kaustubha, and other precious jewels.

Therefore, the topic of the Lord's innate desire for the dust of the feet of the *bhakta* influenced by his submissiveness to the love of the *bhakta* is mentioned in the *Bhāgavata* in the following manner from the Lord's own lips:

> I always follow after the independent, peaceful, enmity-less, sage who sees all as equal so that I may be purified by the dust from his feet.[3]

His activity of following after the *bhakta* is practiced without their knowledge, in the greatest secrecy. This most compassionate and submissive Bhagavān does not want, by his pursuit of the *bhakta*, to be a cause of pain to the mind or to cause the shying away of the *bhakta*. Therefore, this play of the dust is secret so that the *bhakta's* mind is not disturbed. For this reason this sport is carried out without the knowledge of the *bhakta*.

The words "I may be purified" [from the verse above] are glossed in Śrīdhara Svāmin's commentary in this way: "the meaning is that this is done with the feeling 'let me purify all the universes that exist within me.'"[4] In other words, "my following of the *bhaktas* is done with the purpose of purifying all the universes inside me with the dust of their feet."

Just as *bhaktas* possess *bhakti* for Bhagavān, Śrī Bhagavān possesses *bhakti* for his *bhaktas*. That, too, is clearly stated in the *Bhāga*-

---

[2]*Śruti*: एकं सन्तं बहुदा दृश्यमानम्

[3]*Bhāg.*, 11.14.15:

> निरपेक्षं मुनिं शान्तं निर्वैरं समदर्शनम्।
> अनुव्रजाम्यहं नित्यं पूयेयेत्यङ्घ्रिरेणुभिः॥

[4]Śrīdharasvāmin, comm. on Bhāg. 11.14.15: मदन्तर्वर्तिब्रह्माण्डानि पवित्रीकुर्यामिति भावेनेत्यर्थः

vata: "Thus, o king, Bhagavān has *bhakti* for his *bhaktas*."[5] The external manifestation of the internal, mutual affection between Bhagavān and his *bhakta* takes form in the unlimited sports of the Lord.

Apart from fulfilling the wishes of the *bhakta*, Śrī Bhagavān has no other inclinations. The highest expression of Śrī Bhagavān's desire for the dust of the feet of the *bhakta* is found in the dust-game of the sports of Vraja. After herding the cows, at the cow-dust time [the time of the return to the village of the herds], after adorning his curl-circled face and sacred body with the dust of Vraja kicked up by the hooves of the cows, Śrī Hari, the son of Nanda, returns to his house. In the dust of Vraja the dust of the feet of all the *bhaktas* of Vraja is present. Among those again there is a hierarchy and the more desirable dust is the dust of the feet of the cowherd girls. Although the dust of the feet of all the *bhaktas* is dear to him, the highest satisfaction of his desire is found in the dust of the feet of cowherd girls headed by Śrī Rādhā. Therefore, in the words of the Vaiṣṇava poet it has been suggested: "It is not dust, it is not dust—the dust of the feet of the cowherd girls. That dust, Kānu [Kṛṣṇa], the son of Nanda, rubbed on himself."[6] The zenith of the game of dust is found here—in being sprinkled with the dust of the feet of Śrī Rādhā.

Brahmā's austerities lasting for sixty thousand years, performed out of a desire to obtain the dust of the feet of the cowherd women so highly prized by Bhagavān himself, were fruitless. He did not get it:

> Previously, I practiced austerities for sixty thousand years to gain the dust of the feet of the cowherd women of Nandagopa. Still, I did not obtain the dust of their feet.[7]

---

[5] *Bhāg.*, 10.86.59: एवं स्वभक्तयो राजन् भगवान् भक्तभक्तिवान्

[6] Source unidentified:

> ধূলা নয় ধূলি নয় গোপীপদরেণু|
> এই ধূলা মেখেছিল নন্দসূত কানু||

[7] Rūpa Gosvāmin, *Laghu-bhāgavatāmṛta*, 2.31:

> षष्टिवर्षसहस्राणि मया तप्तं तपः पुरा।
> नन्दगोपव्रजस्त्रीणां पादरेणूपलब्धये।
> तथापि न मया प्राप्तास्तासां वै पादरेणवः॥

Therefore, even the best of *bhaktas*, Uddhava, praises the dust of the feet of the cowherd girls:

> I praise in all respects the dust of the feet of Nanda's women of Vraja whose singing of the story of Hari purifies the three worlds.[8]

Just as that dust is the highest desire of every *bhakta* when he recalls that the dust of the feet of Bhagavān along with the dust of the feet of *bhaktas* exists in this dust of Vraja, so is it for Bhagavān in his desire for the dust of the feet of the *bhakta*. Therefore, the highest limit of Śrī Bhagavān's desire is for the dust of the feet of the *bhakta*, and the greatness of the dust of the feet of the *bhakta* culminates in the dust of the feet of the cowherd girls, or rather, in the dust of Śrī Rādhā's feet.

This dust of the feet of the *bhaktas* has for a long time been the Lord's most dear adornment. Therefore, in the Nadīyā sport the golden body of Śrī Gaura was seen to be covered with that dust again and again. For that reason, there was so much rolling on the ground in the dust with his followers. This was not for insignificant earthly dust; it was because of Bhagavān's desire to be decorated by the dust of the feet of his *bhaktas* and it was also because of the *bhaktas*' desire to be ornamented by the dust of the feet of Bhagavān that this rolling on the ground occurred.

Therefore, the *bhakta*, *bhakti* and Bhagavān—wherever these three are united and are of one mind, one life, and in full harmony, dancing in joy together, there is no way to tell which is greater and which is less great in conduct. Thus:

> Love makes Kṛṣṇa dance;
> the *bhakta*, too, it makes dance;
> it itself dances, too;
> the three dance together.[9]

---

[8]*Bhāg.*, 10.47.63:

वन्दे नन्दव्रजस्त्रीणां पादरेणुमभीक्ष्णशः।
यासां हरिकथोद्गीतं पुनाति भुवनत्रयम्॥

[9]Kṛṣṇadāsa Kavirāja, *Caitanya-caritāmṛta*, Antya 18.17:

কৃষ্ণেরে নাচাই প্রেমা ভক্তেরে নাচাই
আপনে নাচয়ে, তিনে নাচে এক থাঞি

Nevertheless, one must remember that in the seed of *dharma* (religious observance) placed in the *bhakta* saints, the holy name and the holy named are present in their true form as the cause of all causes. Since all that has been previously said is joined together in one and the same person, the great *bhakta*: "in determining the source of the birth of *bhakti* for Kṛṣṇa, association with the saints is the foremost of all."[10] Therefore, it has been said:

The dust of the feet of a *bhakta*,
A *bhakta*'s foot-wash, too,
The remnants of a *bhakta*'s food,
These three have great power.[11]

Now we shall reflect on the freedom and independence of the saintly ones. Association with the saints and the attaining of their grace is spontaneous or causeless. In glossing the words *yad-ṛcchayā* [spontaneously] or *yādṛcchika* [spontaneous], Śrī Jīva has written: "by means of the emergence of some kind of good fortune, born of association with the supremely independent *bhakta* of the Lord or of that *bhakta*'s grace."[12]

Moreover, since *bhakti*, too, is independent and self-established, it is capricious. For this reason, attaining the grace and association of the *bhakta*, the support or substrate of *bhakti*, is also unpredictable. For the attainment of *bhakti*, there is no regard for whether someone is a fit or unfit recipient, whether it is the right place or wrong place, whether it is the right time or wrong time or anything like that. Then, too, because of its extreme rarity, there is no certainty about who will get it, who will not get it. For that reason, a manifestation of pure *bhakti* is transmitted sometimes to a man and sometimes to a woman, sometimes to a child and sometimes to an old person, and sometimes to humans and sometimes to plants

---

[10]ibid., Madhya 22.48:

কৃষ্ণভক্তিজন্মমূল হয় সাধুসঙ্গ|

[11]ibid., Antya 16.55:

ভক্তপদধূলি আর ভক্তপদজল
ভক্তভুক্তশেষ এই তিন মহাবল

[12]Śrī Jīva, commenting on Bhāg. 11.20.8: केनापि परमस्वतन्त्रभगवत्भक्तसङ्गतत्कृपाजा-तमङ्गलोदयेन

and animals. Since attaining association with the great ones is rare, pure *bhakti*, too, is very rare.

By the influence of pure *bhakti*, Śrī Bhagavān becomes attainable. Again, since association with saints is the source of the appearance of pure *bhakti*, only by the influence of association with the saintly is Śrī Bhagavān captured. As it is said:

> Yoga does not capture me, nor does Sāṅkhya [cultivation of knowledge], Dharma [good works], study of Veda, penance, renunciation, rites, charity, vows, sacrifices, hymns, pilgrimage, nor restrictions and injunctions, the way I am captured by association with the holy, which dispels all attachments.[13]

If that is so, Śrī Bhagavān is arrested only by association with the saintly. This arrest or being captured in a trap is not a cause of distress for him. Like for a bee which by its own wish becomes stuck in the pod of a lotus, it is the cause of the greatest joy.

Therefore, the establishment of *dharmaśālās* (pilgrimage hotels), guest houses, nursing homes, roads to holy places, ponds, and so forth and especially for householders, the service of guests is recommended for this reason: to set traps to catch saintly persons in order ultimately to capture Bhagavān. If among the general populace who come to such places some saintly person is also in some way caught, then this is the main and hidden objective of the meritorious actions recommended in sacred texts. If that does not happen, at least one obtains some merit as a secondary result of those acts. Still, since the grace of a great saint is random and causeless, once in a while a *bhakta*-saint will allow himself to be caught. Therefore, it is often seen that they are willing to travel on well-traveled or current paths. Then, too, sometimes, they leave aside those well-traveled paths according to their own wills and independent desires and travel the forest paths—paths which have no connection with *dharmaśālās*, ponds, and so forth. Take, for instance, the journey to

---

[13]*Bhāg.*, 11.12.1-2:

> न रोधयति मां योगो न साङ्ख्यं धर्म एव च।
> न स्वाध्यायस्तपस्त्यागो नेष्टापूर्तं न दक्षिणा॥
> व्रतानि यज्ञश्छन्दांसि तीर्थानि नियमा यमाः।
> यथावरुन्धे सत्सङ्गः सर्वसङ्गापहो हि माम्॥

Vṛndāvana on the forest path running through the Jhārikhaṇḍa of Śrīmān Mahāprabhu, who is Bhagavān himself immersed in the feelings of the *bhakta*, or Nārada's journey on the forest path towards Prayāga and his saving of that hunter, or Śrī Dāsa Gosvāmin's rejection of the royal path, the highway, for a lonely, less well known path on his journey to Purī; all of these examples demonstrate the saint's independence. So, too, the hidden objective of the householder's service to guests is said to be the possibility of attaining, in some fashion, association with the saintly. As the sacred text says:

> Since from the mere recollection of such [saints] the houses of humans are made immediately pure, what more [needs be said about] actually seeing them, touching them, washing their feet, offering them places to sit, and so forth.[14]

Śrī Jīva Gosvāmin has given a lengthy discussion of this subject of association with the saintly in his *Bhakti-sandarbha*. The following subjects are recorded here very briefly from that. The accomplished or perfected *bhakta* is of three types: one whose impurities or sins are inactive (that is, *mūrchita*, fainted, unconscious, present but inactive), one whose impurities have been thoroughly cleansed away, and one who has obtained the body of a companion of Bhagavān.

One with inactive impurities is one in whom some semblance of inclinations for the sense objects remain, but they are like someone who has completely lost consciousness and thus they no longer have an active nature.

One cleansed of impurities is one in whom the inclinations for sense objects in the mind have been completely washed away.

One who has obtained the body of a companion of Bhagavān is one who has rejected his current body and attained companionship with the Lord in a consciousness body in the world of Bhagavān.

Among them, from association with saints of the first and the second types, pure *bhakti* is infused into the hearts of living beings. As a result of that:

---

[14]*Bhāg.*, 1.19.33:

येषां संस्मरणात्पुंसां सद्यः शुध्यन्ति वै गृहाः।
किं पुनर्दर्शनस्पर्शपादशौचासनादिभिः॥

1. The beginninglessly obstructed state of facing toward Kṛṣṇa (*kṛṣṇonmukhatā*) arises in the heart of the living being, and along with that, the self-conceit of being the enjoyer, the doer, the master, the placing of one's identity in the body, and the investing of one's sense of ownership in one's house and other things is eliminated; faith arises, and gradually one's taste for sense objects begins to diminish. Other than in this way, the living being's timeless aversion towards Kṛṣṇa can not be destroyed.

2. By listening to the showers of the nectar of pure *bhakti* in the form of presentations of stories about Hari (that is, discussions of his names, forms, qualities, and sports) from the mouths of those saintly *bhaktas*, practical *bhakti* (*sādhana-bhakti*) is infused into the hearts of living beings. That brings about the rise of the highest goal, the *bhakti* of love, starting with faith, association with the saintly, active engagement in worship, and so forth.

If one has association with other kinds of saintly persons, apart from the primary and very rare association with saints of the two types described above, it *is* possible to attain good results from their association according to the degree to which fondness for sense objects has diminished and *bhakti* for Bhagavān has developed in them.

Previously, we discussed the thread-possessing *bhakti* (*saguṇa-bhakti*) that is the true cause of success in the practices of ritualism, cultivation of knowledge, and so forth, which are undertaken out of some selfish desire or out of self interest. That kind of *bhakti* (received from the mouths of people other than the accomplished saint), being easily attainable, is spread throughout the world in many forms. From the mouths of reciters, singers, actors in traveling plays, in the descriptions of professional storytellers, in the songs of alms-beggars, in the performances of priests, and in the instructions of teachers—the current of this thread-possessing *bhakti* flows unbroken throughout social and family life. By the influence of this threaded *bhakti* sins are destroyed, the progression of worldly birth and rebirth is stopped, merit is accrued, and even liberation is achieved. But, without the infusion of pure *bhakti* by the great ones, love for Śrī Kṛṣṇa does not arise.

> One in whose mouth is found one name of Kṛṣṇa
> is a Vaiṣṇava and I pay that one the highest respect."[15]

The understanding of this statement's meaning depends on a lengthy consideration. One, however, can say this briefly on this subject: this statement is about another age, one that is free of offenses to the holy names, or it applies to the time of the salvation of the whole collective of living beings when Śrī Gaura was present. At the present time, however, in a world overrun by offenses to the holy names impelled by the Age of Kali, the literal meaning of this statement is not true. When, by the uncaused influence of association with the great, the mental operations of outward-looking living beings are turned within or rather are turned towards Kṛṣṇa, when in place of threaded faith thread-free faith in the Lord arises, then such persons because of that condition can be referred to by the words *bhakta* or Vaiṣṇava. Therefore, in the *Caitanya-caritāmṛta* it has been said: "One who has faith is a candidate for *bhakti*, according to the highest, the middlemost, and the lowest faiths."[16]

In other words, from the time that faith related to the Lord arises, a person is qualified for *bhakti*, or is called a *bhakta*—which quality of being a *bhakta* rises, according to the hierarchy of kinds of faith, from lowest to highest in a *bhakta*. From the moment of becoming the lowest kind of *bhakta*, defined as having faith related to the Lord, one is a *bhakta* or a Vaiṣṇava. When one is in a state of offense to the holy names, though, even though reciting the holy names, since the name is displeased it is not possible to reach easily the stage of

---

[15]Cc., 2.15.107:

> —যার মুখে এক কৃষ্ণনাম|
> সে বৈষ্ণব—করি পরম সমান||

But the reading in Dr. Radhagovinda Nath's edition is:

> প্রভু কহে—যার মুখে শুনি একবার|
> কৃষ্ণনাম, পূজ্য সেই শ্রেষ্ঠ সভাকার||
>
> The Master said: one in whose mouth I hear once
> The name of Kṛṣṇa is to be honored as the best of all.

[16]ibid., 2.22.38:

> শ্রদ্ধাবান জন হয় ভক্ত্যে অধিকারী|
> উত্তম, মধ্যম, কনিষ্ঠ শ্রদ্ধা অনুসারি||

being even the lowest kind of *bhakta*. Previously, though, that was possible by reciting the name of Kṛṣṇa just once.

What more than this can be said? It is heard that by offenses to the holy name even a *bhakta* falls into hell. As Śrī Jīva says:

> According to rule, even someone who possesses *bhakti* for the Lord, but who has an offense to the holy name, must experience the result in the form of falling below.[17]

At the present time those offenses to the holy name, caused by the Age of Kali, are spread practically everywhere. On this subject, a lengthy discussion in another book is required.

Therefore, that from which emerges faith related to the Lord and as a result of that faith pure *bhakti* or the mode of being or existence (*vṛtti*) that is related to the Lord, the gaining of association with the great thread-free *bhaktas* is by its very nature very rare. Thus, statements like "among billions of liberated beings, rare is one who is a *bhakta* of Kṛṣṇa"[18] are found. We have spoken previously on the subject.

---

[17] Śrī Jīva, *Śrī Krama-sandarbha*, 2.1.11: नामापराधयुक्तस्य भगवद्भक्तिमतोऽपि अधःपात-लक्षणभोगनियमाच्च।

[18] Cc., Madhya 19.131: কোটি মুক্ত মধ্যে দুর্লভ এক কৃষ্ণভক্ত

Chapter Five

Even the *śruti* texts praise, in an indirect way (*parokṣa-bhāva*), the greatness of the superior freedom from desire of the *bhakta*. All subjects established by *śruti* are covered by the veil of the highest secrecy, since the seers are indirect speakers (*parokṣa-vādin*), as it is said: "the seers are indirect speakers and indirection is dear to me."[1] Śrī Kṛṣṇa himself favors the indirect or cryptic approach. And to please him the seers resort to indirect speech in establishing him. In other words, for particular purposes that are for the ultimate benefit of living beings, they conceal their descriptions by not speaking enigmatically. Now on the subject of the desirelessness of the *bhakta* there are indirect statements in the sacred texts like:

> When all the desires that are sheltered in the heart of a living being are released, then the mortal becomes immortal and reaches Brahman even while here.[2]

Because of the reference to Brahman in this statement from *śruti*, one thinks it is about the liberation of the pursuer of knowledge or "gnostic" (the *jñānin*, that is, those who follow the path of liberating knowledge). But, if one analyzes the meaning of the verse carefully one can understand that it is really a reference to the *bhakta*. That

---

[1] *Bhāg.*, 11.21.35:

परोक्षवादा ऋषयः परोक्षञ्च मम प्रियम्।

[2] *Kāṭhaka Upaniṣad*, 6.14:

यदा सर्वे प्रमुच्यन्ते कामा येऽस्य हृदि श्रिताः।
अथ मर्त्योऽमृतो भवत्यत्र ब्रह्म समश्नुते॥

immortality is obtained by means of the direct experience of Brahman and Higher Self (Paramātman) is agreed upon in sacred texts such as the Vedas and so forth. But, if one grasps the expanded meaning of the words, for the *bhakta* the meaning of "becoming immortal (*amṛta*)" does not just mean the knower's liberation from worldly existence. Beyond that, it communicates the attaining of the ocean of ambrosia (also signified by *amṛta*) in the form of the service of Bhagavān. In the verse from *śruit*, in the meaning of the words *sarve kāmāḥ* ("all desires") is understood all selfish goals or devotion to one's own selfish purposes, upto and including the [desire for] liberation. In other words, they mean being intent on one's own selfish purposes. In the word *pra-mucyate* ("are released"), the use of the prefix *pra* means "to the highest degree." It means more than just [letting go of] desires for enjoyment. Thus, those for whom even the desire for liberation is destroyed, the desire-free *bhaktas*, have been described here—under the covering of indirect or arcane speech.

Now, in the opinion of the "gnostics," *karma* that is already in motion (*prārabdha-karma*) is not destroyed without experiencing it. It is said, for instance:

> Of necessity it must be experienced, the results of *karma* that has been done, both good and bad. *Karma* that is not experienced is not destroyed even in a hundred billion ages.[3]

In the opinion of Śrīpāda Śaṅkarācārya, too: "*Karma* already fructifying is destroyed only by experiencing it."[4] When *karma* that has manifested itself is depleted death occurs, the end of the body; at the time of death one who is liberated reaches or becomes united with Brahman.

In the quotation from *śruti* above, however, reaching Brahman in this world, even before the end of the body, is mentioned.

---

[3]Source unidentified:

अवश्यमेव भोक्तव्यं कृतकर्मशुभाशुभम्।
माभुक्तं क्षीयते कर्म कल्पकोटिशतैरपि॥

[4]Śrī Śaṅkarācārya, *Tattva-bodha*: प्रारब्धकर्मणां भोगादेव क्षय: [The work is no longer considered to be actually by the original Śaṅkarācārya. See Hacker. Trans.]

It is known that, by means of *bhakti*, a *bhakta's karma*, even that which has started to fructify, is destroyed, and that, too, without having to experience it. Take for instance the statement:

> Those incipient results of *karma* which are not destroyed even by one's being established in the direct experience of Brahman, except through enjoying or suffering them, are destroyed by the appearance of your holy name. So the Veda shouts out loudly.[5]

Not only is the incipient result of *karma* destroyed; it is possible for the *bhakta* in this world and in his or her present body to meet Bhagavān and to enter and leave the eternal sports in Bhagavān's world. That is learned from the behavior of the best of *bhaktas*, Śrī Uddhava. His absorption in trance at the time he was discussing Śrī Kṛṣṇa with Vidura is described in the *Bhāgavata* like this:

> Slowly he returned from the world of Bhagavān to the world of humans. Opening his eyes, Uddhava, smiling, spoke to Vidura with affection.[6]

From this one learns that for the *bhakta* entering and returning from the world of Bhagavān is possible even while still in the present body. Accounts of *bhaktas*' entering and returning from the sports of Bhagavān while absorbed in recollection, while still in their present bodies, in trances of deep emotion are well known from the lives of many *bhaktas*. Take for instance the examples of great realized Vaiṣṇavas like Śrīnivāsācārya, Śrī Rāmacandra Kavirāja, Śrī Narottama Ṭhākura and so forth, as well as those of many other *bhaktas*. In the following pages I will give a few brief examples just as an indication of this subject.

---

[5]Śrī Rūpa Gosvāmin, *Śrī Kṛṣṇanāmāṣṭaka*, 4:

> यद्ब्रह्मसाक्षात्कृतिनिष्ठयापि
> विनाशमायाति विना न भोगैः।
> अपैति नामस्फूरणे तत्ते
> प्रारब्धेति विरौति वेदः॥

[6]*Bhāg.*, 3.2.6:

> शनकैर्भगवल्ँलोकान्नृलोकं पुनरागतः।
> विमृज्य नेत्रे विदुरं प्रीत्याहोद्दव उत्स्मयन्॥

Śrīnivāsa Ācārya Prabhu (last half of the 16th cent.) at some time passed some days absorbed in recollection (*smaraṇa*) in the house of King Vīrahāmvira, the king of Viṣṇupura. His servants, fearing that Prabhu had passed away, became worried and were tormented by feelings of separation. Receiving this news Śrī Rāmacandra Kavirāja quickly came to Viṣṇupura. Sitting by Ācārya Prabhu's side, he, too, became absorbed in deep feeling (*bhāva*) like him, and entering into the eternal sport, he saw that because one of Śrī Rādhā's jewel earrings had fallen into some water and disappeared, all of her girlfriends were searching for it together. Śrī Ācārya Prabhu, too, in his true identity as a *mañjarī*-servant,[7] at the order of his own *guru* in the form of a girlfriend *sakhi-mañjarī*, was also intently searching for it. But, since no one had found it yet, everyone was distressed. Then Śrīpāda Rāmacandra Kavirāja began to search for it in his *mañjarī* identity. A short time later it was found underneath a lotus leaf and returned to Śrī Rādhikā through the girlfriends of the *guru*-succession. Then Ācārya Prabhu and Śrī Rāmacandrapāda returned to the external state and everyone was astonished and overjoyed when they understood what had happened. From this example one can understand that *bhaktas* can come and go from the eternal sports in the world of Bhagavān even while they are in their physical bodies.

On another occasion at his own place of private worship, Śrīla Ācārya Prabhu in a state of recollective absorption was busy fanning Śrīman Mahāprabhu after decorating him with different kinds of flower garlands. His *cakora*-like eyes were filled with joy drinking in the ambrosia of the moon-like face of Mahāprabhu. All of the autonomous reactions, like tears, gooseflesh, and so forth, were beautifying his body. Seeing the agitation of Śrīnivāsa's service, Śrīman Mahāprabhu had one of his servants put one of the garlands from his neck on the neck of Śrīnivāsa. The garland's beauty and fragrance suddenly filled the atmosphere:

> Ācārya at that time returned to consciousness

[7] *Mañjarī* means "flower bud." It is the term used in Caitanya Vaiṣṇavism for the eternal identity of some, but not all, successful pratitioners of spiritual cultivation or *sādhanā* in the tradition. It is the identity of a young female servant-friend of Rādhā in which one joins and participates in the eternal sport of Kṛṣṇa that takes place in the world of Kṛṣṇa, Goloka.

> and saw the garland given by the Master on his neck.[8]

On another occasion like this, Śrīla Ācārya Prabhu was lost in recollection watching the fun of the Holī sports of Śrī Rādhāmādhava. The bodies of the loving couple was reddened by the powders thrown by the girlfriends. Śrīla Ācārya Prabhu, too, with the permission of his *guru* in his form as a girlfriend *mañjarī*, was with great joy throwing powders at the girlfriends in his *mañjarī*-identity.

> The service was over
> and in external consciousness
> he saw his body covered with powder
> and unable was he to hide it.[9]

How distant are these from each other: entering into eternal sports and playing with colored powders and then seeing that clearly on his physical body?

Here is another incident. Śrīla Narottamadāsa Ṭhākura entered into eternal sport in a state of recollective absorption and was watching the love sports of Śrī Rādhā and Kṛṣṇa in their bower cottage. Śrī Rādhā becoming playful asked her girlfriends to bring treats for Śrī Śyāmasundara ("Beautiful Blue," Kṛṣṇa) to eat. Everyone was busy with that. Śrī Ṭhākura Mahāśaya, at the request of his *guru* who was one of Śrī Rādhā's girlfriends, was engaged in stirring milk in his *mañjarī*-servant form.

> Seeing the milk about to boil over he became anxious
> and removed the milk-pot from the stove
> with her [his] bare hands.
> That his hands were burned, he hardly noticed.
> Stirring the milk he gave it to a girlfriend;
> she with joyful heart fed it to Rādhā and Kṛṣṇa.

---

[8]Narahari Cakravartin, *Bhakti-ratnākara*, Sixth Wave:

> আচার্যের বাহ্যজ্ঞান হৈল হেন কালে
> প্রভুদত্ত মালা দেখে আপনার গলে

[9]ibid:

> হৈল সেবা সমাধান, বাহ্য জ্ঞান হৈতে
> দেখে ফাগুময় দেহ, নারে লুকাইতে

As soon as she received their leftovers,
external awareness returned.
He hid them as soon as he saw his burned hands,
But someone nearby knew the truth.[10]

One can discern on basis of the evidence of the experiences of the learned many incidents like this of many other *bhaktas* who go to and return from the eternal play.

Now the enigmatic meaning of the statement of *śruti* that was cited above, which was not easily understandable because it was hidden by vagueness, is clearly revealed in the *Śrī Bhāgavata* which is an expansion of the meanings of the Vedas. That the statement of revelation refers to the *bhakta* who is free from desire can easily be seen:

> The highest of *bhaktas* is one in whose mind the seeds of past action, which issue in desire, are not born. Such a person is the only dwelling place of Vāsudeva.[11]

In the statement "only dwelling place of Vāsudeva" (*vāsudevaikanilaya*) one understands a dwelling or house, or, in other words, a person whose heart is the resting place of Śrī Bhagavān. That such a person, the best of lovers of the Lord (*bhāgavatas*), is the intended meaning of that aforementioned enigmatic statement of *śruti* is thus understood from the *Śrī Bhāgavata*.

Therefore, only by the influence of pure *bhakti* are all past *karma*, upto and including incipient *karma*, and all subconscious desires for

---

[10]ibid.

উথলি পড়যে দুগ্ধ দেখি ব্যস্ত হৈলা
চূল্লী হৈতে দুগ্ধপাত্র হস্তে নামাইয়া
হস্ত দগ্ধ হৈল তাহা কিছু স্মৃতি নাই
দুগ্ধ আবর্তন করি দিলা সখী ঠাই
মনের আনন্দে রাধাকৃষ্ণ ভুঞ্জাইল
অবশেষ লভ্য মাত্রে বাহ্যজ্ঞ=অন হৈল
দগ্ধ হস্ত দৃষ্ট্িত মাত্র কৈলা সংগোপন
জানিলেন মর্ম অন্তরঙ্গ কোন জন

[11]Bhāg. 11.2.50:

न कामकर्मबीजानां यस्य चेतसि सम्भव:।
वासुदेवैकनिलय: स वै भागवतोत्तम:॥

enjoyment (*bhoga-vāsanā*) destroyed, even without their being experienced. Thus, it is possible to have a direct experience of the highest truth even in this world and while still in this present body. On the other hand, by the other means like cultivation of knowledge and so forth, incipient *karma* is destroyed by experiencing it, and one has a direct experience of Brahman only when the body ends. Distinction-less Brahman is only an object of knowing; whereas Bhagavān, possessed of distinctions, is an object visible to the *bhakta*'s senses which have been purified and infused with *bhakti*. By the clear mention of there being a vision or attainment in this life itself in that statement of *śruti*, it is established that it refers to the *bhakta*.

When I spoke before about *bhaktas* whose impurities were either inactive or had been cleansed away, this kind of pure, desireless *bhakta* was meant. And apart from association with that kind of rare, great-souled *bhakta*, one cannot achieve a true turning back towards Kṛṣṇa and a condition of complete absence of desires for enjoyment, liberation, and magical powers.

Bhakti, *bhakta*, and Bhagavān are completely free of the threads. Therefore, apart from a divine faith that is thread-free, a faith that is affected by threads such as transparency (*sattva*) and so forth, cannot produce an inclination towards a thread-free object. The knowledge-pursuer (*jñānī*) and the *yogin* are not inclined towards threadless Brahman or the Highest Self (*paramātman*) either; they are inclined towards their own purposes—liberation. The desire of the pursuer of knowledge to obtain Brahman—is out of a desire for his own liberation. The *yogin*'s desire to obtain the Highest Self—is out of a desire for his own liberation along with the eight supernatural powers (*siddhis*). However, the *bhakta*'s desire to obtain Bhagavān is out of a desire to serve Bhagavān and please him. It is not for his own enjoyment or liberation.

For *bhaktas* who are intent on *bhakti*, a divine mental operation arises that is completely aimed at the happiness of Śrī Kṛṣṇa and completely free of concern for their own happiness. In all other cases, because of the subconscious traces (*vāsanā*) of desire for enjoyment or liberation, there remains a deceit or ignorance that aims at one's own happiness. *Bhakti* alone is untouched by the fraud of desire to please one's own senses. Therefore, except in the case of the forms of worship (*dharma*) related to Bhagavān, one does not find, in any of the other forms, an absence of the deceit of seeking one's own happiness, in its fullest expression. Therefore, at the beginning of its definition of the form of worship (*dharma*) related to Bhagavān or *bhakti*, the just stated uniqueness of *bhakti* is praised in the *Bhāgavata* unabashedly and full-throatedly:

> *Dharma*, completely free of deceit, is here [described],
> the highest [*dharma*] of holy ones who are without envy.[12]

In other words, in the *Bhāgavata*, the highest form of worship of the saintly, who are without envy, has been described. And what kind is that? In reply to this question it is said: "it is the form of worship in which deceitfulness, or fraud in the form of self-interest, has been completely rejected." In the commentary's elucidation of the *pra* prefix of the word *projjhita* (*pra* + *ujjhita*), Śrīdhara Svāmin writes: "because of the *pra* prefix not only is the desire for sense enjoyment rejected; even deceit in the form of the desire for liberation is rejected."[13] That supreme kind of worship is described in this *Bhāgavata*.

In the word "service" (*sevā*) is understood the intention of only bringing about the happiness of the one being served. For this reason the words "service of Bhagavān" are used only for *bhaktas* who are free of all deceit, and the claim that the *bhakta* and Bhagavān share one life force (*prāṇa*) is proven. But on the subject of the objects of worship of other kinds of worshipers, the word "service" is never used. One doesn't hear anywhere of the "service of the demigods," the "service of Brahman," the "service of the Highest Self," and so forth. Morover, Bhagavān is praised as "fond of his *bhaktas*" (*bhakta-vatsala*). But, in relation to other kinds of worshipers, one never hears that he is "fond of selfless actors," "fond of the pursuers of knowledge," "fond of the *yogins*," and so forth. Therefore, pure *bhakti* towards Śrī Bhagavān, who is the object of worship of pure enthusiasts (*bhāgavatas*), since it is purely free of deceit, or absent of any desire for one's own benefit, is self-evidently the highest form of desirelessness.

On attaining the happiness of serving Śrī Kṛṣṇa, there is no longer any need or longing for one's own separate happiness in the heart of the desireless *bhakta*. The heart of the desireless *bhakta* itself is

[12]Bhāg., 1.1.2: धर्मः प्रोज्झितकैतवोऽत्र परमो निर्मत्सराणां सताम्

[13]Śrīdhara Svāmin, *Bhāvārtha-dīpikā* on 1.1.2: प्रशब्देन मोक्षाभिसन्धिरपि निरस्तः

the only playground for the happiness of service to Śrī Bhagavān. As long as the subconscious urges (*vāsanā*) for sense enjoyment and liberation, whose purposes are finding happiness for one's self, are present in the heart, one is not able to find in that heart any trace of the happiness of *bhakti*. Therefore, Śrī Rūpa Gosvāmin has written:

> As long as the witch of desire for sense enjoyment and liberation is in the heart, how can the happiness of *bhakti* arise in it?[14]

Therefore, *bhakti* is weightier than selfless action, the pursuit of knowledge, and yoga. As it is said: "it [*bhakti*] is greater even than selfless action, knowledge, and yoga,"[15]

More specifically, without any connection with *bhakti* selfless action, pursuit of knowledge, yoga, and other spiritual disciples are not complete. This was demonstrated earlier.

Again, although Brahman and the Highest Self are essentially threadless (*nirguṇa*), the practices to attain them, pursuit of knowledge and yoga, are connected with the thread of transparency (*sāttvika*). As it is said: "from the thread of transparency is born knowledge."[16] In the cultivation of knowledge and yoga, a connection with threaded (*saguṇā*) *bhakti* exists as a part of them. When the pursuit of knowledge is renounced, that is, when, prior to the stage of full accomplishment, knowledge is rejected, then only *bhakti* remains. That then becomes pure or threadless and by providing a connection to threadless Brahman and the Highest Self, it becomes the cause of their attainment. But, the main result of pure *bhakti*, the appearance of divine love (*preman*) for Kṛṣṇa, is not given. The reason for that is that *bhakti* has been accepted into the pursuit of knowledge in a secondary way or as a mere part of it. If *bhakti* is accepted as primary, its result is the appearance of divine love; if it is accepted as secondary or as a mere part, then *bhakti*'s secondary results, the four goals of human life (piety, wealth, pleasure, and liberation), are given. In order to obtain the joy of serving Kṛṣṇa,

---

[14]Śrī Rūpa Gosvāmin, *Bhakti-rasāmṛta-sindhu*, 1.2.22:

> भुक्तिमुक्तिस्पृहा यावत् पिशाची हृदि वर्तते।
> तावद्भक्तिसुखस्यात्र कथमभ्युदयो भवेत्॥

[15]*Nārada-bhakti-sūtras*, 25: सा तु कर्मज्ञानयोगेभ्यो ऽप्यधिकतरा

[16]*Bhagavad-gītā*, 14.17: सत्त्वात्संजायते ज्ञानम्

it is necessary to accept only threadless or pure *bhakti* as the main or dominant force—that *bhakti*, which is the best of all, makes possible, as its main result, the appearance of divine love, and as its secondary result it makes possible, after the destruction of sins and stopping the process of rebirth, liberation.

Bhakti is the inseparable union of the essential cores of Śrī Bhagavān's pleasuring-giving (*hlādinī*) and consciousness (*saṃvit*) powers.[17] Therefore, even though *bhakti* is a personal possession of Śrī Bhagavān, the possessor of all powers, one has to receive it by means of *bhakti* itself. Apart from that it is not available from Bhagavān directly. The reason is that the living being is bound up by *māyā* and has no direct connection with Śrī Kṛṣṇa. His flow or stream of *bhakti* is transported by the great ones (*mahat*) who are his own people and thus descends into the world. And then the grace of some supremely independent person who is dear to Bhagavān infuses it directly into a living being, and with the appearance of *bhakti*, preceded by faith and such, in that living being Kṛṣṇa's grace is also obtained. Therefore it is said: "by means of *bhakti* obtained by association with holy ones."[18] In other words "without the grace of the great ones there is no *bhakti* in any action."[19]

It was previously said that when *bhakti* in the form of the pleasure-giving power is present in Śrī Bhagavān, who is the possesser of power, it is called *śakti*. When it appears outside him and illumines the heart of the *bhakta* it is called *bhakti*. That outside-manifesting *bhakti* situated in the heart of the *bhakta* becomes decorated with many feelings, excitants, and so forth and gives joy to Śrī Bhagavān whose very essence is joy. This is one of *bhakti*'s most astonishing glories. Even though a child in the womb is perceived to be a tremendous joy to its mother, after it is born, it gives its mother even greater joy when it plays and moves about as an infant on

---

[17]Baladeva Vidyābhūṣaṇa, *Siddhānta-ratna*, 1.38: ह्लादिनीसारसमवेतसम्वित्साररूपेति, Literally, "[*Bhakti* is] the essence of consciousness inseparably united with the essence of the pleasure-giving power." This charactization is interesting because it makes the core of *bhakti* the *samvit* or consciousness power of Bhagavān. To that core by the relationship of inherence (*samavāya*) is joined the core of the pleasure-giving power. The relationship of inherence signals a connection that is inseparable. This explains and supports Baladeva's interesting claim, given earlier in the same text, that *bhakti* is a form of knowledge or awareness (*jñāna*). [Trans.]

[18]Bhāg., 11.11.24: सत्सङ्गलब्धया भक्त्या

[19]Cc., 2.22.32: মহৎসঙ্গ বিনা কোনো কর্মে ভক্তি নয়

her lap. In the same way, *bhakti*, which is a form of the pleasure-giving power, appears outside of Śrī Bhagavān in the heart of the *bhakta*. That *bhakti* then manifests itself in many varieties of efforts on the part of the *bhakta* to bring about Hari's satisfaction, and after accomplishing the happiness of Śrī Bhagavān through service, the *bhakta* himself also experiences joy by tasting grace-happiness (*prasādī sukha*).[20]

Again, although honey is the possession of the flower, it cannot be obtained directly from a flower—there is no way. Rather, the only way to obtain honey is by means of the honey bee. In the same way flow streams of honey in the form of talks about Hari, oozing from the honeycombed hearts of bee-like *bhaktas*. It is not possible to attain pure *bhakti* apart from having a fortunate connection with them. As it is said:

> Even though the sun has the power to burn, without the medium of a burning glass (a lens) fire is not produced. So, too, only through the medium of the holy man is *bhakti* for Hari instilled.[21]

Because of the tremendous rarity of association with great *bhaktas* of that calibre, it is extremely difficult for a living being to obtain pure *bhakti* through good fortune. And, as for the causes of this tremendous rarity, basically four reasons are cited:

1. The independence or uncontrollable nature of the arrival of *bhakta*-saints.
2. The complete absense of any cause for such association.
3. The extreme rarity of that kind of desireless *bhakta*.
4. Their unrecognizability (that it, the mundane intellect's inability to recognize a such a saint)

---

[20] Grace-happiness, like grace-food, is happiness left for the enjoyment of the *bhakta* by Śrī Bhagavān [Trans.]

[21] Source unidentified:

> सूर्यकान्तरवियोगाद्वह्निस्तत्र प्रजायते।
> एवं वै साधुसंयोगाद्धरौ भक्तिः प्रजायते॥

I have followed the Bengali version of Kanupriya Goswami rather than translate directly from the Sanskrit. His Bengali brings out implications in the verse that a straight translation would not.

Therefore in the sacred texts it is said: "Association with the great ones is rare, unrecognizable, but not without result."[22]

As, by contact with the exceedingly rare water of the constellation of Svātī, a pearl is sometimes infused into the hidden interior of one clam out of millions and millions, so, into the heart of someone, through an extraordinary stroke of good fortune, is infused pure *bhakti* which is born of the grace of some great one, and that person becomes endowed with qualities like greatness and so forth in the form of a *bhakta*.

Both association with great ones and stories about Hari are self-manifesting things beyond the three threads. Therefore, they are very rare. And again the combination of those two things in one place is a mater even more rare.

Since pure *bhakti* appears in the above mentioned way, obtaining it is extremely rare. Therefore, it has been said in the *Śrī Caitanya-caritāmṛta*:

> Out of millions of selfless actors one knower is best. Out of millions of knowers only one is liberated. Out of millions of those who are liberated one rare one is a *bhakta* of Kṛṣṇa.[23]

As a result, since the mode of worship dear to Bhagavān (*bhāgavata-dharma*) or *bhakti*, which is free of the threads and produced by chance association with great ones, is so rare, engagement in the four goals of life, which is favored by the natural thread-bound faiths of embodied beings, is helpful for living beings in general. As it has been said in the sacred texts:

> Liberation is easily gained from cultivation on the path of knowledge; sense enjoyments such as ascending to heaven is easily obtained from pious acts like the sacrifice and such that are detailed in the sacred writ. But,

---

[22]*Nārada-bhakti-sūtra*, 39: महत्सङ्गस्तु दुर्लभो ऽगम्यो ऽमोघश्च

[23]Cc., 2.19.131:

> কোটি কর্মী মধ্যে এক জ্ঞানী শ্রেষ্ঠ
> কোটি জ্ঞানী মধ্যে একজন মুক্ত
> কোটি মুক্ত মধ্যে দুর্লভ এক কৃষ্ণভক্ত

> this self-manifesting, threadless *bhakti* for Hari is extremely difficult to obtain, even by thousands of thread-laden practices.[24]

For this reason it is said that as long as one has not had the good fortune of acquiring *bhakti* from association with the great ones, or in other words, as long as a divine faith has not arisen in the hearts of livings beings, infused into them by the grace of the great ones, and until, as a result of that, the inclination is born to cultivate *bhakti* with a sense of great respect for it and a feeling that it is the best of all, the four goals of life, or the group of four (*caturvarga*), though not as elevated or as good as *bhakti*, are recommended in the sacred texts as alternative paths. They (the four goals) prevent living beings from falling downwards and according to their qualifications, bring about gradual improvements in them. Therefore, Śrī Bhagavān expressed a similar intention when he spoke to Śrī Uddhava:

> As long as you do not become indifferent to worldly things or as long as faith in listening to stories about me and such practices does not arise in you, you should perform your appropriate actions.[25]

If people give up their own *dharmas* or actions in accord with their own faiths and qualifications, they do not gain knowledge or *bhakti*. However, when by the performance of desire-free action, as enjoined by the sacred texts, disinterest in the enjoyment of the

---

[24]Cited in Śrī Rūpa Gosvāmin's *Bhakti-rasāmṛta-sindhu* as a statement from an unidentified tantra:

> ज्ञानतः सुलभा मुक्तिर्भुक्तिर्यज्ञादिपुण्यतः।
> सेयं साधनसाहस्रैर्हरिभक्तिः सुदुर्लभा॥

[25]Bhāg., 11.20.9:

> तावत्कर्माणि कुर्वीत न निर्विद्येत यावता।
> मत्कथाश्रवणादौ वा श्रद्धा यावन्न जायते॥

The Bengali translation in the original book adds a good deal of commentary: "As long as your mind is not purified by desireless action and indifference to wordly things or dispassion towards sense objects does not arise on the path of knowledge, or, as long as threadless faith in my stories, gained by association with the great ones, does not arise in you, you should perform the actions enjoined by the Vedas."

objects of the senses arises, and then qualification for following the path of knowledge is produced, one automatically gives up action. Or, when *bhakti*, preceded by faith, obtained by causeless association with the great ones, arises one automatically gives up one's own *dharma*. Therefore, it is written in the *Śrī Caitanya-caritāmṛta*, in the context of beautifully analyzing different instructions of the *Bhagavad-gītā*:

> His previous orders were
> the *dharma* of the Vedas,
> action, yoga, and knowledge.
> After discussing them all,
> his final order has more force.
> On the strength of this order,
> if faith in *bhakti* has arisen,
> then give up all other actions
> and worsip Kṛṣṇa.[26]

[26]Cc., 2.22.35-36:

> পূর্ব আজ্ঞা বেদধর্ম, কর্ম, যোগ, জ্ঞান
> সব সাধি অবশেষ আজ্ঞা বলবান
> এই আজ্ঞা বলে ভক্ত্যে শ্রদ্ধা যদি হয়
> সর্ব কর্ম ত্যাগ করি সে কৃষ্ণ ভজয়

[Author:] Even after Śrī Bhagavān gave that instruction to give up all action and *dharma* and only worship him (in the *Bhagavad-gītā*, 18.66: सर्वधर्मान् परित्यज्येत्यादि), many people are still engaged in action and such. From this one can understand that without the most rare association of great ones and the stories and instructions about Hari that arise from that, faith in *bhakti* cannot be produced, even if it is taught by Śrī Bhagavān himself. For this reason, Śrī Bhagavān sometimes has to come himself into the universe as a great, great one to bestow *bhakti* in a grand fashion. Therefore, if faith in *bhakti* is infused into one by the unpredictable influence of association of the great ones, one can give up all other actions and become engaged in the worship of Śrī Kṛṣṇa.

Part II

Appendices

Appendix 1

At the present time, which is disturbed by the influence of the Age of Kali and driven by the influence of offenses to the holy name, there is a dearth of top-notch opportunities to associate with the great ones. From another perspective, however, through the special good fortune of the living beings of this age, an excellent opportunity for the attainment of *bhakti* exists, one such as has not been provided by the fortunes of the people of the following ages, headed by the Age of Truth (Satya-yuga).[1] This has been announced in the *Bhāgavata* itself:

> [Śrī Karabhājana said to Nimirāja:] The creatures in the Kṛta Age and the other ages, o king, wish to be born in the Age of Kali.[2]

The reason for this is that in certain Ages of Kali, Bhagavān himself, hiding out as an exemplary *bhakta*, inaugurates the *dharma* of the age, musical recitation of the holy names. Moreover, only at the time of the Lord's "hidden" descent, which is like an eclipse or "swallowing" of the moon in the sky, is there, by his grace, also a "swallowing" (or "taking")[3] of the holy name for ordinary people, a benefit for them not available in other ages. As a result of

---

[1]The Satya-yuga or Kṛta-yuga as it is also known is the first of the four ages in Hindu accounts of cyclical time. It is considered the best of the ages, for people live the longest, are the most illumined, and suffer the least. The other ages, in order of their appearance, are Tretā, Dvāpara, and the last, Kali. Each following age is worse than the one before it. The Kali-yuga or Age of Kali is considered the worst.

[2]Bhāg. 11.5.38: कृतादिषु प्रजा राजन् कलाविच्छन्ति सम्भवम्।

[3]Goswami is playing with the meanings of the word *grahaṇa* here, which means "swallowing" in the context of an eclipse and "taking" or "repeating" in the context of the holy names.

the good fortune produced by hearing the holy name that has been "swallowed" and performed musically, all living beings, including both moving and unmoving life forms, reach the highest goal and along with that achievement comes liberation from repeated birth and death. All this happens simply by the power of singing the holy names which he (Bhagavān) starts.

In his sport in Vraja, Śrī Kṛṣṇa taught the world the highest form of *bhakti*. But, because he was not infused with the feelings of a *bhakta*, though he revealed the nature (*dharma*) of the Supreme Being to all the world, it was not accepted in that way in human society. He himself had given the authority to bestow *bhakti* to his *bhaktas* and since, at that time, his own state of being a *bhakta* was not separated from his state of being the Supreme Person, he was not able to bestow it (*bhakti*), even though it was his intention to give it away in a massive way.

In this unsatisfactory state of affairs in his previous sport, Bhagavān himself, Śrī Kṛṣṇa, the lord of all *rasas*,[4] went to another place and united with Śrī Rādhārāṇī, who is the very essence of *mahābhāva*[5] and the highest example of the *bhakta* and of all forms of *bhakti*, and "hid" himself, taking on her feelings and physical colorings. The time in which he manifested himself along with his holy names in that specific form of Śrī Kṛṣṇacaitanya is the very special, present Age of Kali. This is Bhagavān himself's only descent as an unmatched or unsurpassed *bhakta* and it is hidden in that way (i.e., his name and abode and such are undisclosed); he can only be recognized by the special traits given in a verse from the *Bhāgavata* (11.5.32): *kṛṣṇavarṇaṃ tviṣākṛṣṇam* "having the syllables 'kṛṣ-ṇa' and a not dark complexion ... " And, in the same verse, the words "by means of sacrifice in the form of musical praise (*saṅkīrtana*) using the holy names" prescribe the proper worship of the lord of the sacrifice using the holy names. His is an extremely secret arrangement and it is stated that this secret is only comprehensible to very bright people.

---

[4]*Rasas*, or *bhakti-rasas*, are powerful, transcendent emotional experiences that Kṛṣṇa and his *bhaktas* experience in their loving interations with each other.

[5]*Mahābhāva* is the highest state of *bhakti-rasa* experience possible and it is only experienced by Rādhikā. See Rūpa Gosvāmin's *Blazing Sapphire* (*Ujjvala-nīlamaṇi*), Chap. 15 for a discussion of this state.

The special greatness of musical praise through the holy names that he started in this particular Age of Kali is proclaimed in the following verse of the *Bhāgavata* (11.5.37):

> There is no higher gain than this for those embodied beings who wander here [in the worldly cycle of birth and death], since one may attain the highest serenity and cyclic existence is destroyed.[6]

The meaning is this—here, the results of musical praise through the holy names are described—the highest gain and the highest peace. And an ancillary or secondary result is the destruction of cyclic existence. For a living being, who is part of the liminal power (*taṭastha-śakti*), gaining that *bhakti* is said to be real achievement since attaining the privileges of the essential power, which is the highest of all powers, is accomplished through pure *bhakti*. Therefore, Śrī Bhagavān himself has said: *lābho madbhaktiruttamaḥ* "*Bhakti* for me is the greatest gain."[7] When *bhakti* for Bhagavān is the greatest gain then the highest gain is the highest form of *bhakti*, which is understood as a love like that of [the residents of] Vraja for Bhagavān, which is called passion-motivated *bhakti* (*rāgānuga-bhakti*). For living beings there is no other achievement or goal that equals or surpasses it.

The complete satisfaction (*prasannatā*) of a living being's self is called "peace." Real satisfaction of the self is achieved by gaining *bhakti*: *yayātmā suprasīdati*, "by which the self is well pleased" (Bhāg. 1.2.6). When rule-motivated *bhakti* (*vaidhi-bhakti*) brings an essentially superior peace, there should be no problem in understanding that the peace that comes from attaining the highest *bhakti*, passion-motivated *bhakti* for Bhagavān himself, is what is meant by the words "highest peace."

That being the case, the result of the musical praise through the holy names initiated by Bhagavān himself in this present special Age of Kali is the love of Vraja or passion-motivated *bhakti*, highest

---

[6]Bhāg.

न ह्यतः परमो लाभो देहिनां भ्राम्यतामिह।
यतो विन्देत परमां शान्तिं नश्यति संसृतिः॥

[7]Bhāg. 11.19.40.

form of *bhakti*, a gain than which there is none higher. The highest peace accompanies this highest form of *bhakti*.

When in general cessation of cyclic existence through repeated birth and death is a secondary result of *bhakti* for Bhagavān, it goes without saying that the bonds of that existence also will be broken on gaining the highest form of *bhakti*, the love of Vraja.

Such being the case, the determination that associating with great *bhaktas* is the only cause of attaining pure *bhakti*, as previously described, is a fine reason for the tremendous grandeur of the great ones. Those who according to their essential trait unite *bhakta*, *bhakti* and Bhagavān together in one person and from whom, as their external trait, overflow with beautiful streams of discussions about Śrī Hari's names, forms, qualities, and sports, infuse pure *bhakti*, along with an expectant hope for gaining Kṛṣṇa, into the hearts of living beings who have been from time without beginning turned away from Kṛṣṇa. This is called associating with great ones.

The time when the seed-like final cause of the character of the great souls, namely, the unmatched or unsurpassed three principles at their highest limit—*bhakta*, *bhakti*, and the principle of Bhagavān—becoming united and along with that the main form of praise of Śrī Hari—the thunderlike musical praise of him through his holy names—when they pour down in a ceaseless shower bringing the highest form of passionate *bhakti* and inundating the whole world with a flood of divine love—without any consideration of anyone's suitability or unsuitability, of whether someone is a fit recipient or unfit recipient, of whether the place is a proper or improper one—occuring only once in each *kalpa*, when it is the best opportunity for attaining the highest of gains in the world of living beings and the highest peace for the selves of living being—that time occurs during the manifestation of the sports of Śrī Gaura.

Bhagavān himself, overcoming in the previously described way the previous obstacle to filling the world with the gift of divine love during his Vraja sport, appeared in his Śrī Gaura role in order to fulfill his unprecedented wish to give divine love away without impairment and along with that to taste that *bhakti* for himself.

The essence of that intensely guarded secret of the sacred texts headed by the Vedas is found revealed in the following way in the Immortal Acts of Śrī Caitanya (*Śrī Caitanya-caritāmṛta*):

After enjoying as much as he wanted, Kṛṣṇa disappeared, and after disappearing he began to think to himself: "For a long time I have not given away the *bhakti* of divine love and without such *bhakti* the world cannot remain. The whole world practices rule-motivated *bhakti* towards me. In rule-motivated *bhakti* there does not exist the power to gain feelings like those found in Vraja. The whole world is mixed with knowledge of my godly might and I am not pleased by love weakened by awareness of my godly might ... . I will inaugurate the spiritual practice (*dharma*) for the age—musical praise through my holy names (*nāma-saṅkīrtana*)—and by bestowing *bhakti* in four emotional perspectives I will cause the earth to dance. I will practice it myself accepting the perspective of a *bhakta* and by practicing *bhakti*, I will teach it to everyone. If I don't practice it myself, teaching the practice will not succeed. This conclusion is reached in the *Gītā* and *Bhāgavata*. The practice of the age always can be started by my partial manifestation, but except for me no one else can give the love found in Vraja. Therefore, bringing my *bhaktas* with me, I will descend to earth and engage in many amusements." Thinking all this, in the first juncture of the Age of Kali, Kṛṣṇa himself descended to the town of Nadīyā.[8]

---

[8] Cc., 1.3.11-22:

যথেচ্ছ বিহরি কৃষ্ণ করি অন্তর্ধান|
অন্তর্ধান করি মনে করে অনুমান||
চিরকাল নাহি করি প্রেম ভক্তি দান|
ভক্তি বিনা জগতের নাহি অবস্থান||
সকল জগতে মোরে করে বিধিভক্তি|
বিধিভক্ত্যে ব্রজভাব পাইতে নাহি শক্তি||
ঐশ্বর্য জ্ঞানেতে সব জগত মিশ্রিত|
ঐশ্বর্য শিথিল প্রেমে নাহি মোর প্রীত|| ...
যুগধর্ম প্রবর্ত্তাইমু—নামসঙ্কীর্তন|
চারিভাব ভক্তি দিয়া নাচাইমু ভুবন||
আপনি করিব ভক্তভাব অঙ্গীকারে|
আপনি আচরি ভক্তি শিখাইমু সভারে||
আপনি না কৈলে ধর্ম শিখান না যায়|
এই ত সিদ্ধান্ত গীতা ভাগবতে গায়||

Therefore, though usually extremely rare, pure *bhakti* which is infused sometimes into someone's heart, due to an extraordinary stroke of good luck in gaining association with great ones, now has come within the grasp of all people, as a result of the great celebration of musical praise through the holy names, without discrimination, in the fine days of the flood of the *bhakti* of divine love. Even without depending on associating with great ones, those holy names arise from the very mouth of Śrī Gaurahari, the greatest of great ones, in his disguise, and they have remained behind in the world by the incomprehensible excellence of his grace. There is no easier or better way than in "taking" ("swallowing") the holy names of Śrī Hari to bring about the development, through the stages of faith and so forth, of the nine types of *bhakti* and their result, the arising of divine love. "Musical praise though the holy names is the highest way in the Age of Kali;"[9] this is the point of his own words.

Of all the limbs or parts of *bhakti*, the holy name is the trunk or whole. Therefore it is said: "the nine forms of *bhakti* issue from the complete holy name."[10] Thus, since it is the whole of which all the limbs of *bhakti* and practice (*sādhana* are parts, musical recitation of the holy name (*śrī nāma-saṅkīrtana*) is "the best of all." On this subject Bhagavān himself has spoken:

> Among forms of worship, ninefold *bhakti* is the best.
> It has great power to bestow love for Kṛṣṇa and Kṛṣṇa, too.
> Among those [nine forms], singing the holy name is the best of all.
> From the holy name, without offense, comes the fortune

> যুগধর্ম প্রবর্ত্তন হয় অংশ হৈতে|
> আমা বিনা নারে ব্রজপ্রেম দিতে||
> তাহাতে আপন ভক্তগণ করি সঙ্গে|
> পৃথিবীতে অবতরি করিব নানা রঙ্গে||
> এত ভাবি কলিকালে প্রথম সন্ধ্যায়|
> অবতীর্ণ হৈলা কৃষ্ণ আপনি নদীয়ায়||

[9] Cc., 3.20.8: নামসঙ্কীর্তন কলৌ পরম উপায়

[10] Cc., 2.15.107:

> নববিধা ভক্তি পূর্ণ নাম হৈতে হয়|

of divine love.[11]

At the time of Śrī Gaurāṅga's manifest sport, when, with his companions, love of the holy name was distributed to the world without consideration [of whether one was worthy or not], offenses were not taken into account. "Nitāi and Caitanya did not consider all these [restrictions]. Repeating the holy name, they gave away divine love with tears flowing from their eyes."[12] But when he became unmanifest, all the other rules in relation to the holy name were abandoned except for the one requiring eliminating the ten types of offense in repeating or "taking" the holy name.[13] Only, in

---

[11]Cc., 3.4.65:

> ভজনের মধ্যে শ্রেষ্ঠ নববিধা ভক্তি|
> কৃষ্ণপ্রেম কৃষ্ণ দিতে ধরে মহাশক্তি||
> তার মধ্যে সর্বশ্রেষ্ঠ নাম সঙ্কীর্তন|
> নিরপরাধে নাম হৈতে হয় প্রেমধন||

[12]Cc., 1.8.31:

> নিতাই চৈতন্যে নাহি এসব বিচার|
> নাম লৈতে প্রেম দেন বহে অশ্রু ধার|

[13]Here, the ten offenses to the holy name are listed only briefly. For a more detailed discussion of them see Manindranath Guha's *Nectar of the Holy Name.*

1. Reproaching virtuous, honest people, especially holy men [and women] (*sādhu*).
2. Thinking that Śiva and other gods are independent of Viṣṇu.
3. Disrespecting one's *gurudeva.*
4. Belittling the Vedas and sacred texts that follow them.
5. Hearing of the greatness of the holy name and thinking it is mere praise or eulogy.
6. Considering the greatness of the holy name as secondary or less important. Or, on another interpretation, considering some other method of spiritual cultivation to be greater than the holy name.
7. Engaging in sinful deeds on the strength of the holy name.
8. Thinking the holy name is on the same level as all other pious acts.
9. Trying to teach the stories of Hari and the holy name to people who have no faith or who are averse to Hari.
10. Being displeased when one hears about the greatness of the holy name.

his words, "if one repeats the holy name without offense does the treasure of divine love arise."[14]

Just as from a seed grows the sprout, the stem, branches, sub-branches, flowers, and so forth, until finally the fruit itself appears, so in repeating the holy name, which is the seed of the fruit of divine love, the rise of divine love through the stages of faith and so forth cannot be stopped. Even so, when there are offenses to the holy name, because it is displeased, it does not reveal its own power.

After repeating the holy name, when one does not see the rise of divine love in due time and in due course, one should know for sure that it is useless to search for some cause other than one brought about by offenses. That is because, apart from offenses to the holy name, there is no other cause for the holy name's displeasure and its not revealing its might. The evidence for this is found in a statement of the *Immortal Acts of Śrī Caitanya*:

> One name of Kṛṣṇa destroys all sins
> And manifests *bhakti*, the cause of love.
> When divine love rises, so do love's agitations
> Perspiration, shudders, gooseflesh, stuttering, and tears.
> Easily material life withers and Kṛṣṇa's service swells.
> From one name of Kṛṣṇa one gets so much treasure.
> If one repeats such a name of Kṛṣṇa many times
> And if divine love still does not appear,
> And there are no tears,
> Then we know there are many offenses in it
> The seed of Kṛṣṇa's name has not sprouted.[15]

---

[14]Cc., 3.4.71:

> নিরপরাধে নাম লৈলে হয় [পায়] প্রেমধন|

[15]Cc., 1.8.22-26:

> এক কৃষ্ণনাম করে সর্বপাপ নাশ|
> প্রেমের কারণ ভক্তি করেন প্রকাশ||
> প্রেমের উদয় হয়—প্রেমের বিকার|
> স্বেদ কম্প পুলকাদি গদ্গদাশ্রুধার||
> অনায়াসে ভবক্ষয়-কৃষ্ণের সেবন|
> এক কৃষ্ণ নামের ফলে পাই এত ধন||
> হেন কৃষ্ণনাম যদি লয় বহুবার|
> তবু যদি প্রেম নহে, নহে অশ্রুধার||

That all those names, "Hare Kṛṣṇa" and so forth, which flowed from the lips of Śrī Gaurakṛṣṇa, are to be repeated ("taken") by everyone in the present age and have set in motion the cause that will fill the whole world with divine love, Śrī Rūpa has revealed with his pen, and he has also spread the greatest hope for a world befuddled by the Age of Kali:

> The syllables [of his own name,] "Hare Kṛṣṇa," shouted forth from the lips of Śrī Kṛṣṇacaitanyadeva, have submerged the whole world in divine love. May his names be ever victorious![16]

Therefore, in place of very rare discussions of Hari from the lips of great ones in other ages, the present age's easily available major form of discussion of Hari—the holy name of Hari—from the lips of the greatest of great ones, Śrī Hari himself, is available for everyone and spreads limitless good fortune to the people of this Age of Kali. With regard to the development of the highest peace and the highest *bhakti* through the stages of faith and so forth from the holy name alone, no other impossibility can be found—except for the dependence in the repetition of the holy name on becoming free from the offenses to the holy name, which are reinforced by the influence of the Age of Kali, and being careful. This is so because the one and only reason for experiencing or not experiencing the great power of the holy name is whether one is free from or not free from the offenses.

If one is able to remain single-pointedly sheltered by the holy name which is the best of all practices, Śrī Lord Holy Name, who is fond of those dependent on him, will protect in all respects such a sheltered person from the major chicanery of the Age of Kali in the form of the occurence of offenses to the holy name.

This Age of Kali which was touched by the feet of Śrī Gaura will end in the not too distant future and in its place, for the remainder

---

তবে জানি অপরাধ তাহাতে প্রচুর|
কৃষ্ণনাম বীজ তাহে না হয় অঙ্কুর||

[16]Rūpa Gosvāmin, *Laghu-bhāgavatāmṛta*, 1.4:

श्रीचैतन्यमुखोद्गीर्णा हरेकृष्णेतिवर्णिकाः।
मज्जयन्तो जगत् प्रेम्णि विजयन्तां तदाह्वयाः॥

of the time of this Kali, the rise of a universal age of divine love has become possible. Therefore, the full characteristics and influence of the rest of this Age of Kali are being experienced now, at its beginning. Like a lamp that is out of oil briefly flares up once before it goes out, this, too, is indicative of Kali's farewell. At the opening juncture of this age, beleaguered Kali's best attack or way of spoiling things is infecting them with offenses to the holy name.

Just as this display of the full influence of Kali, as it bids us all farewell, is consented to by the creator himself for the purpose of a better future, and in the same way, on the other side, as a person sheltered by a fortress is protected from his enemies, so, too, has Bhagavān provided throughout the sacred texts the means of protecting oneself from the tumultuous brawl caused by the present Age of Kali—staying safely in the shelter of the holy name. Shelter of the holy name means: with awareness that its might is unsurpassed and that it is the best of all, respecting the holy name as core of all practices and remaining in faithful adherence to it. In this difficult situation in the dreadful Age of Kali, being one "sheltered by the holy name" rather than a mere "repeater the holy name" is much more safe. The sacred texts have this to say here:

> In this dreadful Age of Kali, all those people who are intent on the holy name will achieve their goals. Kali cannot harass them.[17]

If someone has to stir or move fire, it is possible that that person may get burned, if he or she is not constantly careful while doing it. The offenses to the holy name and subjects connected with those offenses are the concern of everyone. In not taking care with respect to the offenses of the holy name, the possibility of the occurrence of offenses to the holy name, caused by the influence of Kali, is far greater in the society of people who practice religion in the pious land of Bhārata (India), home of Sanātana Dharma, than it is for those who are completely indifferent and unconcerned in this matter, i.e., the residents of other countries. For the general populace of

[17] *Bṛhannāradīya Purāṇa*:

> हरिनामपरा ये च घोरे कलियुगे नराः।
> त एव कृतकृत्याश्च न कलिर्बाधते तान्॥

other countries the possibility of that [offenses] happening in that way cannot be imagined.

In the manifestation of the unfailing power of the holy name, it does not matter whether awareness of the nature and might of the holy name is present or not—except for the requirement that there be no offense. If a child who is completely ignorant of the power of fire touches it, there will not be even a moment's delay of the child's experience of fire's power to burn. In the same way, when there is no offense, whether one hears, sings, remembers the holy name, no matter whether one is aware or unaware of its power, without regard for whether one is a suitable or unsuitable recipient, the inconceivable, unfailing power of the holy name suddenly becomes manifest for all people without distinction. As the sacred text says:

> As whether touched through inadvertence or ignorance, a spark of fire shows its power to burn, so, too, even if through inadvertence the holy name touches the space between the lips, all sins are burned.[18]

If, even though this kind of holy name is being repeated, the result is not found to develop, then, in that case, one must infer the necessary existence of offenses to the holy name.

Therefore, the in the *Immortal Acts of Śrī Caitanya* it is said:

> If one repeats such a name of Kṛṣṇa many times
> And if divine love still does not appear,
> And there are no tears,
> Then we know there are many offenses in it
> The seed of Kṛṣṇa's name has not sprouted.[19]

---

[18] Gopāla Bhaṭṭa Gosvāmin, *Hari-bhakti-vilāsa*, 11.324:

> प्रमादादपि संस्पृस्टो यथाऽनलकणो दहेत्।
> तथौष्टपुटसंस्पृष्टं हरिनाम दहेदघम्॥

[19] Cc., 1.8.25-26:

> হেন কৃষ্ণনাম যদি লয় বহুবার|
> তবু যদি প্রেম নহে, নহে অশ্রুধার||
> তবে জানি অপরাধ তাহাতে প্রচুর|
> কৃষ্ণনাম বীজ তাহে না হয় অঙ্কুর||

In the present world, the thing most desired is "superior peace," which is indicated in sacred text as the highest gain of living beings and which was previously mentioned. In bringing about this highest peace, of all the other ways it is possible to adopt, engaging in the universal singing of the holy names of Hari is the best way.[20]

Therefore, from this comes—not only in human society—for all living beings the greatest possibility of bringing about the greatest peace and the greatest gain—in those cases not infected with the offenses to the holy name.

Since with respect to the body there is a difference between one human being and another, distinctions of class and country in human society cannot be avoided. For this reason, characteristics related to the body are necessarily based in difference. Therefore, physical natures cannot be the same for everyone. But, between the possessors of the body (the embodied or *dehin*) or the living selves (*jīvātman*) there is no such difference. All living selves are of one type—of one intent. The living being is sheltered by the single cause of all, the shelter of all, the Higher Self (*Paramātman*) or Supreme Lord (*Parameśvara*)—for the sheltered, serving and cultivating affection for the one sheltering, and for the one sheltering supporting and protecting in all ways the one sheltered. That is the natural ultimate state in the unfolding of the true nature of the self.

But, for the living being, floating in the current of beginningless worldliness, apart from the perception of the non-self or the gross world produced by ignorance caused by *māyā*, experience of the "self" or the conscious reality does not exist. As a result, the living being, though it is itself "self" (*ātman*), has long forgotten, along with itself, the Higher Self which is its long-time foundation and dear one. A result of that is that for the living being, becoming possessed or gobbled up by *māyā*, the cause occurs for its thinking the body is "I," and things related to the body—son, wealth, wife, house and so forth, all illusory or gross objects—are "mine," from time immemorial. A necessary conclusion of being turned away from the Lord is being turned towards the gross world, its altered state being thinking the body is the self and gross objects like the house and so forth belong to it.

---

[20] Cc., 3.20.7: নামসঙ্কীর্তন কলৌ পরম উপায়

That which is the reverse of the condition related to the body and bodily things, which are rooted in difference, is the condition of the self. With the appearance of the condition of the self, in the living being's heart is awakened an awareness of that ancient relationship the living being has with the Higher Self and the greatest way of bringing about the rise of the highest peace is singing the holy name.

Therefore, it is found that in the practice of all other religious and spiritual practices, humans merely have selected them. Then, too, not all people are qualified for those without regard for birth and caste. Rites, knowledge, yoga, austerity, and the rest, or in the case of any of the religious practices in other countries, at the very least, the seat of religious practice is seen to be reserved for only humans or the human self. But if it were an essential condition or property of the self, all living creatures—all living selves would be qualified for it; they would be called to take part in it; the salvation of all living selves would be considered. But, instead of that, we find them to be limited to only the human self. Therefore, even if the essential nature of the self is in it, one cannot say that it is the complete or finest property of the self.

The superior competence, as established in the sacred texts, of the singing of the holy name advocated by Śrī Caitanya in bringing about the liberation of all living selves from the ropes of *māyā* and their achievement of the highest peace, was demonstrated in all respects in his [Śrī Caitanya's] earthly sport. Therefore, we are able to discover that the singing of the holy name is necessarily the highest means of unfolding the topmost condition of the selves of all living beings—not just for the purpose of unfolding human selves. A sufficient clue is given in the conversation of Śrī Kṛṣṇacaitanya Mahāprabhu with Śrī Brahma-Haridāsa Ṭhākura,[21] the very image of the power of the holy name:

> Śrī Mahāprabhu's question:
>
> On earth there are many living beings, moving and unmoving.
> In what manner will all of these be liberated?
>
> Śrī Haridāsa Ṭhākura's answer:

[21] Haridāsa Ṭhākura is considered in the Caitanya tradition to have been a descent of Brahmā, the Hindu creator god.

Haridāsa said; Lord! But, this is your grace!
Unmoving and moving beings you saved first
The loud singing [of the holy name] you have done,
Unmoving and moving beings hear that.
On hearing it, moving beings' worldly existence was destroyed.
That sound strikes the unmoving—by that an echo is created.
That is not an echo—they sing in response.
By your grace the speechless speak.
In whole world there is loud singing
Hearing it, moving and unmoving beings dance in love's thrall.
Like you did in Jhāḍikhaṇḍa on your way to Vṛndāvana;
Balabhadra Bhaṭṭācārya told me about it.
Vāsudeva petitioned for living beings;
Then you agreed to liberate them.
Your descent is to liberate the world.
First the bhakta [asked], then you agreed.
You spread loud singing [of the holy name].
Of still and moving living beings you cracked the worldly plight.[22]

---

[22] Cc., 3.3.62-71:

পৃথিবীতে বহু জীব স্থাবর জঙ্গম।
ইহা সভার কি প্রকারে হৈবে মোচন।

হরিদাস কহে প্রভু যাতে এ কৃপা তোমার।
স্থাবর জঙ্গমে প্রথম করিয়াছ নিস্তার॥
তুমি যেই করিয়াছ উচ্চ সঙ্কীর্তন।
স্থাবর জঙ্গমের সেই হয় তো শ্রবণ॥
শুনিতেই জঙ্গমের হয় সংসার ক্ষয়।
স্থাবরে সে শব্দ লাগে—তাতে প্রতিধ্বনি হয়॥
প্রতিধ্বনি নহে সেই—করয়ে কীর্তন।
তোমার কৃপায় এই অকথ্য কথন॥
সকল জগতে হয় উচ্চ সঙ্কীর্তন।
শুনি প্রেমাবেশে নাচে স্থাবর জঙ্গম॥
যৈছে কৈলে ঝাড়িখণ্ডে—বৃন্দাবনে যাইতে।
বলভদ্র ভট্টাচার্য কহিয়াছে আমাতে॥
বাসুদেব জীব লাগি কৈল নিবেদন।
তবে অঙ্গীকার কৈলে জীবের মোচন॥

It is clearly understood from this whole statement that singing the holy name is introduced for the highest benefit of all living beings, not just for human beings. Again, along with that, in the statement that it [singing the holy name] pervades the whole world, we hear that the earth-felicitating sound of singing the holy name creates sound waves in the sky and by the touch of those sound waves the living beings of the world are delivered. In that claim we find a reflection of the modern science of wireless radios through statements like "sound strikes," "echo arises," and "in the whole world." At a time when wireless-science was beyond the scope of even dreams or was situated in the state of deep sleep, when the subject of it was not even a seed of an idea in the heads of mankind, in that condition for those three statements to give some indication of it? Well, what more can be said? Certainly whatever else is necessary in connection with science can be accomplished by the mere wish or will of the creator of the universe, the highest person, who possesses all knowledge and science. Mentioning this is unnecessary.

In the unrestricted courtyard of the singing of the holy name, which is the best of all practices and was initiated by Śrī Gaurahari, it is remarked that everyone, regardless of birth or religion, has the same right of entrance. Since it is the ultimate way to awaken the true state of the self in the heart of all living beings, in the meeting place of singing of the holy name, in the midst of the transcendent tumult that rises up from the self, the living beings, free from any distinctions from one another, become sheltered in the Higher Self. In that state, the external dependence of the awareness of physical distinctions such as being higher or lower or of the awareness of birth and so forth no longer remains. Therefore, it is then seen that:

> Laughing, crying, stuttering in love,
> His body covered with goosebumps,
> Low caste or high, he embraces them all

জগৎ নিস্তারিতে এই তোমার অবতার|
ভক্তগণ আগে তাতে করিয়াছ অঙ্গীকার||
উচ্চ সঙ্কীর্তন তাতে করিলা প্রচার|
স্থিরচর জীবের সব খণ্ডাইলে সংসার||

Oh when before has this fun taken place?[23]

By influence of the highest means of unfolding the true nature of the self in the form of singing the holy name as promoted by Śri Gauracandra, not just is the human self pleased and completely satisfied, but, for all living selves, still or moving, through the influence of singing the holy name the possibility remains of bringing about the cause of their attaining the highest good, provided the recipient is free of offenses to the holy name.

That is the all-encompassing greatness of Ṭhākura Śrī Brahma-Haridāsa's sacrifice of the holy name in the field of practice. He clearly made known to some unknown person that the singing of the name of Hari, the highest means of developing the true nature of the self to its utmost, is not just for delivering the human self from the material prison of body, house, and so forth. It is the highest means for the attainment of the highest good, namely, supreme peace, that is attainable by all living selves, still or moving, from animals, birds, bugs, and so forth to trees, vines and the rest:

Animals, birds, bugs and the rest
Who are not able to speak,
If they hear the name of Hari,
They all will be saved.[24]

Therefore, the intention of raising up the true nature of self is not only for human selves—it is for all living selves and the satisfaction or happiness that is mentioned in it, that is called the true nature of the self [*ātma-dharma*] and singing the holy name is the highest way of attaining that.

---

[23]Premānanda Dāsa, *Manaḥśikṣā*:

হাসিয়া কাঁদিয়া প্রেমে গড়াগড়ি,
পুলকে ব্যাপিত অঙ্গ|
চণ্ডালে ব্রাহ্মণে করে কোলাকুলি
কবে বা ছিল এ রঙ্গ||

[24]Vṛndāvanadāsa, *Caitanya-bhāgavata*, 1.11:

পশু পক্ষী কীট আদি বলিতে না পারে|
শুনিলে সে হরিনাম তারা সব তরে||

For all living selves, he who is the highest form of the suitably dear Higher Self is Śrī Bhagavān himself. Natural affection or love for him is called divine love (*prema*). The full unfolding of the true nature of the self is accomplished by the rising up of divine love (*prema*).

With the rise of divine love all complaints of privation, all incompleteness, all dissatisfaction completely cease. The living self, scorched by the three sufferings, finds a home in the cooling lotus forest of the highest peace in the form of the topmost satisfaction. Attaining shelter and enjoying him in the shade of the lotus-like feet of Śrī Bhagavān, free from fear and enduringly peaceful, is for the bee-like living self a cooling lotus forest.

When divine love rises in the heart of the living being, there is no more room for occurrences of harm, hatred, and so forth for one another because of the body and things related to the body. In relationship to that one dear-to-all Higher Self-Supreme Lord the world becomes full of happiness.[25] Since between each living being, then, there is no sense of difference, there is the inclination or possibility for each to be bound to the other by bonds of affection. Only in the heart of the living being does the true nature of the self in the form of the rise of divine love unfold. Therefore we find it described in the *Bhāgavata* as the highest nature of the living self:

> The nature from which *bhakti* for Bhagavān, free of motive and obstacles, is set in motion is the highest nature of embodied beings or living selves.[26]

The best way of unfolding the highest nature of the self as the *bhakti* of divine love is singing the holy name.

"The nine forms of *bhakti* issue from the fullness of the holy name."[27] Therefore, in the present world, the father and initiator of the culture of divine love and of the best means of cultivating it, singing the holy name, Śrī Kṛṣṇacaitanya Mahāprabhu, has taught the essence of the essence of all sacred texts in his own words:

---

[25] Prabodhānanda Sarasvatī, *Śrī Caitanya-candrāmṛta*: विश्वं पूर्णं सुखायते

[26] Bhāg., 1.2.6:

स वै पुंसां परो धर्मो यतो भक्तिरधोक्षजे।
अहैतुक्यप्रतिहता ययात्मा सुप्रसीदति॥

[27] Cc., 2.15.107: নববিধা ভক্তি পূর্ণ নাম হৈতে হয়|

Singing the holy name
Is the highest way
In the Age of Kali.[28]

He did not leave off with merely giving an instruction. Practicing it himself and along with that flooding the country with the powerful storm of singing the holy name and its downpour of divine love, he caused direct experience of the great power of singing the holy name. That was not just limited to human beings—when he went to Vṛndāvana by the forest path through Jhāḍikhaṇḍa, by his inconceivable grace, at the touch of the ambrosia of the holy name, "Hare Kṛṣṇa," pouring from his lips, deer, tigers, elephants, rhinosceros, and other forest animals, forgetting their wild enmity towards each other, began to singing the holy names loudly and gave proof, by their behavior, of the amazing greatness of the holy name. After obtaining human births suitable for performing worship, they did not have to perform worship by the special dispensation of his inconceivable grace.

When Śrī Gauracandra and his companions were present, without taking into account offenses to the holy name, the holy name and divine love were distributed like a deluge without regard for who was deserving or not. Therefore, then: "Nitāi and Caitanya did not consider all these things. While repeating the holy name they gave out divine love, their eyes flowing with tears."[29] For that reason, at that time, through any kind of connection with the holy name, divine love would arise, all the physical agitations called the *sāttvika-bhāvas*, like tears, gooseflesh, and so forth, would appear, and people would suddenly become known as possessors of divine love. Therefore, during his [Gauracandra's] time here, every house was alive with the sounds of numerous performances of the singing of the holy name, and as a result of that, suddenly every body, every person, would be decorated with tears, goosebumps, and the other *sāttvika-bhāvas*. Seeing that with his own eyes, the lion of *paṇḍitas*, Śrī Prabodhānanda Sarasvatī, wrote:

---

[28]Cc., 3.20.8: নামসঙ্কীর্তন কলৌ পরম উপায়

[29]Cc., 1.8.31:

নিতাই চৈতন্যে নাহি এসব বিচার|
নাম লৈতে প্রেম দেন বহে অশ্রু ধার|

> When Śrī Gauracandra descended into this world, in every house rose the tumultuous sounds of singing Hari's name; in every body appeared tears, goosebumps, and all the other physical agitations (*sāttvika-bhāvas*); every affection and sense of possession rose to the level of the most sweet, divine love of Vraja and granted living beings an ambrosia beyond the ken of the Vedas.[30]

After the departure of Śrī Gaurasundara and his companions, the influence of the emerging Age of Kali increased day by day and at present has almost reached its ultimate state:

> As much time as has passed since Caitanya was here, that much has the the Age of Kali's influence grown in severity.[31]

The truth of this great-soul's statement has now become quite clear in the eyes of those with subtle vision.

The best way for the Age of Kali, which is advancing outside of its proper time, to cause injury is infecting the people of the land of piety (*dharma*), Bhārata, with numerous offenses to the holy name, The reason for that has been previously discussed, Now, since the people of Bhārata have been specially infected with offenses to the holy name under the influence of the Age of Kali, the holy name, being displeased, has nearly stopped manifesting its power in the enormous and open-handed way (i.e., without regard for worthiness) it did before. Therefore, [though] it is possible at the present time for the influence of the holy name to be nearly unnoticable among the people of Bhārata, since that sort of causation does not exist for people of other countries, who are indifferent, it is hoped that it is possible to notice the influence of the holy name among them.

---

[30]Prabodhānanda Sarasvati, Śrī Caitanya-candrāmṛta, 30:

> अभूद्गेहे गेहे तुमुलहरिसङ्कीर्तनरवो
> बभौ देहे देहे विपुलपुलकाश्रुव्यतिकरः।
> अपि स्नेहे परममधुरोत्कर्षपदवी
> दवीयस्याम्नायादपि जगति गौरेऽवतरति॥

[31]Prabodhānanda Sarasvatī, *Śrī Vṛndāvana-mahimāmṛta*, 4.29:

> दूरे चैतन्यचरणाः कलिराविरभून्महान्।

Thus, for people of other countries, though they are completely ignorant about the truth and greatness of the holy name, if somehow they come into contact with the holy name, in the hearts of those living selves the long slumbering eagerness for the Higher Self will awaken and the true nature of the self will appear and an unprecedented tranquility and blossoming will unfold in the self. As a result of that they will taste the highest joy, and though they are unable to understand the real cause of that, because of that complete satisfaction in their inner selves, attraction to and enjoyment of all the worldly forms of happiness and fortune will become insignificant in comparison to it. No longer will any uproar produced by the clash of wordly self-interest, any violence and hatred, be able to find a place in the hearts of those living selvses. In this way, there is a possibility that the highest nature of the self will become manifested, in the form of blossoms of divine love, in the hearts of all humans that have become strung together by the thread of the holy name. Then, in the not too distant future, like an unbroken garland of pure *pārijāta* flowers, it [the hearts of humankind strung together], after making this unpeaceful and unsatisfying world peaceful, beautiful, and delightfully decorated, will be able to brighten this world with the sweet aroma of the happiness of the highest peace, if, that is, the introduction and spread of the singing of the holy names to every country in the world is possible—by the auspicious wish and inspiration of the Higher Self-Supreme Lord.

Therefore, only by the spreading of the singing of the holy names in offenseless arenas does there remain a possibility of seeing quickly its inconceivable and unfailing power everywhere. And since this is determined in the sacred texts, too, as the supreme way of bringing about the greatest peace in the world, there is no hope of attaining that kind of well-being by adopting any other path.

For all of humankind in the not too distant future—taking shelter of whatever names of the Lord they personally prefer and understanding the single thread of connection running through and between all living beings and the Higher Self-Supreme Lord, there remains the possibility of becoming bound by bonds of oneness within all of humankind, through the process of singing the holy names in all countries. Even though not too many days remain before the rise of the good days of the world's greatest peace and highest achievement, before that, the full and final influence of the Age of Kali, which is facing premature dismissal, will, like a dying crocodile, take on its fiercest features, in all directions, in all ways, and by means of the terrible war-dance of externality (*bahirmukhatā*).

At the end of the deep darkness of night, the first light of dawn introduces the impending rise of the sun. In the same way, at the end of the influence of the present Age of Kali, an enormous, world-wide age of divine love will necessarily appear. Its indication will be noticed before too long—even from the midst of the dreadful, frantic dance of Kali. In this problematic condition at the juncture of the ages, the best means of protecting oneself from the fear of being swallowed up by Kali is none other than situating oneself in the shelter of the holy name without offense.

When, through the inconceivable greatness of contact with the singing of the names of Kṛṣṇa, people from various countries, the differences in their hearts cast aside and bound to one another by bonds of affection, as a vast flood from many countries will come to the field of *dharma*, India, to offer their heartfelt offerings of affection to the supreme deity—the great initiator of the highest cultivation of the self in the form of divine love of the holy name, then finding us in this condition, our spiritual lives and consciousnesses damaged by the poison of offenses to the holy names, with astonished and disturbed minds. they will again enliven us and wake us up by the sight of the inconceivable power of the holy name and by sprinkling us with the nectar of their love.

In that state, that is, on the return, in this way, of India's consciousness of the loftiest truths which was carried away by offenses to the holy name, the development of the highest peace, long wished for throughout the world, will take place through the great coming together of all human beings, and from that the highest achievement of the world of living beings will occur, such as has not happened before this in the vast period of a *kalpa*[32] and will not happen again after this. That which the crown jewel of sacred texts, the *Bhāgavata Purāṇa*, has proclaimed, I recall here again—to support my statement.

> Than this there is no higher gain
> For embodied beings wandering here
> From which they gain the highest peace

---

[32]A period said to last three hundred and twenty million years.

And transmigration is destroyed.[33]

For embodied beings wandering around in the cycle of worldly existence undergoing repeated birth and death, there is no higher gain than obtaining the highest peace and destroying worldly existence through singing the holy names.

Finally, with joined hands, I make the following humble submission: though it is hardly necessary to say so, the future prognostications of a lowly living being like me, who cannot even perceive his own present condition, cannot possibly be appropriate or of any worth.

Nevertheless, all of my previous statements are only echoes of predictions from the lips of Śrī Bhagavān himself who has been confirmed by sacred writ as the highest reach of the supreme truth, under whose governance the wheel of creation, maintenance, and destruction has been spun, and who is all-knowing, all-seeing, of endless knowledge, and of great glory.

There is a possibility in the not too distant future of the fulfillment, within the bounds of the present, of the prediction that was given during the time of his sport—that the holy name that he promoted will be spread among and infused into all living beings not just in India, but throughout the entire world.

In all the towns and countries
That there are all around the world
Everywhere my name will be spread.[34]

These words from his lips are the basis of all my previously mentioned possibilities.

Once again, when there are no offenses, by the unfailing greatness of the singing in praise of the holy names that he (Caitanya) spread, there will awaken on its own in the hearts of all human

---

[33] Bhāg., 11.5.37:

न ह्यत: परमो लाभो देहिनां भ्राम्यतामिह।
यतो विन्देत परमां शान्तिं नश्यति संसृति:॥

[34] Vṛndāvana Dāsa, *Caitanya-bhāgavata*, 3.4.126:

পৃথিবী পর্য্যন্ত যত আছে দেশ গ্রাম|
সর্বত্র সঞ্চার হইবে মোর নাম||

beings—that is, of all living beings—a joyful meeting with the highest form of the most dear Supreme Self (Paramātman) and a desire to serve him. This desire to serve, widely known by the name "divine love" (*preman*), after revealing itself as the best characteristic of the self, supplying all the needs of the human self, and completing all forms of incompleteness, will cause the universal rise of the most peaceful and most fine equality. This, too, was predicted during the time of Caitanya's sports:

> The Master said, "My name is World-filler.[35]
> My name will be meaningful if
> I fill the world with divine love.[36]

The day for seeing the fulfillment of that statement is not too distant. This is the inference of an insignificant person like me.

On that day, among all the discoveries in the world of living beings, the greatest and the most astounding discovery will be when the present human beings of the world discover their creator himself; the intelligence of human beings will achieve its fullest purpose, and all human beings will fill creation with songs of his glory. May all of the torments of the Age of Kali be cast aside, may the sandalwood breeze of the highest peace waft forth, and may that auspicious day soon arise in this world! This is our plaintive prayer at his (Śrī Caitanya's) lotus-like feet

> I bow to the Vaiṣṇavas
> Who are like wish-fulfilling trees,
> Oceans of compassion indeed,
> And rescuers of the fallen.[37]

---

[35] Viśvambhara

[36] Kṛṣṇadāsa Kavirāja, *Caitanya-caritāmṛta*, 1.9.5:

> প্রভু কহে আমি বিশ্বম্ভর নাম ধরি|
> নাম সার্থক হয় যদি প্রেমে বিশ্ব ভরি||

[37] Traditional:

> वाञ्छाकल्पतरुभ्यश्च कृपासिन्धुभ्य एव च।
> पतितानां पावनेभ्यो वैष्णवेभ्यो नमो नमः॥

Appendix 2: On the Author (by Rasikamohana Śarmā)

After a long period of inactivity and apathy, or of the sleep of illusion in some society, when a sign of awakening is perceived, in most cases its first appearance is noticeable in its literature. At such times literature has to reshape itself by means of many different states or conditions. Through many blows and counter-blows, actions and counter-actions, creatings and breakings, the life of a literature can be unfolded and nourished. At the present time one can perceive signs of a new awakening of Vaiṣṇava literature in Bengali. Even though many deficiencies are visible at this time,[1] it is a subject of hope and joy that now the body of society is being stirred by vibrations of life and is starting to blossom again. Life has begun; a living self has entered the body of society. It is natural that some deficiencies are seen at this energetic, uncontrollable time.

It is an occasion for even greater happiness that the descendents of all those great beings, who at the time of the appearance of the Lord himself, Śrī Kṛṣṇa Caitanyadeva, surrounded him on all sides like stars in the evening sky and who brightened the life-force of society with the light of *prema-bhakti* (sacred love), have been revived now by remembering who they are, and their senses of their duty have blossomed. In the flood of the nectar of sacred love, their pure

[1] This essay is dated 1340 Baṅgābda or 1933 C.E.

ancestors created on the dry bones of a dead society a magnificent flowering garden possessed of the sweetness and beauty of sacred love. With the wealth of Vṛndāvana poetry those ancestors gave dead Bengali literature a new life, a new beauty, a new sweetness, and drew the eyes of the world to it. Those ancestors raised Bengali poetic literature to a position of respect and honor in world literature. Now their descendents, realizing their hereditary responsibilities, have entered onto the field of action. Among the writers of this order the name of Śrīmat Kānupriya Gosvāmī Mahāśaya is particularly noteworthy. Before starting any discussion of this book[2] by him I think it necessary to give a bit of an introduction to him.

Five hundred years ago, even before the appearance of Śrī Kṛṣṇa Caitanya Mahāprabhu, from time to time in certain villages of Bengal many deeply experienced, great souls used to descend into the world and beautify the breast of mother earth, the nurse of living beings. They used to illumine the hearts of men and women with the shining light of their sharp knowledge. They used to sprinkle the hearts of men and women who were scorched by the heat of the three types of suffering with a Yamunā-Jāhnavī-like current of sacred love (*prema-bhakti*). They used to establish the power of all kinds of good instruction in the hearts of men and women by the affectionate and warm glow of their own good examples. This author is a virtuous, fortunate descendent of one of those great souls.

Of all the names, that have been received with *bhakti*, of the great souls who were eternally perfected companions of Śrī Kṛṣṇa Caitanya Mahāprabhu, who descended to purify this Age of Kali, the names of three persons have been specially honored in the Gaudiya Vaiṣṇava society as eternally perfected companions: Śrī Sadāśiva Kavirāja, his son Śrī Puruṣottama Dāsa, and his son Śrī Kānu Ṭhākura or Ṭhākura Kānāi. They are introduced in Vaiṣṇava texts like the *Caitanya-caritāmṛta*, the *Caitanya-bhāgavata* and so forth:

> Śrī Sadāśiva Kavirāja was truly great
> And Śrī Puruṣottamadāsa was his son,
> Who from birth was immersed in Nityānanda's feet.
> He ceaselessly performed childhood sports with Kṛṣṇa.

---

[2]This introduction was written for another, previous book of Śrī Kanupriya Goswami called *Jīver Svarūpa o Svadharma*, or, *The True Form and Function of the Living Being.*

> His son was the great soul, Śrī Kānu Ṭhākura,
> In whose body stayed the nectar of love for Kṛṣṇa.[3]

In the *Śrī Laghu-bhāgavatāmṛta* (Smaller Nectar of Things Relating to the Lord), Section Two entitled *Bhaktāmṛta* (Nectar of the *Bhakta*) it is determined: among all of the *bhaktas* of Hari, Prahlāda is the best; but even better than Prahlāda are the Pāṇḍavas and even better than the Pāṇḍavas are some of the Yādavas; once again, among all of the Yādavas Uddhava is the best and yet even better than Uddhava are the ladies of Vraja since even Śrī Uddhava begs for the dust from the feet of the ladies of Vraja; moreover, among those ladies of Vraja Śrī Rādhikā and Śrī Candrāvalī are the best of all. That is made known in the *bhakti* texts:

> There, too, the two best [group leaders] in all respects
> are Rādhā and Candrāvalī. Moreover, in their two groups
> are millions of doe-eyed ladies.[4]

Between those two, once again Śrī Rādhikā is Śrī Kṛṣṇa's dearmost lover. Only Śrī Rādhikā is the crown-jewel of all *bhaktas*.

We see in the works of Vaiṣṇavas that Śrī Sadāśiva Kavirāja is determined to be that Candrāvalī in the previous sport:

> Candrāvalī, who is equal to his life-breath, is Kavirāja Sadāśiva.[5]

> She who was previously Candrāvalī in Vraja, foremost beloved of Kṛṣṇa is now in Gauḍa [Bengal] Kavirāja Sadāśiva.[6]

---

[3]Kṛṣṇadāsa Kavirāja, *Caitanya-caritāmṛta*, 1.11.35-37:

শ্রীসদাশিব কবিরাজ বড় মহাশয়|
শ্রীপুরুষোত্তমদাস তাঁহার তনয়||
আজন্ম নিমগ্ন নিত্যানন্দের চরণে|
নিরন্তর বাল্য লীলা করে কৃষ্ণ সনে||
তাঁর পুত্র মহাশয় শ্রীকানু ঠাকুর|
যাঁর দেহে রহে কৃষ্ণ প্রেমামৃতপুর||

[4]Rūpa Gosvāmin, *Ujjvala-nīlamaṇi*, 4.1:

तत्रापि सर्वथा श्रेष्ठे राधाचन्द्रावलीत्युभे।
यूथयोस्तु ययो: सन्ति कोटिसङ्ख्या मृगीदृश:॥

[5]*Ananta-saṃhitā*: चन्द्रावली प्राणतूल्या कविराज: सदाशिव:।

[6]Kavikarṇapūra, *Śrī Gaura-gaṇoddeśa-dīpikā*, 156:

Śrī Sadāśiva Kavirāja's son, Śrī Puruṣottama Dāsa, was, like his father, famous in the Vaiṣṇava world as a repository of *bhakti*. In the sport of Śrī Gaura, some companions of Śrī Nityānanda—the great souls known as the twelve Gopālas—brought a flood of holy names and divine love to Bengal. Śrī Puruṣottama Dāsa Ṭhākura was one of those great beings. He has been described in the Vaiṣṇava texts as the famous Stokakṛṣṇa among the dear friends of Śrī Kṛṣṇacandra, the Supreme Person.

> He who was [Kṛṣṇa's] friend Stokakṛṣṇa before is [now] Dāsa Śrī Puruṣottama.[7]

> He who was Stokakṛṣṇa became Dāsa Puruṣottama.[8]

The famous author of *Praise of Vaiṣṇavas*, Śrī Devakīnandana took shelter [became a disciple] of this Śrī Puruṣottama Dāsa and became most pure and fortunate. This the author himself has related in his book.

The son of Śrī Puruṣottama Dāsa, Śrī Kānu Ṭhākura, was respected, like his father and grandfather, in Gauḍīya Vaiṣṇava society as an eternally accomplished companion of Bhagavān. When he was very young his name was "Baby Kṛṣṇadāsa." At a very early age the sweetness of transcendent divine love appeared in his heart. Among the friends of Śrī Kṛṣṇa, the dear playmates occupy the highest place and among them Subala and Ujjvala are considered the foremost: "Among the dear playmates the chief are Subala and Ujjvala."[9] Śrī Vṛndāvana Dāsa Ṭhākura in his book named the *Śrī Caitanya-candrodaya*[10] describes him as the friend named Ujjvala of Vraja:

पुरा चन्द्रावली यासीद्व्रजे कृष्णप्रियापरा।
अधुना गौडदेशे ऽसौ कविराज: सदाशिव:॥

[7]ibid., 130: स्तोककृष्ण: सखा प्राग्यो दास: श्रीपुरुषोत्तम:।

[8]*Bhaktamāla*: स्तोककृष्ण येँहो तेँहो दास पुरुषोत्तम

[9]Śrī Rūpa Gosvāmin, *Bhakti-rasāmṛta-sindhu*, : प्रियनर्मवयस्येषु प्रवरौ सुबलोज्ज्वलौ

[10]The *Śrī Caitanya-candrodaya* by Śrīmat Vṛndāvanadāsa Ṭhākura was edited and published in CA 429 (1915 CE) from a handwritten manuscipt by the late Śrī Surendranath Goswami. Later (1962) Sundarānanda Vidyāvinoda Mahodaya published another edition of it.

> The son of Puruṣottama was Baby Kṛṣṇadāsa Gosvāmī. He was really Ujjvala; this much I know by experience.[11]

As a youth he went to Vṛndāvana with Śrīmatī Jāhnavā Devī. At that time, seeing his sweetness as he played the flute in addition to his supernatural beauty and unparalleled dancing expressions, Śrīpāda Jīva Gosvāmin and the other teachers then residing in Vraja were astonished. From that time forth he became known as "Śrī Kānu Ṭhākura." This event was witnessed personally by the author of the *Śrī Caitanya-bhāgavata*, Śrī Vṛndāvanadāsa Ṭhākura and recorded as follows:

> When he was a teenager then in Vṛndāvana I saw his great realization with my own eyes. In *saṅkīrtana* he was like a second Madanagopāla. With a pearl necklace swinging from his neck and a garland of forest flowers, the sound of his flute stole everyone's heart. The Vrajavāsīs said he was Kṛṣṇa become visible. Śrī Jīva Gosvāmin and the rest of the Vrajavāsīs saw his beauty and offered praise. From that time on his name became Śrī Kānu Ṭhākura. What more can I say about his vast greatness? Whomever that friend Ujjvala showed his grace easily attained Rādhā and Kṛṣṇa.[12]

It is said that when he danced the ankle-bells on his swift moving feet broke and landed in Bodhkhānā in the district of Yaśohar. For that reason, he later selected Bodhkhānā as his home. There, the sacred images he established, Śrī Śrī Rādhā-Prāṇavallabha are still present[13] and in honor of his fifth swing, every year in that place there is a festival. On that day, an amazing *kadamba* tree blossoms.

Some of the Gosvāmī descendants of Kānāi Ṭhākura moved from Bodhkhānā to the village of Bhājanaghāṭa in the District of Nadīyā

---

[11] Vṛndāvana Dāsa, *Śrī Caitanya-candrodaya*:

> পুরুষোত্তমসুত শিষু কৃষ্ণদাস গোস্বামী|
> উজ্জ্বল স্বরূপ অনুভবে জানি আমি||

[12] Śrī Vṛndāvanadāsa Ṭhākura, *Śrī Caitanya-candrodaya*, 2.115-120.

[13] In the turmoil of the creation of Pakistan, the images were moved and at present are in Kolkata, in Barāhanagar, at 1/2 Pāṭhabārī Lane, in the temple established by Śrīmat Gaurahari Gosvāmī Prabhu.

to live. There the sacred images named Śrī Śrī Rādhāvallabha, Śrī Śrī Rādhāvṛndāvanacandra, and Śrī Śrī Rādhāgovinda were revealed and established. They are still serving them to this day. Śrīla Ṭhākura Kānāi was the last of the eternally accomplished in that family, which, nevertheless, is pure and possesses the highest *bhakti* of divine love. For that reason, they are known in the community of Vaiṣṇavas as Gosvāmīs of the family of Ṭhākura Kānāi.

The Vaidya community of Bengal is famous for its genius from ancient times. Learning, intelligence, discrimination, renunciation, knowledge, concentration, *bhakti*, and divine love, for these and other spiritual virtues they have been respected in society at large for a long time. Beyond this, from time to time, many accomplished persons (*siddha-puruṣa*) have appeared among them. Not just in the Vaiṣṇava community, in the Śākta and Śaiva communities, too, many renunciant Vaidya practitioners and accomplished persons' names have come to our attention. Among the hagiographers of Śrī Kṛṣṇacaitanya Mahāprabhu many great beings like Śrīla Murārigupta, Śrī Narahari Ṭhākura, Śrīla Kavikarṇapūra, Śrīla Locana Dāsa, Śrīla Kṛṣṇadāsa Kavirāja Gosvāmī, and others have, by their lives, brought fortune to the Vaidya community. By the appearance of three eternally accomplished persons in a row, from Śrīla Sadāśiva Kavirāja to Ṭhākura Kānāi, the excellence of the Vaidya community has been illuminated.

After the time of Śrī Kānu Ṭhākura many pious, learned, and saintly persons have been born in this family. Many of them have been respected in society for the excellence of their learning and the power of their *bhakti*. Among the pious and learned persons born in this family, the names of Śrī Bihārīlāla Gosvāmī, author of the book *Śrī Kānutattvanirṇaya* (*An Inquiry into the Truth About Śrī Kānu*), and Śrī Hārādhana Gosvāmī, who had an uncommon expertise in *bhakti*-texts like the *Bhāgavata*, are specially worthy of note. Nearly half a century ago someone created a massive flood of joy with *bhakti-rasa* in Eastern Bengal (now Bangladesh) through his songs and poetry. That celebrated and deeply faithful person was Śrī Kṛṣṇakamala Gosvāmiī Mahodaya who was born in this same, pure family at Bhājanaghaṭa. I met him personally in Dhaka. I was then a young man and he was elderly. My mind was drawn by his poetic genius; I had memorized many of the songs from his *Svapna-vilāsa*, *Vicitra-vilāsa*, *Rāi Unmādinī*, and *Bharata Milana*. Even now those songs are in my memory. I myself saw in him the good habits, honest modes of interaction, civility, and humility of those Vaiṣṇavas possessed of good character of the days of old.

The author of this book's late father, the most honorable and sagelike Śrī Surendranātha Gosvāmī Mahāśaya (BA., L.M.S.), was a special object of my affection. From the time we first met, a deep feeling of friendship existed between us. In age he was much junior to me, but because of his stolidness, profundity, sweetness, passion for knowledge, acceptance of renunciation, firmness in truth, measured speech, straight-forwardness, and above all his Vaiṣṇavism I always had faith in him. I loved him—had a deep affection for him, but that affection was not exactly like the affection one has for someone who is younger; it was an affection mixed with deep faith. I, with deep faith in my heart, felt affection for him. When he entered the eternal home, I experienced the flames of intense grief for a long while.

I have known the author of this book, Śrīmān Kānupriya Gosvāmī, since he was a child. His firmness in the truth, purity of character, passion for *dharma*, and concern for maintaining proper etiquette developed in childhood. I had noticed those traits in him then, too. But, that he would attain the proficiency to increase the honor of his already universally honored family by becoming so highly regarded and respected in Vaiṣṇava society and by attaining such eminence in the world of Vaiṣṇava literature, that I could not foresee. Control over the senses, self-control, life-long celebacy, rejection of desire for enjoyment, and other fine virtues developed in special measure in him from his early youth. Just as in the tiniest Banyan seed all the qualities of being a huge tree are hidden and just as in time in the bossom of the earth the gradual development of those traits become visible and enlarged in a regular fashion, so too from his very childhood I watched the unfolding of his limitless fine qualities. But, that the current of this accomplished family would become so much more highly developed in him, that was beyond my ability to infer back then. He was not educated in any school, college or traditional school (*catuṣpaṭhi*), but the kind of excellence in sagacity and learning and in *bhakti* and knowledge that he attained by the power of his keen intelligence, which he accrued from previous births, and by the grace of the Lord, all those qualities are rarely seen even among well-educated people. The current of the force of his oratorial eloquence is immense like the currents of the Gaṅgā or Yamunā and is full of both purity of word and purity of feeling. In his oratory nothing like irrelevant speech, loss of direction, harshness to the ear, pointless use of language, and so forth are even in the slightest degree noticeable. Even after hearing many of his lectures, there remain in the ears of his well-educated listeners, those who are sensitive to feelings and *rasa*, the emotionally packed, sweet resonances of his words.

Now I shall talk about his writing ability. In this connection, this book is a shining example.[14] People in general think that writing essays on Vaiṣṇava texts is easy, but actually it is completely the reverse. All the works written by his eternal companions, the Gosvāmins of Vṛndāvana, by the grace of Śrī Kṛṣṇa Caitanya Mahāprabhu are vast treasure troves of settled teaching filled with the most subtle analyses. Without the grace of the Lord we lack qualification to enter into that treasury of teaching on the strength of our own laboriously accumulated intellects and learning. Works on the teachings of *bhakti* by those who write only on the strength of their keen intellects may have skillful writing in them. They may be pleasant to read because of their clever choice of words and charming use of language, but in reading those kinds of books by writers who do not practice *bhakti*, *bhakta* readers do not find even a drop of enjoyment.

In this little book[15] extremely difficult philosophical issues have been discussed. The author, by the divine eye of his *bhakti*, has seen the hidden, secret essence of all of those truths and in a natural and simple way made those easily available to the general public. His language is lucid and well polished. Each and every subject reveals his thoughtfulness, and because of his skillful writing, even women with little education can easily understand him. The essays are filled with philosophical thought and yet because of the beauty and sweetness of their poetry and the charm of their language they are attractive to readers in general. One other special feature of this book is that whenever the author takes up whatever work, the freshness of his feelings and the fundamental nature of his thinking are extremely clearly noticeable. Freshness and funda-

[14] This essay appeared as a preface to Kānupriya Goswami's *The True Form and Function of the Living Being* (*Jīber Svarūp o Svadharma*), first published in 1934.

[15] *The True Form and Function of the Living Being* (*Jīber Svarūp o Svadharma*)

mental thinking are quite rare in others. Even those teachings that contain extraordinarily subtle truths have become comprehensible to the general public through his skillful explanations. One of his major distinguishing traits is in making his essays attractive to the general reader through use of similes, examples, and so on, and by the beauty of his quite charming and sweet language.

In some specific places and for some specific topics, there is a need for repetition. For some readers this may seem unjustified. But, if one is going to make some of those hidden, profound truths comprehendible by general readers, they have to be reflected into the budlike minds of readers whose intelligences are soft in many ways, in many manners, by many methods, and with many examples. In certain circumstances the method of "[repeatedly] pounding the post" is not to be regarded as a fault, but instead as an ornament. Critics must keep all subjects in their gaze in order to reveal the author's intention. Just as a human being's physical appearance and type is a matter of individual independence, independence in one's mental vision, one's assessment of arguments and operation of intellect and analysis are also due to one's distinctive nature. I am expressing my own individual opinion here. I think that among all of the books that are available at the present time in Gauḍīya Vaiṣṇava literature, this book will attain a very high standing. Its language is pure, its taste is highly refined, its conception is elevated, it is decorated with clarity and skillfulness of explanation and with use of similes and examples, and it is filled with the settled teachings of the Vaiṣṇava sacred texts. The language of this book is charming throughout, its feeling and flavor are sweet, and its clear demonstration of expertise in explaining the genuine teachings shines through most brightly.

I pray at the tips of the feet of the most compassionate Śrī Gaurāṅgasundara that, by his grace, this author obtains a healthy body, a peaceful mind, and a long life, that he shine in human society as an example of the condition of the *bhakta*, and that, becoming an eternal resident of his (Śrī Gaurāṅga's) home world, which is illumined by the light of the bliss of his sweet nectar as though scattered everywhere through the rays of moonlight from his toe nails, he sprinkles nectar, through his explanations of the *bhakti* sacred texts, on all living beings who are scorched by the three sufferings. *alamiti vistāreṇa* ("Enough said on this subject.")

1340 Sāla (1934 C.E.)
12th Agrahāyaṇa, Mahādvādaśī

Śrī Rasikamohana Śarmā (Vidyābhūṣaṇa)
25 No. Bagbazar Street,
Kolkata

Appendix 3: The Guru and Divine Name

In the context of association with great ones or saints, the question of the importance and role of the *guru* or spiritual guide naturally arises. While association with the saints of a tradition, when it can be had, is certainly indispensable for one who wants to advance on the path to sanctity envisioned by that tradition, in India this association most often occurs in the context of finding, testing, asking for acceptance by, and then living under the protection and guidance of a religious teacher who belongs to the tradition. Thus, it is important to understand the role of the guru as understood in the Caitanya tradition as an extension of belief in the sacred power of association with the great *bhaktas*.

Surprisingly perhaps, while the position of the guru is discussed in sections of many books, there is only one book that I am aware of that is devoted entirely to the subject of the guru. That is Sundarānanda Dāsa's (a.k.a., Sundarananda Vidyavinode) book in Bengali called *The Nature of the Guru in Vaiṣṇava Teaching* (*Vaiṣṇava-siddhānte Śrīgurusvarūpa*). The learned author discusses many of the important issues relating to the guru in the twelve chapters of his book: (1) The Necessity of the Guru, (2) The Mantraguru and Initiation (*dīkṣā*), (3) The General Characteristics of the Guru, (4) The Suitableness of the Guru and the Disciple, (5) The Testing of the Guru and the Disciple, (6) The Temporal, Family, and Lineage-perfected Gurus, (7) The Collective and Distributive Gurus, (8) The Non-difference of the Guru from Śrī Kṛṣṇa, (9) Offenses to the Guru, (10) The Rejection of the Guru, (11) The Duties of the Initiated Disciple, and finally (12) Service of and Association with the Guru. This thorough treatment of the principle of the guru is too detailed for inclusion in this book. It really requires a separate monograph and it is my hope that in the near future I will be able to translate and document Sundarānanda's fine work. For the present book, however, I decided to include a chapter from an early Caitanya Vaiṣṇava text, little known outside the tradition, that discusses briefly, in the scope of some twenty-five verses with occasional commentary, the role of the guru.

The text presented here in both Sanskrit and English is the third chapter of a work called the *A Collection of the Essentials of Bhakti for the Lord* (*Śrī Bhagavad-bhakti-sāra-samuccaya*) by Lokānandācārya, a disciple of Narahari Sarkar, who was an important and close companion of Śrī Caitanya.[1] When the book was written is not known, but we can assume that it was composed within a generation of Śrī Caitanya's time. There is a story told about the author in a work devoted to praising the initiation lineage of Narahari Sarkar called *The Discernment of the Branch of Narahari* (*Narahari-śākhā-nirṇaya*) by a Gopāla Dāsa. The date and authenticity of this text are uncertain, but the following account has become part of the tradition of Lokānandācārya:

> I call the branch of Narahari the victor of all directions.
> I now describe a learned man named Lokānandācārya.
> He once told Śrī Gaurāṅga, "I have this certain bug.
> Whoever shall defeat me, I will take shelter of him."[2]
> He was defeated by Ṭhākura [Narahari];
> therefore, he took shelter of him in Nīlācala.
> His book is the *Bhakti-sāra-samuccaya*,
> which explains the doctrines of Gaurāṅga in [on the basis of] the Purāṇas.[3]

[1]There are three editions of the work in my possession, two by Haridas Sastri (1979 in Devanagari and with Hindi translation and again in 1979 in Bengali script and with Bengali translation) and that of Haribhakta Das (1982 in Bengali script with a Bengali translation).

[2]That is, I will accept him as my *guru* and become his disciple.

[3]As cited in both Haridas Sastri's and Haribhakta Das' introductions:

> *digvijayī nāma kari ṭhākurera śākhā*
> *lokānānandācārya nāma paṇḍite kari lekhā*
> *śrīgaurāṅge kahe mora ei kīṭa haẏa*

The work of Lokānandācārya contains eight chapters: (1) Determining the Nature of the Object of Worship, (2) Determining the Nature of Bhakti, (3) Taking Shelter With a Guru, (4) The Greatness of the Holy Name, (5) The Characteristics of Worship of Bhagavān and of the Bhāgavata [the follower of Bhagavān], (6) Determining the Nature of the Greatness of Grace, (7) Determining the Nature of Aversion to Śrī Kṛṣṇa and the Vaiṣṇavas, (8) Determining the Nature of Detachment. The book is not a long one. It contains only two hundred and seventy-six verses, mostly culled from the Purāṇas and the *Bhāgavata*. Between the verses are connecting passages introducing the verses and in addition some of the verses have a commentary on them. These commentarial passages appear to be the work of the author and it may be that some of the unidentified verses are also his. Thus, the work appears to be a concise presentation of the essentials of the beliefs and practices of the early Caitanya movement, from a source other than the companionship of the Gosvāmins of Vṛndāvana. It represents the viewpoint of bhaktas of Bengal as distinct from the viewpoint of the Vṛndāvana school.

The first verse makes it clear that this is the work of an avid follower of Śrī Caitanya and the second verse recognizes the author's indebtedness to Narahari Sarkar:

> A pure lotus-like face, golden-skinned,
> eyes like lotus petals as well,
> the sweetest of sweet laughs,
> charming cupid-like his attire,
> praised by god, man and sage,
> the moon-like Kṛṣṇacaitanya,
> possessed by the power of the dance,
> him, image of love, do I worship.[4]

---

ye more jinibe tāre kariba āśraẏa
ṭhākurer sthāne teṃho hailā parājaẏa
nīlācale kailā tāṃra caraṇa āśraẏa
bhaktisāra samuccaẏa grantha yāṃhāra
gaurāṅgera siddhānta purāṇe vyākhyā tāṃra

[4]Lokānānandācārya, *Bhagavad-bhakti-sāra-samuccaya*, 1:

अमलकमलवक्रं गौरमम्भोजनेत्रं
मधुरमधुरहासं चारुकन्दर्पवेशम्।
सुरनरमुनिवन्द्यं कृष्णचैतन्यचन्द्रं

> I, blinded by the darkness of ignorance,
> take shelter in the moon of the ocean
> of knowledge, Śrī Narahari,
> my *guru*, who is so kind to the fallen.[5]

After seeking shelter with his *guru*, Lokānandācārya describes the power of associating with the *bhaktas* of the Lord, revealing how closely connected association with great ones and surrendering to a *guru* are:

> I praise the two feet of the *bhakta*
> which counteract all obstacles;
> by the mere hearing of a *bhakta's* name
> all the worlds are immediately purified.[6]

Anticipating a question from prospective readers, Lokānanda in his fifth verse raises the question himself: "why should inquisitive people put their efforts into reading this book when they could busy themselves with studying the many Purāṇas headed by the Bhāgavata?" In response, he wrote a little verse that identifies and describes the audience he had in mind for his book. It is an interesting and realistic characterization of the community Lokānanda saw before him at a time shortly after the disappearance of Śrī Caitanya, a snapshot of some segments of Bengali society in the middle and last part of the 16th century:

> Those whose minds are confused by attachment
> arising from unhealthy past impressions
> and who are lazy about listening to

कलितनटनशक्तिं तं भजे प्रेममूर्तिम्॥

[5]ibid., 2:

अज्ञानतिमिरान्धो ऽहं ज्ञानार्णवसुधाकरम्।
आश्रये श्रीनरहरिं श्रीगुरुं दीनवत्सलम्॥

[6]ibid., 3:

वन्दे भक्तपदद्वन्द्वं सर्वविघ्ननिवारकम्।
यन्नामश्रुतिमात्रेण लोकाः सद्यः पुणन्ति च॥

and studying the many Purāṇas,
yet curious about the lotus-like feet of Kṛṣṇa
and above all good-hearted, they will make
the best effort in [reading] this book.[7]

Lokānandācārya's audience was ordinary people involved in or attached to the world, society, and their families, their spiritual visions, in his opinion, clouded by karmic results called *samskāras* or *vāsanās*, subtle, surviving impressions left by experiences undergone in past existences which manifest in present lives as desires for or wishes to avoid certain things or actions. Another characteristic that Lokānandācārya recognizes in his audience is a certain lack of enthusiasm for studying and listening to the various Purāṇas, especially to the *Bhāgavata Purāṇa*. This is understandable, perhaps, since the Purāṇas are vast and parts of the them are difficult to understand. Moreover, the *Bhāgavata* is no doubt one of the most challenging of them. Thus, in the following short paragraph in which Lokānandācārya unpacks the name of his book, "A Collection of the Essentials of Bhakti for the Lord," he says his work is "a collection of statements in the form of verses that are essential to the awakening of *bhakti*." The last two characteristics of his audience are that its members have some interest in or curiosity about Śrī Kṛṣṇa and that they be *sādhu*, essentially virtuous people.

With this brief introduction to the *A Collection of the Essentials of Bhakti for the Lord* of Lokānandācarya, let us now turn to the third chapter which focuses on seeking shelter with an authentic guru. In addition, since one of Kanupriya Goswami's major areas of reflection was the theology of the divine name, I also include the fourth chapter of Lokānandācārya's book which is entitled "The Greatness of the Holy Name." It is perhaps the earliest treatment of the beliefs and practices surrounding the divine names in the Caitanya tradition.

[7] ibid., 5:

दुर्वासनासक्तिविमूढबुद्धयो नानापुराणश्रवणेक्षणालसाः।
जिज्ञासवः कृष्णपदारविन्दयोः कुर्वन्ति यत्नं परमत्र साधवः॥

Taking Shelter With a Guru

अथ श्रीगुरुचरणाश्रयणम्

अथ तावद्भगवद्भजने गुरुरेव प्रधानकारणमित्येव दर्शयितुमाह भगवद्वाक्येन —

नृदेहमाद्यं सुलभं सुदुर्लभं प्लवं सुकल्पं गुरुकर्णधारम्।
मयानुकूलेन नभस्वतेरितं पुमान्भवाब्धिं न तरेत्स आत्महा॥ १॥[8]

एवं कीदृशो गुरुरुपासनीय इत्याह भगवद्वाक्येन —

यमानभीक्ष्णं सेवेत नियमान्मत्परः क्वचित्।
मदभिज्ञं गुरुं शान्तमुपासीत मदात्मकम्॥ २॥[9]

एतदेव स्पष्टयन्नाह —

तस्माद्गुरुं प्रपद्येत जिज्ञासुः श्रेय उत्तमम्।
शाब्दे परे च निष्णातं ब्रह्मण्युपशमाश्रयम्॥ ३॥[10]

तत्र प्रयोजनमाह—

तत्र भागवतान्धर्मान् शिक्षेद्गुर्वात्मदैवतः।
अमाययानुवृत्त्या यैस्तुष्येदात्माऽऽत्मदो हरिः॥ ४॥[11]

[8]भाग. ११.२०.१७
[9]भाग. ११.१०.५
[10]भाग. ११.३.२१
[11]भाग. ११.३.२२

Now, taking shelter with a blessed ***guru*****:**

Now, first, to show that the *guru* is the chief cause of the worship of Bhagavān he says by means of a statement of Bhagavān:

> The human body is primary, easily attained, and yet very rare; it is like a boat with the *guru* at the helm that I push along with a favorable wind. If a person does not cross the ocean of becoming under these conditions, that person is like a killer of the self.[12] (1)

Now what sort of guru should be worshiped? To this he replies with another statement of Bhagavān:

> One who is devoted to me should observe constantly the *yamas* and *niyamas*[13] at some point and honor a *guru* who knows me well, who is peaceful, and who thinks of me as the very self.[14] (2)

He makes this even more clear:

> Therefore, someone who is inquisitive about the highest good should resort to a *guru* who is deeply immersed in the sacred texts and in supreme *brahman* [Śrī Kṛṣṇa] and who tranquil.[15] (3)

And the purpose in that is—

> One whose *guru* is his very self and deity should learn from him the characteristics of the Lord by which through sincere cultivation Hari, who gives himself, is pleased.[16] (4)

---

[12]Bhāg., 11.20.17.

[13]The *yamas* and *niyamas* are the first two limbs of the eight-limbed practice of yoga. The *yamas* or restraints are: nonviolence, truthfulness, no stealing, celibacy, and non-acquisitiveness (*Yoga-sūtra*, 2.30). The *niyamas* or obligations are: cleanliness, being satisfied, austerity, study, and devotion to God. (*Yoga-sūtra*, 2.32). An expanded and somewhat different list is given later in the text from the *Bhāgavata* (11.19.33-4).

[14]Bhāg., 11.5.5.

[15]Bhāg., 11.3.21.

[16]Bhāg., 11.3.22.

एवं तत्फलमाह —

इति भागवतान्धर्मान् शिक्षन्भक्त्या तदुत्थया।
नारायणपरो मायामञ्जस्तरति दुस्तराम्॥ ५॥[17]

ननु तावदाचार्यस्य वेदपाठनद्वारा, पितुर्जनकत्वात्, मातुर्गर्भधारणपोषणत्वाच्च गुरुत्वमस्ति। तत्र कुत्र भक्तिः कार्येत्याह —

गुरुर्न स स्यात्स्वजनो न स स्यात्
पिता न स स्याज्जननी न सा स्यात्।
दैवं न तत्स्यान्न पतिश्च स स्यात्
न मोचयेद्यः समुपेतमृत्युम्॥ ६॥[18]

ननु तावद्भगवान् श्रीकृष्ण सर्वेषामीश्वरः स्वतन्त्रस्तस्य साक्षात्सेवया भक्तिर्भविष्यति। तत्कथं भक्ताश्रयणं कार्यमित्यत्राह वैकुण्ठनाथवचनेन —

अहं भक्तपराधीनो ह्यस्वतन्त्र इव द्विज।
साधुभिर्ग्रस्तहृदयो भक्तैर्भक्तजनप्रियः॥ ७॥[19]

ननु देवतान्तराराधनेन भगवान्प्राप्तव्यः, किं भक्तैः इत्यत्राक्रुरं प्रति भगवद्वचनमाह—

भवद्विधा महाभागाः निषेव्या अर्हसत्तमाः।
श्रेयस्कामैर्नृभिर्नित्यं देवाः स्वार्था न साधवः॥ ८॥[20]

---

[17]भाग्. ११.३.३३
[18]भाग्. ५.५.१८
[19]भाग्. ९.४.६३
[20]भाग्. १०.४८.३०

Now, he describes the result of that—

> Thus, as one learns the truths relating to Bhagavān by the *bhakti* that arises from that, one becomes intent on Nārāyaṇa and quickly crosses over *māyā* which is difficult to get beyond.[21] (5)

Now then, the vedic teacher (*ācārya*) by teaching the Vedas, the father by begetting one, the mother by carrying one in her womb and raising one are all *gurus*. Towards which of them should one perform *bhakti*? To this he replies—

> One is not a *guru*, one is not a relative, one is not a father, one is not a mother, one is not a god, nor is one a husband who cannot free one from imminent death.[22] (6)

Here is another doubt. Bhagavān Śrī Kṛṣṇa is the Lord of All, fully independent. By direct service to him *bhakti* arises. Therefore, why must one seek the support of a *bhakta* of his? To this he replies with a statement of the Lord of Vaikuṇṭha (Nārāyaṇa)—

> I am under the control of my *bhaktas*, as if I, o twiceborn, were not independent. My heart is held by my good *bhaktas* and I am dear to them.[23] (7)

Now, too, Bhagavān can be obtained by worshiping the gods. What need is there for his *bhaktas*? To this he replies with a statement of Bhagavān to Akrūra—

> Greatly fortunate ones like you, who are most noble and good, are to be constantly served by human beings who desire the supreme good. The gods are only interested in their own goals, but not so the holy ones.[24] (8)

---

[21] Bhāg., 11.3.33.
[22] Bhāg. 5.5.18.
[23] Bhāg., 9.4.63.
[24] Bhāg. 10.48.30.

देवताराधनापेक्षया सद्यः फलत्वाच्च सत्सङ्ग एव श्रेयानिति मुचुकुन्दवचनेनाह —

भवापवर्गो भ्रमतो यदा भवेत्
जनस्य तर्ह्यच्युत सत्समागमः।
सत्सङ्गमो यर्हि तदैव सद्गतौ
परावरेशे त्वयि जायते मतिः॥ ९॥[25]

अतएव सद्यः फलत्वं स्पष्टयति—

न ह्यम्मयानि तीर्थानि न देवा मृच्छिलामयाः।
ते पुनन्त्युरुकालेन दर्शनादेव साधवः॥ १०॥[26]

वैष्णवाल्लभते भक्तिं भक्त्या मां लभते नरः।
तस्मात्तु वैष्णवो विष्णुः कलेर्मध्ये विशेषतः॥ ११॥[27]

एवं प्रकरणार्थभगवद्वचनमाह चतुर्भिः —

अन्नं हि प्राणिनां प्राणा आर्तानां शरणं त्वहम्।
धर्मो वित्तं नृणां प्रेत्य सन्तो ऽर्वाग्बिभ्यतो ऽरणम्॥ १२॥[28]

सन्तो दिशन्ति चक्षूंषि बहिरर्कः समुत्थितः।
देवता बान्धवाः सन्तः सन्त आत्माहमेव च॥ १३॥[29]

प्रायेण भक्तियोगेन सत्सङ्गेन विनोद्धव।
नोपायो विद्यते सम्यक्प्रायणं हि सतामहम्॥ १४॥[30]

---

[25]भाग. १०.५१.५३
[26]भाग. १०.४८.३१
[27]?
[28]भाग. ११.२६.३३
[29]भाग. ११.२६.३४
[30]भाग. ११.११.४८

And, because it produces an immediate result in comparison to worshiping the gods, associating with the holy is better. This he says through the words of Mucukunda:

> When release from material existence is to occur for someone spinning in the cycle of rebirth, then, o Acyuta, that person meets someone holy. When there is association with someone holy, faith in you, who are lord of the higher and lower and the goal of the holy, is born.[31] (9)

Therefore, he makes clearer its immediate results:

> Not places of pilgrimage on the banks of sacred streams, nor gods made of mud and stone, they only purify one after a long time. Holy ones purify one on sight.[32] (10)
>
> From a Vaiṣṇava one obtains *bhakti*. By *bhakti* a person obtains me. Therefore, a Vaiṣṇava is Viṣṇu, especially in this Age of Kali.[33] (11)

Thus, he cites four statements of Bhagavān that are relevant to the topic:

> Food is indeed the life-breath of living beings and I am the shelter of those who suffer. *Dharma* is the livelihood of humans after they pass on and the holy ones are the shelter of one who fears while in this world.[34] (12)
>
> The holy ones give eyes. Outside only the sun rises. The holy ones are [your real] gods and friends. Holy ones are [your] Self and me as well.[35] (13)
>
> As a rule, apart from the yoga of *bhakti* and associating with holy ones, o Uddhava, no way [to freedom] exists. I am the complete shelter of the holy ones.[36] (14)

---

[31] Bhāg., 10.51.53.
[32] Bhāg. 10.48.31.
[33] Source unknown.
[34] Bhāg. 11.26.33.
[35] Bhāg., 11.26.34.
[36] Bhāg., 11.11.48.

इष्टापूर्तेण मामेवं यो यजेत समाहितः।
लभते मयि सद्भक्तिं मत्स्मृतिं साधुसेवया॥ १५॥[37]

तस्माद्गुरुत्वेन भगवद्भक्ताश्रयणमेव भगवद्भक्तिप्राप्तौ मूलं कारणमिति। अत्र केचिदाहुर्गुरुभक्तिरेव कृष्णभक्तिः, तस्या अपृथगायाससाध्यत्वात्। अथ तावद्गुरुभक्तिरेव किं नाम। उच्यते कायवाङ्मनोभिः सद्यः शक्याशक्याविचारेणाज्ञापालनपूर्वकगुरुचित्तबोधनं गुरुभक्तिरिति। एतदपि शरणापन्ने सति भवति। तत्र शरणापन्नस्य लक्षणमाह प्रथमतो गुरोर्गोप्तृत्वस्वीकार आनुकूल्यकरणं प्रातिकूल्यपरित्यागः सर्वस्वनिःक्षेपस्तत्प्रसादलेशग्रहणमात्मनो निरभिमानित्वाचरणम्। एतेन सर्वं निरवद्यम्। यद्येवं भगवन्नामादिश्रवणकीर्तनस्मरणपादसेवनादिकं कर्तव्यं न वेत्याशङ्क्य मैवम्, यतः तदाज्ञावशादेव भगवत्परिचर्यातन्नामादिश्रवणवैष्णवसेवादिकं कर्तव्यमिति गुरुचित्तबोधनमुपपन्नमिति साधूक्तम्। एवं गुरोः सर्वमयत्वमाह भगवद्वचनेन —

आचार्यं मां विजानीयान्नावमन्येत कर्हिचित्।
न मर्त्यबुद्ध्यासूयेत सर्वदेवमयो गुरुः॥ १६॥[38]

एवं प्रपञ्चयति —

गुरुर्ब्रह्मा गुरुर्विष्णुर्गुरुर्देवो महेश्वरः।
गुरुरेव परं ब्रह्म तस्मादादौ तमर्चयेत्॥ १७॥[39]

---

[37]भाग. ११.११.४७
[38]भाग. ११.१७.२७
[39]गुरुगीता 32

> Whoever may worship me with a concentrated mind in order to fulfill his desired aims obtains true *bhakti* for me, [but] by service to the holy ones one obtains remembrance of me.[40]

Therefore, the primary cause of obtaining *bhakti* to the Lord is taking shelter with a *bhakta* of the Lord in the form of the *guru*. Here some say that *bhakti* for the *guru* **is** *bhakti* for Kṛṣṇa. Now then, what exactly is *bhakti* for the *guru*? It is said that *guru-bhakti* is knowing the mind of the *guru* as a result of observing the *guru*'s orders with one's body, words, and mind, without considering whether or not one is able to do it. This, too, occurs when one has surrendered to the *guru*. Here the characteristics of one who is surrendered are: first of all, accepting the *guru* as one's protector, acting favorably towards the *guru*, rejecting unfavorable things, giving up one's possessions, accepting a little of the *guru*'s grace (*prasāda*), and behaving without conceit or egotism. In this way everything becomes free of blemish. If one wonders whether things such as hearing, repeating, remembering, serving of the Lord's names and so forth are to be performed or not, have no doubt. By the very force of the *guru*'s orders, the service of Bhagavān, hearing his names, serving the Vaiṣṇavas and the rest are to be performed. Therefore, defining *guru-bhakti* as "knowing the mind of the guru" is justified.

Thus, he states that the *guru* is everything with a statement from Bhagavān—

> One should know me to be the teacher and should never disrepect the teacher. One should not envy him as if he were an ordinary mortal. The *guru* is composed of all the gods.[41]

And this he makes more clear:

> The *guru* is Brahmā; the *guru* is Viṣṇu; the *guru-god* is Maheśvara. The *guru* is supreme Brahman. Therefore, one should worship him first.[42]

---

[40] Bhāg., 11.11.47.

[41] Bhāg., 11.17.27.

[42] This is similar to the verse from the *Guru-gītā*: 32.

गुरौ प्रसन्ने सति फलमाह —

प्रसन्ने तु गुरौ सर्वसिद्धिरुक्ता मनीषिभिः॥ १८॥[43]

अप्रसन्ने फलमाह —

हरौ रुष्टे गुरुस्त्राता गुरौ रुष्टे न कश्चन।
तस्मात्सर्वप्रयत्नेन गुरुमेव प्रसादयेत्॥ १९॥[44]

पूजाकरणे ऽमङ्गलफलमाह —

गुरौ सन्निहिते यस्तु पूजयेदग्रतो न तम्।
स दुर्गतिमवाप्नोति पूजा च विफला भवेत्॥ २०॥[45]

विद्याद्यभावे ऽपि स एव परमेष्टदेव इत्याह —

अविद्यो वा सविद्यो वा गुरुरेव तु दैवतम्।
मार्गस्थो वाप्यमार्गस्थो गुरुरेव सदा गतिः॥ २१॥[46]

अत्र विमुखे ऽनिष्टमाह —

प्रतिपद्य गुरुं यस्तु मोहाद्विप्रतिपद्यते।
स कल्पकोटीं नरके पच्यते पुरुषाधमः॥ २२॥[47]

---

[43]Source unknown.
[44]Source unknown.
[45]Source unknown.
[46]Source unknown.
[47]Source unknown.

He describes the result when the *guru* is pleased:

> The wise say that when the *guru* is pleased all things are successful.[48] (18)

And he describes the result when the *guru* is not pleased:

> When Hari is angered the *guru* is one's savior; when the *guru* is angered no one can save one. Therefore, one should make every effort to make the *guru* happy.[49] (19)

He describes the inauspicious result of not worshiping the *guru*:

> But one who does not honor the *guru* first when he is present obtains a bad end and his worship, too, becomes fruitless.[50] (20)

He now adds that even if one's *guru* does not have knowledge, the *guru* is still the highest desired deity:

> Whether without knowledge or with knowledge, the *guru* is one's deity. Whether on the path or not on the path, the *guru* is always one's goal.[51] (21)

Now the unwanted result when one turns against one's *guru*:

> One who, after having surrendered to a *guru*, then out of delusion turns against him is the lowest of humans and burns in hell for a billion ages.[52] (22)

---

[48] Unknown source.
[49] Unknown source.
[50] Unknown source.
[51] Unknown source.
[52] Unknown source.

तत्सन्निधौ व्यवहारमाह —

आयान्तमग्रतो गच्छेद्गच्छन्तं तमनुव्रजेत्।
आसने शयने वापि नो तिष्ठेदग्रतो गुरोः॥
अनुज्ञां प्राप्य यस्तिष्ठेन्नैवं पापमवाप्नुयात्॥ २३॥[53]

गुरौ दूरस्थे निकटस्थे च भोजनव्यवहारमाह —

यत्किञ्चिदन्नपानादि प्रियं द्रव्यं मनोरमम्।
समर्प्य गुरवे पश्चात्स्वयं भुञ्जीत प्रत्यहम्॥ २४॥[54]

प्रकरणार्थमुपसंहरति —

महान्धकारमध्येष्वादित्यश्च प्रकाशकः।
अज्ञानतिमिरान्धेषु गुरुरेव प्रकाशकः॥ २५॥[55]

श्रीभक्तिसारसमुच्चये गुरुचरणाश्रयनं तृतीयं विरचनम्॥

[53]Source unknown.
[54]Source unknown.
[55]Source unknown.

He describes proper behavior when the *guru* is near:

> When the *guru* is arriving one should walk before him and when the guru is leaving one should walk behind him. In sitting or in lying down one should not sit or lie down in front of the *guru*. One who has received the *guru*'s permission may do so and thus obtains no sin.[56] (23)

He describes proper behavior for eating when the *guru* is far away and when the *guru* is nearby:

> Everyday any food and drink or any object that is dear to one and pleasing, one should offer first to one's *guru* and then afterwards enjoy it oneself.[57] (24)

He wraps up the subject of this section:

> And in the great darknesses the sun is the bearer of light. In the darknesses of ignorance the *guru* is the bearer of light.[58]

Thus ends the Third Chapter entitled "Taking Shelter with a Guru" in the *Collection of the Essentials of Bhakti for the Lord* of Lokānandācārya.

---

[56] Unknown source.
[57] Unknown source.
[58] Unknown source.

The Greatness of the Divine Name

अथ नाममाहात्म्यम्

अथ तावत्सर्वधर्मसाध्यत्वात्परममङ्गलरूपं भगवन्नामैव सर्वश्रेष्ठतममिति तन्महिमानं दर्शयितुमाह —

नाम्नो ऽस्य यावती शक्तिः पापनिर्हरणे हरेः।
तावत्कर्तुं न शक्नोति पातकं पातकीजनः॥ १॥

वर्तमानञ्च यत्पापं यद्भुतं यद्भविष्यति।
तत्सर्वं निर्दहत्याशु गोविन्दानलकीर्तनात्॥ २॥

एवं परममङ्गलत्वं दर्शयति त्रिभिः —

कृष्णेति मङ्गलं नाम यस्य वाचि प्रवर्तते।
भस्मीभवन्ति राजेन्द्र महापातककोटयः॥ ३॥

गायन्ति वैष्णवाः सर्वे कृष्णेति नाममङ्गलम्।
सर्वत्र मङ्गलं तेषां कुतस्तेषाममङ्गलम्॥ ४॥

सकृदुच्चारणे ऽपि परममङ्गलमाह —

मधुरमधुरमेतन्मङ्गलं मङ्गलानां
सकलनिगमवल्लीसत्फलं चित्स्वरूपम्।
सकृदपि परिगीतं हेलया श्रद्धया वा
भृगुवर नरमात्रं तारयेत्कृष्णनाम॥ ५॥

Now the Greatness of the Divine Name:

Now, first of all, in order to show that since it is the goal of all *dharma*, the name of the Lord, which is the form of the highest beneficence, is the best of all , he says:

> No sinner is capable of commiting as much sin as there is power in the divine name of Hari to remove it. (1)
>
> The sin that currently exists as well as that which is past and that which will be, all of it is quickly burned up by the repetition of the fire-like [name of] Govinda. (2)

Now he demonstrates how the divine name is the highest benefaction:

> Of one in whose speech is found the beneficient name "Kṛṣṇa" all great sins are turned into ashes, o King of Kings. (3)
>
> All Vaiṣṇavas sing the auspicious name "Kṛṣṇa." For them there is always good. Where is there ever anything inauspicious for them? (4)

The highest good comes even when the divine name is pronounced only once:

> Sweet among things sweet is this, auspicious among things auspicious. It is the real fruit of the vine of all the Vedas, consciousness in its essence, which if sung even once, neglectfully or with faith, the name of Kṛṣṇa causes any human to cross beyond, o best of Bhṛgus![59] (5)

---

[59] *Prabhāsa-khaṇḍa*, ?. Also cited in the *Haribhakti-vilāsa* at 11.451

एतत्सदृशं किमपि नास्तीत्याह —

न नाम सदृशं ज्ञानं न नाम सदृशं व्रतम्।
न नाम सदृशं ध्यानं न नाम सदृशं फलम्॥ ६॥

न नाम सदृशस्त्यागो न नाम सदृशं तपः।
न नाम सदृशा मुक्तिर्न नाम सदृशः प्रभुः॥ ७॥

एवं नाम ग्रहणमात्रेण भगवत्प्रीतिर्जायते —

कामादिगुणसंयुक्ता नाममात्रैकबान्धवाः।
प्रीतिं कुर्वन्ति ते पार्थ न तथा जितषड्गुणाः॥
ये गृह्णन्ति हरेर्नाम त एव जितषड्गुणाः॥ ८॥

एवं तस्य विशेषफललाभमाह —

मम नाम सदाग्राही मम नाम प्रिय सदा।
भक्तिस्तस्मै प्रदातव्या न च मुक्तिः कदाचन॥ ९॥

एवं विशेषफलमाह —

श्रद्धया हेलया नाम वदन्ति मम जन्तवः।
तेषां नाम सदा पार्थ वर्तते हृदये मम॥ १०॥

मानवाः ये हरेर्नाम सेवन्ते नित्यमेव च।
भक्त्या सह गमिष्यन्ति यत्र योगेश्वरः प्रभुः॥ ११॥

To demonstrate that there is nothing similar to this [divine name], he says:

> Liberating knowledge is not equal to the divine name, nor are vows; meditation is not equal to the divine name, nor is any other result. Renunciation is not equal to the divine name, nor is austerity; liberation is not equal to the divine name, nor is any other master. (6-7)

Thus, simply by repeating the divine name the pleasure of the Lord is born:

> Those whose only friend is the divine name, though they possess the six mundane traits of desire, and so forth,[60] please me more than those who have conquered those traits. Those who repeat the divine name of Hari have indeed conquered the six mundane traits. (8)

And he describes the special result that one [who repeats the divine name] obtains:

> One who always repeats my name and to whom my name is dear, to such a one *bhakti* is to be given, never liberation (*mukti*). (9)

Thus, he describes the special result:

> The names of my creatures who speak my name whether with faith or frivolity are always in my heart, o Pārtha. (10)
>
> And humans who regularly repeat the name of Hari will go with *bhakti* to wherever the Master, the Lord of Yoga, is. (11)

[60]The six traits are: desire, anger, greed, illusion, pride, and envy.

एवं रामनाम्नो विशेषमहिमाहमाह —

राम रामेति रामेति राम रामे मनोरमे।
सहस्रनामभिस्तुल्यं रामनाम वरानने॥ १२॥

एवं नामादिप्रसङ्गात्सर्वतीर्थसम्भावना भवतीत्याह —

तत्रैव गङ्गा यमुना च तत्र गोदावरी तत्र सरस्वती च।
सर्वानि तीर्थानि वसन्ति तत्र यत्राच्युतोदारकथाप्रसङ्गः॥
१३॥

विशेषमाह —

मन्नामस्मरणात्किञ्चित्कलौ नास्त्येव पातकम्।
मद्भक्ता यत्र गायन्ति तत्र मे पार्थिव स्थितिः॥ १४॥

जगनाथनाम्नो महिमानमाह सप्तभिः वैदिकतन्त्रे इन्द्रद्युम्नं प्रति ब्रह्मवाक्यम्

पूजयस्व जगन्नाथं सर्वतन्त्रेषु गोपितम्।
गुह्याद्गुह्यतरं नाम कीरतयस्व निरन्तरम्॥ १५॥

यस्तु संकीर्तयेन्नित्यं जगन्नाथमतन्द्रितः।
निर्मुक्तः सर्वपापेभ्यो मुक्तबन्धः परं व्रजेत्॥ १६॥

विष्णुयामले कूर्मध्वजोत्तरणप्रस्तावे महादेवं प्रति भगवद्वाक्यम् —

जगन्नाथेति नाम्ना ये कीर्तयन्ति च ये नराः।
अपराधशतं तेषां क्षमिष्ये नात्र संशयः॥ १७॥

Thus, he describes the special greatness of the name of Rāma:

> O mind-pleasing Rāmā [Pārvatī], "Rāma, Rāma, and Rāma, and Rāma," the name of Rāma is equal to a thousand names, O lady with a gorgeous face. (12)

Now he claims that because of connection with the divine names and such, all the holy places appear together with them:

> There indeed is the Gaṅgā, the Yamunā, the Godāvarī, and the Sarasvatī. All the holy places reside wherever there is connection with the exalted stories of Acyuta. (13)

In particular he says:

> Because of remembering my name there is no sin in the Age of Kali. Wherever my bhaktas are singing, there am I present, o king! (14)

In the next seven verses he describes the greatness of the name of Jagannātha. In the *Vaidika-tantra* is found Brahmā's statement to Indradyumna:

> Worship Jagannātha who is hidden away in all the *tantras*. Praise ceaselessly his name which is more secret than secret things. (15)
>
> One who loudly praises Jagannātha constantly and without tiring is liberated from all sins and being freed of bondage goes to the supreme. (16)

In the *Viṣṇu-yāmala* on the topic of the salvation of Kūrmadhvaja, there the Lord's statement to Mahādeva:

> Those humans who sing praise with the name "Jagannātha," a hundred of their offenses do I forgive. In this there is no doubt. (17)

ब्रह्मरहस्ये शूरशर्मब्राह्मणं प्रति नारदवाक्यम् —

> सकृदुच्चारयेद्यस्तु जगन्नाथेति हेलया।
> ब्रह्महत्यादिपापेभ्यो मुच्यते नात्र संशयः॥ १८॥
>
> सर्वाअचारविहीनो ऽपि तापक्लेशादिसंयुतः।
> जगन्नाथं वदन् विप्र याति ब्रह्मसनातनम्॥ १९॥

मेरुतन्त्रे ब्रह्मणो नामकीर्तनप्रस्तावे वैष्णवान् प्रति नारदवाक्यम् —

> नाम्नां मुख्यतरं विष्णोर्जगन्नाथमुदीरितम्।
> नातः परतरं नाम त्रिषु लोकेषु विद्यते॥ २०॥
>
> न गङ्गास्नानमेतादृङ्न काशीगमनं तथा।
> जगन्नाथेति सङ्कीर्त्य नरः कैवल्यमाप्नुयात्॥ २१॥

एवं विशेषमहिमानमाह —

> विष्णोर्नामैव पुंसः समलमपहरत्पुण्यमुत्पादयच्च
> ब्रह्मादिस्थानभोगाद्विरतिमथगुरोः श्रीपदद्वन्द्वभक्तिम्।
> तत्त्वज्ञानञ्च विष्णोरिहमृतिजननभ्रान्तिबीजञ्च दग्ध्वा
> सत्यज्ञानन्दबोधे महति च पुरुषे स्थापयित्वा निवृत्तम्॥
> २२॥

There is the following statement of Nārada to Śūraśarma, the *brāhmaṇa*, in the *Brahmarahasya*:

> But one who once says "Jagannātha" even frivolously is liberated from sins like the killing of a *brāhmaṇa* and so forth. Of this there is no doubt. (18)
>
> A person afflicted by sufferings, pains, and so forth, even though lacking all good behavior, by saying "Jagannātha" goes to eternal Brahman, O Brāhmaṇa. (19)

In the *Merutantra*, in the section praising the recitation of the names of Brahman, Nārada tells the Vaiṣṇavas:

> It is said that more primary among the names of Viṣṇu is "`Jagannātha." No higher name than this exists in the three worlds. (20)
>
> Bathing in the Ganges is not comparable to this, nor is visiting Kāśī. By saying loudly "Jagannātha" a person can reach ultimate singularity (*kaivalya*, liberation). (21)

Thus does he describe the special magnificence [of the divine names]:

> Viṣṇu's name itself removes a person's sins and creates for that person merit, detachment from the pleasures of abodes like that of Brahmā and others, *bhakti* for the two lotus-like feet of the guru, and knowledge of the truth. Then, after burning up the seeds of one's roaming from birth to death in this world and after truly establishing one in the experience of bliss of the great person (Mahāpuruṣa, Bhagavān), it rests. (22)

तस्माद्गुरुसन्निध्यात्कृष्णोपदेशं गृहीत्वा भक्तिसाधनं कार्यमिति। नन्वत्र गुरोरुपदेशे कर्तव्ये दक्षिणादीक्षापुरश्चरणविधिनियमो ऽस्तीति कथं न स्यादित्यत्राह भगवद्वाक्येन —

आकृष्टिः कृतचेतसां सुमहतामुच्चाटनं चांहसाम्
आचण्डालममुकलोकसुलभो वश्यश्च मोक्षश्रियः।
नो दीक्षां न च दक्षिणां न च पुरश्चर्यां मनागीक्षते
मन्त्रो ऽयं रसनास्पृगेव फलति श्रीकृष्णनामात्मकः॥ २३॥

यथा पाद्मे —

कृष्णाय नम इत्येष मन्त्रः सर्वार्थसाधकः।
भक्तानां जपतां भूप स्वर्गमोक्षफलप्रदः॥ २४॥

एवं स्मरणादौ कालदेशादिनियमो नास्तीत्यत्राह भगवच्छ्रीकृष्णचैतन्याज्ञाया द्वाभ्याम्—

नाम्नामकारि बहुधा निजसर्वशक्ति-
स्तत्रार्पिता नियमितः स्मरणे न कालः।
एतादृशी तव कृपा भगवन्ममापि
दुर्दैवमीदृशमिहाजनि नानुरागः॥ २५॥

न कालनियमस्तत्र न देशनियमस्तथा।
नोच्छिष्टादौ निषेधः स्यात्कृष्णनामानुकीर्तने॥ २६॥

Therefore, after accepting instruction about Kṛṣṇa from one's *guru*, one should perform the practices of *bhakti*. Now, at this point someone may ask: when the instruction of the *guru* is necessary, rules concerning *guru*-gift, initiation, and rites of purification are required. Why is this not so here? To this he replies with a statement of Bhagavān:

> It attracts great ones whose minds are pure, irradicates sins, is easily available to small folk upto and including Caṇḍālas, and controls the good fortune of liberation. It does not depend on initiation, nor donations, nor preparatory rites. This *mantra* made of the names of Śrī Kṛṣṇa produces results as soon as it touches the tongue.[61] (23)

As in the *Padma Purāṇa*:

> The *mantra*, "*kṛṣṇaāya namaḥ*," accomplishes all objectives and gives to those *bhaktas* who chant it, o king, the results: heaven and liberation. (24)

Thus, he says here that there are no rules concerning time, place, and so forth in the remembering [of the holy names] with two stanzas of the order of Bhagavān Śrī Kṛṣṇacaitanya:

> Many are your names and all of your own power was placed in them. There is no restriction on the time for remembering them. So great is your grace, o Bhagavān, and yet such is my misfortune that my love for them was not born.[62] (25)
>
> In the repetition [or singing] of the names of Kṛṣṇa, there is no rule regarding proper time nor one regarding proper place, and no prohibition in matters of impurity caused by contact with leftovers and such. (26)

---

[61] Śrī Rūpa Gosvāmin, compilor, *Padyāvalī*, 29.
[62] Śrī Caitanya, *Śikṣāṣṭaka*, 2.

इदानीं प्रकरणार्थमुपसंहरति शुक्राचार्यवाक्येन —

मन्त्रतस्तन्त्रतश्छिद्रं देशकालार्हवस्तुतः।
सर्वं करोति निश्छिद्रं नामसङ्कीर्तनं हरेः॥ (भाग्., ८.२३.१६)
२७॥

श्रवणं कीर्तनं ध्यानं विष्णोरद्भुतकर्मणः।
जन्मकर्मगुणानाञ्च तदर्थे ऽखिलचेष्टितम्॥ (भाग्., ११.३.२७)
२८॥

को ऽयं नामापराध इत्याह —

सतां निन्दा नाम्नः परममपराधं वितनुते
यतः ख्यातिं यातं कथमुत्सहते तद्विगरिहाम्।
शिवस्य श्रिविष्णोर्य इह गुणनामादिसकलं
धिया भिन्नं पश्येत्स खलु हरिनामाहितकरः॥ २९॥

गुरोरवज्ञा श्रुतिशास्त्रनिन्दनं
तथार्थवादो हरिनाम्नि कल्पनम्।
नाम्नो बलाद्यस्य हि पापबुद्धि-
र्न विद्यते तस्य यमैर्हि शुद्धिः॥

Now, he wraps up the content of this section with a statement of Śukrācārya:

> All the flaws arising from *mantra*, rites, the appropriateness of time, place, and material, the repetition of the the names of Hari removes.[63] (27)
>
> Hearing about, praising, and meditating on Viṣṇu, whose actions are wondrous, and on his births, actions, and qualities and performing all actions for his sake [with *bhakti* produced by *bhakti*, one maintains one's ecstatic body].[64] (27) (28)

Thus, by the repeating, hearing, and so forth of the the names of Śrī Kṛṣṇa *bhakti* arises. This is its meaning. If there is offense it does not arise.

What are these offenses towards the divine names? To this he replies:

> Defamation of holy ones (1) causes the most serious offense to the divine name. How can he tolerate the defamation of those from whom the name is made famous. One who sees with his intellect all the qualities, names, and so forth of Śiva and Viṣṇa as different is indeed an offender of the divine names (2). (29)
>
> Disrespect for the *guru* (3), defamation of revealed and reasoned texts (4), as well as considering [the greatness of] the divine names to be mere praise (*artha-vāda*) (5), and one who intends to sin on the strength of the divine names is not made pure even by the restraints (*yama*) (6).[65]

---

[63]Bhāg., 8.23.16.

[64]Bhāg., 11.3.27.

[65]Lokānandācārya gives in his commentary the following example of *arthavāda* with regard to the divine names: "*arthavāda* is thinking: 'is it really possible that repeating the divine name only once destroys sins accumulated over many births? It does not have the power to destroy all sins.'"

अथ यमाः —

अहिंसा सत्यमस्तेयमसङ्गो ह्रीरसञ्चयः।
आस्तिक्यं ब्रह्मचर्यञ्च मौनं स्थैर्यं क्षमाभयम्॥ (भाग्., ११.१९.
३३) ३१॥

प्रसङ्गान्नियमा लिख्यन्ते —

शौचं जपस्तपोहोमः श्रद्धातिथ्यं मदर्चनम्।
तीर्थाटनं परार्थेहातुष्टिराचार्यसेवनम्॥ (भाग्., ११.१९.३४)
३२॥

धर्मव्रतत्यागहुतादिसर्वशुभक्रियासाम्यमपि प्रमादतः।
अश्रद्दधाने विमुखे ऽप्यशृन्वति यश्चोपदेशः शिवनामाप-
राधः॥ ३३॥

श्रुत्वापि नाममाहात्म्यं यः प्रीतिरहितो ऽधमः।
अहं ममादिपरमो नाम्नि सो ऽप्यपराधकृत्॥ ३४॥

ननु नामापराधयुक्तानां केन निस्तारः स्यादित्याह —

नामापराधयुक्तानां नामान्येव हरन्त्यघं।
अविश्रान्तं प्रयुक्तानि तान्येवार्थकराणि च॥

इतिश्रीभक्तिसारसमुच्चये नाममाहात्म्यं नाम चतुर्थं विरचनम्॥ ४॥

Now the restraints (*yama*)—

> Non-violence, truth, not stealing, not associating [with the worldly], modesty, non-accumulation, faithfulness, celibacy, silence, steadfastness, tolerance, and fearlessness.[66]

Because of the context the obligations (*niyama*) are also listed:

> Cleanliness, silent recitation, austerity, ritual offerings, faith, hospitality, worship of me, visiting the holy places, effort for the sake of others, satisfaction, and serving the teacher.[67] (32)
>
> Mistakenly [thinking the divine names are] the same as auspicious actions like dharma, vows, renunciation, fire offerings, and so forth (7). And instructing someone who is faithless, hostile, or not listening, is an offense to the auspicious name (8). (33)
>
> After hearing of the greatness of the divine name one who has no attraction for it is vile (9). One who is intent on himself and what belongs to him is also an offender of the divine name (10). (34)

Now, to the question "how might an offender of the divine name be saved?" he says:

> The divine names themselves remove the sin of those who are offenders of the names. They themselves, when repeated without ceasing, bring about the goal. (35)

Thus ends the Fourth Chapter, called the "Greatness of the Divine Name," in the *Śrī Bhakti-sāra-samuccaya*.

---

[66]Bhāg., 11.19.33
[67]Bhāg., 11.19.34.

Bibliography

Bharati, Premananda. *Śrī Kṛṣṇa: the Lord of Love*. Kirksville, MO, USA: Blazing Sapphire Press, 2007, 2nd edition. New edition with introductions and scholarly apparatus and appendices of the 1912 edition published by William Ryder and Son, Ltd.

Blackmore, Susan. *The Meme Machine*. Oxford: Oxford University Press, 1999, 1st edition.

Bābājī, Kuñjabihāri Dāsa. *Bhakti-kalpa-latā*. Radhakund, U.P., India: Anantadāsa Bābājī, G. 498 [1984], 3rd edition. In Bengali. A work on the process of attaining *bhakti* by a previous abbot (*mahānta*) of Radhakund.

Dāsa, Haridāsa. *Śrī Śrī Gauḍīya Vaiṣṇava Jīvana, Dvitīya Khaṇḍa*. Navadvīpa, India: Haribol Kuṭīra, 489 GA [1975], 3rd edition. In Bengali. On the lives of the famous saints and practitioners of the Caitanya Vaiṣṇava tradition.

Dāsa, Vinoda Vihārī. *Bhakti-krama-vikāśer Antarāya*. Vṛndāvana, India: Śrī Murārī Dāsa, 1995, 1st edition. In Bengli. Binode Bihari Das Bābājī's earlier book on the obstacles to the development of *bhakti*.

———. *Prabhupāda Śrī Śrī 108 Kiśorīkiśorānanda Bābā, Tinkaḍi Bābā*. Keśīghāṭa, Vṛndāvana, India: Śrī Murārī Dāsa Bābājī, 1999, 1st edition. In Bengali. On the life of a great practitioner and saint of the Caitanya tradition. Translated as *Sādhu Sādhu: a Life of Tinkaḍi Bābā*. See the separate entry.

———. *Sādhu Sādhu: a Life of Tinkaḍi Bābā.* Kirksville, MO, USA: Blazing Sapphire Press, 2008, 1st edition. A translation of *Prabhupāda Śrī Śrī 108 Kiśorīkiśorānanda Bābā, Tinkaḍi Bābā.*

Dawkins, Richard. *The Selfish Gene.* Oxford: Oxford University Press, 1976, 1st edition.

Dennett, Daniel. *Breaking the Spell.* London: Penguin Books, 2006, 1st edition.

Ṭhākura, Narottama Dāsa. *Sri Sri Prema Bhakti Candrika.* Rādhākuṇḍa, India: Śrī Ananta Dāsa Bābājī Mahārāja, [n.d.], 1st edition. With the commentaries of Vishvanatha Chakravartipada and Srila Ananta Dasa Babaji Maharaja. Translated into English by Advaita Dasa.

Dāsa, Sundarānanda. *Śrī Śrī Caitanyacandrodaye Viśiṣṭa Tārakātraya.* Navadvīpa, India: NavīnaKṛṣṇa Dāsa Vidyālaṅkāra, 1961, 1st edition. In Bengali. On three of Caitanya's early followers: Sadāśiva Kavirāja, his son, Puruṣottama Dāsa Ṭhākura, and his son, Kānu Ṭhākura. These are ancestors of Kanupriya Goswami.

Ghose, Shishir Kumar. *Lord Gouranga or Salvation for All,* volume 1-2. Calcutta, India: Piyush Kanti Ghose, 1923, 3rd edition.

Gosvāmin, Gopāla Bhaṭṭa. *Śrī Hari-bhakti-vilāsaḥ.* Mayamanasiṃha (now in Bangla Desh): Śacīnātharāya-caturdhurīṇa, 1946, 1st edition. Edited by Purīdāsa Mahāśaya with the commentary of Sanātana Gosvāmin. In Sanskrit (Bengali script).

Gosvāmin, Jīva. *Śrībhakti-śrīprīti-nāmaka-sandarbhadvayam.* Vṛndāvana, India: Haridāsa Śarmā, 1951a, 1st edition. Edited by Purīdāsa Mahāśaya. In Sanskrit (Bengali script).

———. *Śrītattva-śrībhagavat-śrīparamātma-śrīkṛṣṇākhya-sandarbha-catuṣṭayam.* Vṛndāvana, India: Haridāsa Śarmā, 1951b, 1st edition. Edited by Purīdāsa Mahāśaya. In Sanskrit (Bengali script).

———. *Śrī Śrī Sarvasaṃvādinī.* Vṛndāvana, India: Haridāsa Śarman, 1953, 1st edition. In Sanskrit (Bengali script). A commentary on the authors first four *sandarbhas: Tattva, Bhagavat, Paramātma,* and *Kṛṣṇa.*

———. *Śrī Bhagavatsandarbha.* Vṛndāvana, India: Sadgranthaprakāśaka, 1983, 1st edition. In Sanskrit (Devanāgarī script) with a Hindi trans. The second of the six *sandarbhas* or treatises by Śrī Jīva that make up the Caitanya tradition's major set of theological dogmas. Edited with the autocommentary *Sarvasaṃvādinī* by Haridāsa Śāstrī.

Gosvāmin, Raghunātha Dāsa. *Stavāvalī.* Mūrśidābād (West Bengal, India): Rādhāramaṇa Yantra, 1329 [1923], 2nd edition. In Sanskrit with the commentary of Vaṅgeśvara Vidyābhūṣaṇa and a Bengali translation.

Gosvāmin, Rūpa. *Śrī Padyāvalī.* Vṛndāvana, U. P., India: Rāghavacaitanyadāsa, 1959, 1st edition. In Sanskrit (Devanāgarī) with a Hindi translation. Edited by Vanamālidāsa Śāstrī.

———. *Ujjvala-nīla-maṇi.* Varanasi, India: Chaukhamba Sanskrit Pratishthan, 1985, reprint edition. Edited with the commentaries of Jīvagosvāmin and Viśvanātha Chakravarty by M. M. Pandit Durga Prasad & Vasudev Lakshaman Shastri Panashikar. In Sanskrit (Devanāgarī script).

———. *The Bhakti-rasāmṛta-sindhu of Rūpa Gosvāmin.* New Delhi, India: Indira Gandhi Center for the Arts, 2003, 1st edition. Translated with introduction and notes by David L. Haberman.

———. *Śrī Śrī Bhakti-rasāmṛtra-sindhuḥ.* Mathurā, India: Śrī Kṛṣṇajanmasthāna, 495 [1981], 3rd edition. Edited with the commentaries of Śrī Jīva, Mukundadāsa, and Viśvanātha Cakravartin and a Bengali translation by Haridāsa Dāsa. In Sanskrit and Bengali.

———. *Ujjvala-nīla-maṇiḥ.* Navadvīpa, West Bengal, India: Mukundadāsa, G. 478 [1964], 2nd edition. Edited with the commentary of Viṣṇudāsa Gosvāmin by Haridāsa Dāsa, In Sanskrit (Bengali script) with a Bengali translation.

Gosvāmin, Sanātana. *Bṛhad-bhāgavatāmṛta.* Mayamanasiṃha (now in Bangla Desh): Śacīnātharāya, G. 458 [1944], 1st edition. Edited with the author's own commentary by Purīdāsa. In Sanskrit (Bengali script).

Gosvāmī, Kānanavihārī. *Bāghnāpāṛā-sampradāya o Baiṣṇava Sāhitya*. Kalakātā, India: Ravīndrabhāratī Viśvavidyālaya, 1993, 1st edition. In Bengali.

Goswami, Kanupriya. *Jīver Svarūpa o Svadharma*. Kalikātā (Kolkata), India, 1934, 1st edition. In Bengali. On the true nature and function of the living being.

———. *Mahat-saṅga-prasaṅga*. Kalikātā (Kolkata), India: Śrī Kiśorasāya Gosvāmin, B, 1376 [1970], 1st edition. In Bengali. On the benefits of associating with the great ones, holy men and women who are *bhaktas*. This is the Bengali original of this translation.

———. *Śrī Nāma-cintāmaṇi*. Kalikātā (Kolkata), India: Śrī Kiśora Rāya Goswami, B. 1378 [1972], 3rd edition. In Bengali. On the theology and practice of repeating the holy name.

Guha, Manindranath. *Nectar of the Holy Name*. Kirksville, MO, USA: Blazing Sapphire Press, 2006, 1st edition. An English translation of the author's Bengali work, *Śrīman-nāmāmṛta-sindhu-bindu*.

Hacker, Paul. *Philology and Confrontation: Paul Hacker on Traditional and Modern Vedanta*. Albany, New York, USA: State University of New York Press, 1995, 1st edition. Essays of the Indologist Paul Hacker translated and edited by Wilhelm Halbrass.

Kapoor, Dr. O. B. L. *The Saints of Bengal*. Radhakunda, India: Srila Badrinarayana Bhagavata Bhushana Prabhu, 1995, 1st edition.

———. *The Companions of Sri Chaitanya Mahaprabhu*. Radhakunda, India: Srila Badrinarayana Bhagavata Bhushana Prabhu, 1997, 1st edition.

———. *The Saints of Vraja*. New Delhi, India: Aravali Books International (P) LTD, 1999, 2nd edition.

———. *Experiences in Bhakti: the Science Celestial*. Kirksville, MO, USA: Blazing Sapphire Press, 2006, 2nd edition.

Kavirāja, Kṛṣṇadāsa. *Caitanya-caritāmṛta*, volume 1-6. Kalikātā: Sādhanā Prakāśanī, [1963], 4th edition. Edited with commentary by Dr. Rādhāgovinda Nātha. In Bengali and Sanskrit.

———. *The Caitanya Caritāmṛta of Kṛṣṇadāsa Kaviraja.* Cambridge, MA: Department of Sanskrit and Indian Studies, Harvard University, 1999, 1st edition. A translation and commentary by Edward C. Dimock, Jr. Edited by Tony K. Stewart.

Lokānandācārya. *Śrī Bhagavad-bhakti-sāra-samuccaya.* Kālidaha, Brindaban, India: Haridāsa Śāstrī, 1979a, 1st edition. In Sanskrit (Devanāgarī script) with Hindi trans.

———. *Śrī Bhagavad-bhakti-sāra-samuccaya.* Kālidaha, Brindaban, India: Haridāsa Śāstrī, 1979b, 1st edition. In Sanskrit (Bengali script) with Bengali trans.

———. *Śrī Bhagavad-bhakti-sāra-samuccaya.* Brindaban, India: Haribhaktadāsa, 1982, 1st edition. In Sanskrit (Bengali script) with Bengali trans.

Mahāprabhu, Śrī Caitanya. *Śrī Caitanya-śikṣāṣṭakam.* Vṛndāvana, India: Śrī Sāvitrī Guha, 1984, 2nd edition. In Sanskrit (Bengali script) and Bengali. Eight verses said to have been composed by Śrī Caitanya. Translated with the Bengali commentary of Śrī Maṇīndranātha Guha.

———. *Śrī Śrī Śikṣāṣṭakam.* Rādhākuṇḍa, India: Śrī Ananta Dāsa Bābājī Mahārāja, 2003, 1st edition. Eight verses said to have been composed by Śrī Caitanya. With the commentary of Śrī Ananta Dāsa Bābājī Mahārāja. Translated into English by Advaita Das.

Nāth, Nīradprasād. *Narottama o Tāñhār Racanāvalī.* Kalikātā (Kolkata), India: Kalikātā Viśvavidyālaya, 1975, 1st edition. In Bengali. On the life and works of Narottama Dāsa Ṭhākura. Contains editions of all his major works and many attributed to Narottama Dāsa.

Purīdāsa, editor. *Śrīmad-bhāgavatam,* volume 1-3. Mayamanasiṃha, Bangla Desh: Śacīnātharāya-caturdhurīṇa, 1945, 1st edition. In Sanskrit. No commentaries.

Śāstrī, Bhagavat Kumar. *The Bhakti Cult in Ancient India.* Varanasi, India: The Chowkhamba Sanskrit Series Office, 1965, 2nd edition.

Stein, William Bysshe. *Two Brahman Sources of Emerson and Thoreau*. Gainesville, FL.: Scholar's Facsimiles & Reprints, 1967.

Tarkabhūṣaṇa, Mahāmahopādhyāya Pramathanātha, editor. *Śrīmadbhagavadgītā*. Kalikātā, India: Deva Sāhitya Kuṭīra Prāibheṭa Limiṭeḍ, 2001, 7th edition. In Sanskrit [Bengali script] with the comms. of Śaṅkara and Ānandagiri. Edited with a Bengali translation by Mahāmahopādhyāya Pramathanātha Tarkabhūṣaṇa.

Vidyābhūṣaṇa, Baladeva. *Prameyaratnāvalī*. Calcutta, India: Saṃskṛtasāhityapariṣat, 1927a, 1st edition. In Sanskrit (Devanāgarī) with the comms. of Kṛṣṇadeva Vedāntavāgīśa and Akṣayakumāra Śarma Śāstrī and a Bengali trans. of the primary text. Edited by Akṣayakumāra Śarmā Śāstrī.

———. *Siddhāntaratna*, volume 1-2. Benares, India: Government Sanskrit Library, 1927b, 1st edition. In Sanskrit (Devanāgarī) with the autocomm. of Baladeva. Edited by Gopīnātha Kavirāja in the Princess of Wales Saraswati Bhavana Texts series (no. 10).

———. *Vedānta-syamantakaḥ*. Vṛndāvana, India: Title Page, G 456 [1942], 1st edition. In Sanskrit (Devanāgarī) with the Hindi trans./comm. by Śrī Bālakṛṣṇa Gosvāmī. This publication identifies the author of the text as Baladeva Vidyābhūṣaṇa instead of his guru Rādhādāmodara Gosvāmin.

———. *Prameyaratnāvalī*. Vṛndāvana, India: Sadgranthaprakāśaka, G. 485 [1971], 1st edition. In Sanskrit (Devanāgarī) with the comm. of Kṛṣṇadeva Sārvabhauma (Vedāntavāgīśa)and a Hindi trans. of the primary text. Edited by Haridāsa Śāstrī. Included the *Navaratna* of Harirāma Vyāsa with Hindi trans.

Vopadeva. *Muktāphala*. Calcutta, India: Calcutta Oriental Series, 1944, 1st edition. In Sanskrit (Devanāgarī script) with the comm. of Hemādri. Introduction by Narendranath Law.

Introduction to the Devanāgarī Script

Learn Sanskrit! Or, at least learn the alphabet and how to pronounce it. It is not hard and it is the first step towards learning the Sanskrit language. The following guide will help you. If you wish to learn more, there are a number of resources on the internet with the help of which one can learn to read the "language of the gods."

Vowels: Svara

The sounds of the Sanksrit alphabet are divided among the different places in the mouth; a and ā are pronounced in the throat, i and ī at the palate, u and ū with the lips, ṛ and ṝ with the tongue curled upward at the roof of the mouth, ḷ and ḹ at the teeth, e at the palate, ai sliding from throat to palate, o at the lips, au sliding from throat to lips, and aḥ at the throat. (ă is a nasal sound)

अ — a, pronounced like "a" in "Roman,"[68]

आ — ā, pronounced like "a" in "father,"

इ — i, pronounced like "i" in "it" or "pin,"

[68]Many of these pronunciation examples s have been taken from the fine introduction to Sanskrit called *Sanskrit: an easy introduction to an enchanting language* by Ashok Aklujkar. (Richmond, British Columbia: Svādhyāya Publications, 1992)

ई — ī, pronounced like "i" in "police,"

उ — u, pronounced like "u" in "push,"

ऊ — ū, pronounced like "u" in "rude,"

ऋ — ṛ, pronounced like "er" in "fiber,"

ॠ — ṝ, pronounced like "ree" in "reel,"

ऌ — ḷ, pronounced like "le" in "angle,"

ॡ — ḹ, pronounced like "lea" in "leash,"

ए — e, pronounced like "ay" in "way,"

ऐ — ai, pronounced like "ai" in "aisle,"

ओ — o, pronounced like "o" in "note,"

औ — au, pronounced like "ow" in "now,"

आं — āṃ, pronounced like "awng" in "wrong,"

आः — āḥ, pronounced like "awha,"

Consonants: Viṣṇujana/Vyañjana

The ka-varga (ka-group)

These velar consonants are all pronounced in the throat.

क् — k, pronounced like the "k" in "sky,"

ख् — kh, pronounced like "c" in "cat,"

ग् — g, pronounced like the "g" in "gum,"

घ् — gh, pronounced like the "gh" in "doghouse,"

ङ् — ṅ, pronounced like "ng" in "sung,"

The ca-varga (ca-group)

These palatal consonants are all pronounced at the palate.

च् — c, pronounced like the "ch" in "church,"

छ् — ch, pronounced like the "ch" in "chew,"

ज् — j, pronounced like "j" in "jump,"

झ् — jh, pronounce this like "j" with a strong outward breath,"

ञ् — ñ, pronounced like "n" in "canyon,"

The ṭa-varga (ṭa-group)

These retroflex consonants are all pronounced with the tip of the tongue curled upward touching the roof of the mouth.

ट् — ṭ, pronounced like the "t" in "art" or "stop,"

ठ् — ṭh, pronounced like the "th" in "boathouse,"

ड् — ḍ, pronounced like "d" in "ardent" or "bird,"

ढ् — ḍh, pronounce this like "dh" in "hardhat,"

ण् — ṇ, pronounced like "n" in "yarn," "land" or "tint,"

The ta-varga (ta-group)

These dental consonants are all pronounced at the teeth.

त् — t, pronounced like the "th" in "the," "them" or the french word "*tete* (head),

थ् — th, pronounced like the above letter `t', but with more aspiration,

द् — d, pronounced like in the french word "*donner*" (to give),

ध् — dh, pronounce this like "d" with a strong outward breath,

न् — n, pronounced like "n" in "no,"

The pa-varga (pa-group)

These labial consonants are all pronouced with the lips.

प् — p, pronounced like the "p" in "spin,"

फ् — pha, pronounced like the "ph" in "tophat,"

ब् — b, pronounced like "b" in "boat,"

भ् — bh, pronouned like "bh" in "abhor,"

म् — m, pronounced like "m" in "mud,"

The Semivowels

The sounds are divided thus; y is produced at the palate, r at the roof of the mouth, l at the teeth, and v at the lips.

य् — y, pronounced like the "y" in "yoga,"

र् — r, pronounced like the "r" in "relic,"

ल् — l, pronounced like "l" in "land,"

व् — v, pronounced like "v" in "vote,"

The Sibilants

The sounds are divided thus; ś is produced at the palate, ṣ at the roof of the mouth, s at the teeth, and h at the throat.

श् — ś, pronounced like the "sh" in "Swedish-chocolate,"

ष् — ṣ, pronounced with tongue curled upward touching the roof of the mouth,

स् — s, pronounced like "s" in "sun,"

ह् — h, pronounced like "h" in "house,"

Combining Vowels and Consonants

Most vowel consonant combinations follow the pattern shown here.

क्	+	अ	=	क
क्	+	आ	=	का
क्	+	इ	=	कि
क्	+	ई	=	की
क्	+	उ	=	कु
क्	+	ऊ	=	कू
क्	+	ऋ	=	कृ
क्	+	ॠ	=	कॄ
क्	+	ऌ	=	कॢ
क्	+	ॡ	=	कॣ
क्	+	ए	=	के
क्	+	ऐ	=	कै
क्	+	ओ	=	को
क्	+	औ	=	कौ

ग्	+	अ	=	ग
ग्	+	आ	=	गा
ग्	+	इ	=	गि
ग्	+	ई	=	गी
ग्	+	उ	=	गु
ग्	+	ऊ	=	गू
ग्	+	ऋ	=	गृ
ग्	+	ॠ	=	गॄ
ग्	+	ऌ	=	गॢ
ग्	+	ॡ	=	गॣ
ग्	+	ए	=	गे
ग्	+	ऐ	=	गै
ग्	+	ओ	=	गो
ग्	+	औ	=	गौ

And so forth.

Compound Consonants

क्क kka	क्ख kkha	क्च kca	क्ण kṇa	क्त kta
क्त्य ktya	क्त्र ktra	क्त्र्य ktrya	क्त्व ktva	क्न kna
क्न्य knya	क्म kma	क्य kya	क्र kra	क्र्य krya
क्ल kla	क्व kva	क्व्य kvya	क्ष kṣa	क्ष्म kṣma
क्ष्य kṣya	क्ष्व kṣva	ख्य khya	ख्र khra	ग्य gya
ग्र gra	ग्र्य grya	घ्न ghna	घ्न्य ghnya	घ्म ghma
घ्य ghya	घ्र ghra	ङ्क ṅka	ङ्क्त ṅkta	ङ्क्त्य ṅktya
ङ्क्य ṅkya	ङ्क्ष ṅkṣa	ङ्क्ष्व ṅkṣva	ङ्ख ṅkha	ङ्ख्य ṅkhya
ङ्ग ṅga	ङ्ग्य ṅgya	ङ्घ ṅgha	ङ्घ्य ṅghya	ङ्घ्र ṅghra
ङ्ङ ṅṅa	ङ्न ṅna	ङ्म ṅma	ङ्य ṅya	च्च cca
च्छ ccha	च्छ्र cchra	च्ञ cña	च्म cma	च्य cya
छ्य chya	छ्र chra	ज्ज jja	ज्झ jjha	ज्ञ jña
ज्ञ्य jñya	ज्म jma	ज्य jya	ज्र jra	ज्व jva
ञ्च ñca	ञ्च्म ñcma	ञ्च्य ñcya	ञ्छ ñcha	ञ्ज ñja
ञ्ज्य ñjya	ट्ट ṭṭa	ट्य ṭya	ठ्य ṭhya	ठ्र ṭhra
ड्ग ḍga	ड्ग्य ḍgya	ड्घ ḍgha	ड्घ्र ḍghra	ड्ढ ḍḍha
ड्म ḍma	ड्य ḍya	ढ्य ḍhya	ढ्र ḍhra	ण्ट ṇṭa
ण्ठ ṇṭha	ण्ड ṇḍa	ण्ड्य ṇḍya	ण्ड्र ṇḍra	ण्ड्र्य ṇḍrya
ण्ढ ṇḍha	ण्ण ṇṇa	ण्म ṇma	ण्य ṇya	ण्व ṇva
त्क tka	त्क्र tkra	त्त tta	त्त्य ttya	त्त्र ttra
त्त्व ttva	त्थ ttha	त्न tna	त्न्य tnya	त्प tpa
त्प्र tpra	त्म tma	त्म्य tmya	त्य tya	त्र tra
त्र्य trya	त्व tva	त्स tsa	त्स्न tsna	त्स्न्य tsnya
थ्य thya	द्ग dga	द्ग्र dgra	द्घ dgha	द्घ्र dghra
द्द dda	द्द्य ddya	द्ध ddha	द्ध्य ddhya	द्न dna
द्ब dba	द्भ dbha	द्भ्य dbhya	द्म dma	द्य dya
द्र dra	द्र्य drya	द्व dva	द्व्य dvya	ध्न dhna
ध्न्य dhnya	ध्म dhma	ध्य dhya	ध्र dhra	ध्र्य dhrya
ध्व dhva	न्त nta	न्त्य ntya	न्त्र ntra	न्द nda
न्द्र ndra	न्ध ndha	न्ध्र ndhra	न्न nna	न्प npa
न्प्र npra	न्म nma	न्य nya	न्र nra	न्स nsa
प्त pta	प्त्य ptya	प्न pna	प्प ppa	प्म pma
प्य pya	प्र pra	प्ल pla	प्व pva	प्स psa
प्स्व psva	ब्घ bgha	ब्ज bja	ब्द bda	ब्ध bdha
ब्न bna	ब्ब bba	ब्भ bbha	ब्भ्य bbhya	ब्य bya
ब्र bra	ब्व bva	भ्न bhna	भ्य bhya	भ्र bhra
भ्व bhva	म्र mra	म्प mpa	म्प्र mpra	म्ब mba

म्भ mbha	म्म mma	म्य mya	म्न mna	म्ल mla
म्व mva	य्य yya	य्व yva	ल्क lka	ल्प lpa
ल्म lma	ल्य lya	ल्ल lla	ल्व lva	ल्ह lha
व्न vna	व्य vya	व्र vra	व्व vva	श्च śca
श्च्य ścya	श्न śna	श्य śya	श्र śra	श्र्य śrya
श्ल śla	श्व śva	श्व्य śvya	श्श śśa	ष्ट ṣṭa
ष्ट्य ṣṭya	ष्ट्र ṣṭra	ष्ट्र्य ṣṭrya	ष्ट्व ṣṭva	ष्ठ ṣṭha
ष्ण ṣṇa	ष्ण्य ṣṇya	ष्प ṣpa	ष्प्र ṣpra	ष्म ṣma
ष्य ṣya	ष्व ṣva	स्क ska	स्ख skha	स्त sta
स्त्य stya	स्त्र stra	स्त्व stv	स्थ stha	स्न sna
स्न्य snya	स्प spa	स्फ spha	स्म sma	स्म्य smya
स्य sya	स्र sra	स्व sva	स्स ssa	ह्ण hṇa
ह्न hna	ह्म hma	ह्य hya	ह्र hra	ह्ल hla
ह्व hva				

Pronunciation Table

	guttural	palatal	retroflex	dental	labial
1.	अ (a)	इ (i)	ऋ (ṛ)	ऌ (ḷ)	उ (u)
2.	आ (ā)	ई (ī), ए (e)	ॠ (ṝ)	ॡ (ḹ)	ऊ (ū), ओ (o)
3.	क (ka)	च (ca)	ट (ṭa)	त (ta)	प (pa)
4.	ख (kha)	छ (cha)	ठ (ṭha)	थ (tha)	फ (pha)
5.	ग (g)	ज (ja)	ड (ḍa)	द (da)	ब (ba)
6.	घ (gha)	झ (jha)	ढ (ḍha)	ध (dha)	भ (bha)
7.	ङ (ṅa)	ञ (ña)	ण (ṇa)	न (na)	म (ma)
8.		य (ya)	र (ra)	ल (la)	व (va)
9.	ह (ha)	श (śa)	ष (ṣa)	स (sa)	

ऐ slides from guttural to palatal.
औ slides from guttural to labial.

1. Short vowels
2. Long vowels
3. Unvoiced, unaspirated
4. Unvoiced, aspirated
5. Voiced, unaspirated
6. Voiced, aspirated
7. Nasals
8. Semivowels
9. Sibilants

Other Books by Blazing Sapphire Press

1. *Experiences in Bhakti: the Science Celestial* by Dr. O. B. L. Kapoor. This book is on the empirical dimensions of the Vaiṣṇava religious tradition centered around the worship of the Hindu god Kṛṣṇa. It uses stories from the lives of the saints of the tradition, large and small, to suggest that Vaiṣṇavism has many similarities with modern science and can be thought of as a kind of science. (ISBN: 978-0-9817902-6-8 soft; 978-0-9747968-6-4 hard)

2. *Fundamentals of Vedānta*, Part 1: *The Vedānta-sāra* of Sadānanda Yogīndra and the *Prameya-ratnāvalī* of Baladeva Vidyābhūṣaṇa (trans. by Neal Delmonico). *Fundamentals of Vedānta*, Part One, is a translation, with a detailed introduction and notes, of two short Sanskrit texts, the *Vedānta-sāra* (Essence of Vedānta) of Sadānanda and the *Prameya-ratnāvalī* (Necklace of Truth-Jewels) of Baladeva, from opposite ends of the Vedāntic spectrum. Each has been used in India for centuries to introduce beginning students to the fundamental ideas of Vedānta. (ISBN: 978-0-9747968-3-3)

3. *The Life and Teachings of Krishna Das Baba of Radhakund* by Zakrent Christian. This is a work on the life and teachings of a 20th century saint from the Caitanya Vaiṣṇava tradition. Krishna Das Baba was a well known practitioner and guide who lived in a community of renunciants nestled around a holy lake in North India called Radhakund (the Pond of Śrī

Rādhā). His story is typical of many stories of modern Indian men and women who gave up participation in modern society to pursue religious and spiritual goals. It thus presents insight into the yearnings of many modern Indians who when faced with the challenges of modernity haved turned towards tradition. (ISBN: 978-0-9747968-5-7)

4. *Nectar of the Holy Name* by Manindranath Guha (trans. Neal Delmonico). This is a translation of Manindranath Guha's classic Bengali book (*Hari-nāmāmṛta-sindhu-bindu*) on the beliefs and practices centering around the "holy names" (the names of Kṛṣṇa and of his consort Rādhā) of the Caitanya Vaiṣṇava tradition. Guha's book is a good introduction to an area of theological reflection in Caitanya Vaiṣṇavism called the "theology of the holy name." (ISBN: 978-0-9747968-1-9 soft; 978-0-9747968-2-6 hard)

5. *Sādhu Sādhu: a Life of Baba Śrī Tinkudi Gosvami* by Binode Bihari Dasa Babaji. This is an English translation of Śrī Binode Bihari Das Babaji's short Bengali work on the life of Baba Tinkudi Goswami, one of the great Vaiṣṇava practitioners and saints of the 20th century. This work is translated by Neal Delmonico with an introduction and annotations. It also contains two Bengali songs by his disciples remembering Tinkudi Goswami's life and some short recollections of him by some of his American disciples. (ISBN: 978-0-9747968-8-8)

6. *The Song Divine, or Bhagavad-gītā: a Metrical Rendering (with Annotations)* (English and Sanskrit edition), trans. by C.C. Caleb. This is a new edition of the delightful English metrical translation by C.C. Caleb of the Hindu classic, the *Bhagavad-gītā*, with an introduction, annotations, and an appendix. The original Sanskrit text, in both Devanāgarī and transliteration, of the *Gītā* has been included on the left hand pages for easy access and comparison with the translation. An appendix has been added containing short summaries of the teachings of the *Gītā* by many of the great commentators on the text: Śaṅkara, Yamunā Muni, Rāmānuja, Madhusūdana Sarasvatī, Viśvanātha Cakravartin, and Baladeva Vidyābhūṣaṇa. (ISBN: 978-0-9817902-3-7)

7. *The Song Divine, or Bhagavad-Gita: A Metrical Rendering (with Annotations) (English-only Edition)* trans. by C.C. Caleb. This is an edition of the metrical English translation by C.C. Caleb of the great Hindu classic, the *Bhagavad-gītā*, or The Song Divine. It includes an introduction to the text, annotations drawn from the commentary of Śaṅkara, and an appendix containing some of the traditional summaries of the text from different schools of interpretation. This edition does not include the original Sanskrit text of the *Gītā*. (ISBN: 978-0-9817902-8-2)

8. *Śrī Kṛṣṇa the Lord of Love*, Premananda Bharati. Premananda Bharati's classic work, *Sri Krishna: the Lord of Love*, was originally published in 1904 in New York. It is the first full-length work presenting theistic Hindu practices and beliefs before a Western audience by a practicing Hindu "missionary." Premananda Bharati or Baba (Father) Bharati had come to the USA as a result of the encouragement of his co-religionists in India and of a vision he received while living in a pilgrimage site sacred to his tradition. He arrived in the USA in 1902 and stayed until 1911 with one return journey to India in 1907 with several of his American disciples. His book was read and admired by numerous American and British men and women of the early 20th century and captured the attention of the great Russian writer Leo Tolstoy through whom Mahatma Gandhi discovered it. This new edition contains two introductions, one by Gerald T. Carney, PhD, a specialist on Premananda Bharati's life and work and another by Neal Delmonico, PhD, a specialist on Caitanya Vaiṣṇavism, the religious tradition to which Baba Bharati belonged. In addition, the text has been edited, corrected, annotated, and newly typeset. Appendices have been added containing supporting texts and additional materials bearing on Baba Bharati's sources for some of the ideas in his book and on his life and practices in India before his arrival in the USA. (ISBN: 978-0-9747968-7-1)

9. *Śrīmad-Bhagavad-Gītā (Sanskrit Edition)* ed. and introduced by Neal Delmonico. This is an edition of the *Bhagavad-gītā* in the original language of the text, Sanskrit. No translation of the text is given in this book. Only a Roman transliteration is provided alongside the Devanāgarī version and a number

of the most common variant readings in footnotes. There are hundreds of translations of the *Gītā* in various of the languages of the world and some of them include the text in either its native script, which is called Devanāgarī (the city of the gods), or in some transliterated format. A few even include word-by-word translations. But, many translations include neither text nor word equivalences. This edition is for those who would like to have access to and get to know the text itself better. It can be paired with any of the translations available in any language, including our own companion volume called the *The Song Divine*, which is a reprint/re-edition of the old classic verse translation of C. C. Caleb completed in India in 1911. (ISBN: 079-1-936135-00-4)

10. *Vaishnava Temple Music in Vrindaban: the Radhavallabha Songbook* by Guy L. Beck. This is a collection of 108 songs from the Radhavallabha tradition, a major North Indian *bhakti* tradition dating from the 16th century. The songs have been collected by ethno-musicologist Guy L Beck over a period of thirty years during which time he paid many visits to the religious headquarters of the sect, in Vrindaban, UP, India. In the book, Beck analyzes each song, discussing its rhythmic characteristics and its melodic structure within the raga system of classical Indian music. The verbal text for each song is given along with a faithful translation into English. In a long introduction, Beck discusses the development of religious music in India with reference to the special history and contributions of the Radhavallabha tradition. Two CDs filled with recordings of sample music are available free to purchasers of the book and the entire collection of recordings covering 18 expertly mastered CDs is available for purchase separately. (ISBN: 978-0-9817902-4-4)

Coming soon:

1. *The Blazing Sapphire (Ujjvala-nīlamaṇi)* by Rūpa Gosvāmin (translation by Neal Delmonico). In three volumes. In Sanskrit and English with introduction, notes, and the commen-

tary of Śrī Jīva Gosvāmin.

2. *My Gurudeva: a short biography of Siddha Manohara Dāsa Bābājī* by Navadvīpa Dāsa with excerpts from the original works of Siddha Bābā. Translation, introduction, and annotation by Neal Delmonico.

3. *In Praise of Śrī Kṛṣṇa's Sports (Śrī Kṛṣṇa-līlā-stava)*, the first theological/meditational text of the Caitanya Vaiṣṇava tradition, by Sanātana Gosvāmī. Translation, introduction, and annotation by Neal Delmonico.

4. *Sacred Rapture: a Study of the Religious Aesthetic of Śrī Rūpa Gosvāmin* by Neal Delmonico.

5. *The Eight Instructions of Śrī Caitanya (Śrī Caitanya-śikṣāṣṭaka)* with the Bengali commentary of Manindranath Guha. Translated, introduced, and annotated by Neal Delmonico.

6. *Holy Name—Thought Jewel (Nāma-cintāmaṇi)* by Kānupriya Gosvāmī. In three volumes. Translated, introduced, and annotated by Neal Delmonico

7. *Mahāmantra (The Great Mantra)* by Sundarānanda Dāsa Vidyāvinoda. Translated, introduced, and annotated by Neal Delmonico.

8. *Moonlight on the Daily Acts of Kṛṣṇa*, the earliest meditation/visualization (*līlā-smaraṇa*) text of the Caitanya tradition, by Kavikarṇapūra. Translated, introduced, and annotated by Neal Delmonico.

Introducing Golden Avatar Press

1. *Gosvāmins of Vṛndāvana* by Dr. O.B.L. Kapoor. (coming soon)

2. *Lord Gaurāṅga, or Salvation for All* by Shishir Kumar Ghosh. 2 vols. (coming soon)

www.ingramcontent.com/pod-product-compliance
Lightning Source LLC
Chambersburg PA
CBHW052020290426
44112CB00014B/2316
* 9 7 8 0 9 8 1 7 9 0 2 9 9 *